Mathematics Olympiad

Highly useful for all school students participating
in Various Olympiads & Competitions

Series Editor Keshav Mohan
Author Sanmeen Kaur

Class
7

arihant

ARIHANT PRAKASHAN, MEERUT

ARIHANT PRAKASHAN, MEERUT

All Rights Reserved

卐 **Administrative & Production Offices**

Corporate Office   'Ramchhaya' 4577/15, Agarwal Road, Darya Ganj New Delhi -110002
Tele: 011- 47630600, 43518550; Fax: 011- 23280316

Head Office   Kalindi, TP Nagar, Meerut (UP) - 250002
Tele: 0121-2401479, 2512970, 4004199; Fax: 0121-2401648

All disputes subject to Meerut (UP) jurisdiction only.

卐 **Sales & Support Offices**

Agra, Ahmedabad, Bengaluru, Bhubaneswar, Bareilly, Chennai, Delhi, Guwahati, Haldwani, Hyderabad, Jaipur, Jalandhar, Jhansi, Kolkata, Kota, Lucknow, Meerut, Nagpur & Pune

卐 **ISBN**   978-93-5203-396-6

卐 **Price**   ₹75

Typeset by Arihant DTP Unit at Meerut
Printed & Bound by Arihant Publications (I) Ltd. (Press Unit)

Production Team

Publishing Manager	Mahendra Singh Rawat	*Page Layouting*	Diwakar Gaur
Project Head	Karishma Yadav	*DTP Operator*	Amit Agarwal
Project Coordinator	Divya Gusain	*Cover Designer*	Syed Darin Zaidi
Proof Reader	Reena Garg	*Inner Designer*	Deepak Kumar

For further information about the products from Arihant
log on to www.arihantbooks.com or email to info@arihantbooks.com

Preface

Mathematics Olympiad Series for Class 6th-10th is a series of books which will challenge the young inquisitive minds by the non-routine and exciting mathematical problems.

The main purpose of this series is to make the students ready for competitive exams. The school/board exams are of qualifying nature but not competitive, they do not help the students to prepare for competitive exams, which mainly have objective questions.

- **Need of Olympiad Series**
  This series will fill this gap between the school/board and competitive exams as this series have all questions in Objective format. This series helps students who are willing to sharpen their problem solving skills. Unlike typical assessment books, which emphasis on drilling practice, the focus of this series is on practicing problem solving techniques.

- **Development of Logical Approach**
  The thought provoking questions given in this series will help students to attain a deeper understanding of the concepts and through which students will be able to impart Reasoning/Logical/Analytical skills in them.

- **Complement Your School Studies**
  This series complements the additional preparation needs of students for regular school/board exams. Along with, it will also address all the requirements of the students who are approaching National/State level competitions or Olympiads.

We shall welcome criticism from the students, teachers, educators and parents. We shall also like to hear from all of you about errors and deficiencies, which may have remained in this edition and the suggestions for the next edition.

Editor & Author

Contents

Chapter 1

Integers

A Representation of Integers on Number Line and Their Addition & Subtraction Properties

1. Use the suitable properties and choose the greatest positive integer.

    a $-(+100)$ b $-(-2)$

    c $|-48|$ d $+(-101)$

2. Pick the odd one out.

    a -4 and -7 b $+11$ and -22

    c -5 and -6 d -2 and -10

3. Integer used to represent the depreciation of machine by ₹ 2000 is

    a depreciate ₹ 2000   b $+$ ₹ 2000

    c $-$ ₹ 2000   d -2000

4. Opposite of going above sea level to 20 km in integer form is

    a $+20$ km   b -20 km

    c rise in 20 km   d descending 20 km

5. Choose the correct statement.

    a Integers are closed under addition but not under subtraction.

    b Integers are closed under subtraction but not under addition.

    c Integers are closed both under addition and subtraction.

    d None of the above

6. The absolute value of $-28 + 12 + 42 - 63$ is

    a 37   b -36 c 145   d -145

7. Fill in the box with appropriate integer.

$$\boxed{-6} \xrightarrow{+} \boxed{-24} \xrightarrow{-} \boxed{48} = \boxed{x}$$

    a 78   b -78 c 6   d -6

8. Choose the correct statement.

    a 0 is the number which is neither positive nor negative.

    b Negative of a negative number is a positive number.

    c Absolute value of x is always positive.

    d All of the above

9. Which of the following properties is wrong?

    a $a + b = b + a$ b $a - b = b - a$

    c $a + 0 = a = 0 + a$ d $a - 0 = a \neq 0 - a$

10. Marnold travels to Paris which is 760 km North from his city and then from Paris to Spain which is approximately 1100 km South from Paris. What is his position with respect to his city?
  a 340 km South
  b 340 km North
  c 1860 km North
  d 1860 km South

11. Shreya cycles 4 km to North and takes rest. She again starts cycling and travels a distance of 8 km to North. Determine which of the following options will represent her starting position from end position.
  a +4 km
  b −8 km
  c +8 km
  d −12 km

12. The six-day forecast for the Antartica lists the low temperatures (in Celsius) as $-52°C, -53°C, -40°C, -58°C, -70°C, -79°C$. Which choice shows the temperatures in order from lowest to highest?
  a $-79°C, -70°C, -52°C, -53°C, -48°C, -58°C$
  b $-52°C, -53°C, -58°C, -70°C, -79°C, -48°C$
  c $-79°C, -70°C, -58°C, -53°C, -52°C, -48°C$
  d $-48°C, -52°C, -53°C, -58°C, -70°C, -79°C$

13. Fill in the blanks with the help of options, given in the box.

> (i) addition, (ii) $-x$, (iii) $+a$, (iv) positive,
> (v) negative, (vi) $-a$, (vii) Subtraction,
> (viii) 0, (ix) 1, (x) $+x$

  I. ...... of integers is not commutative.
  II. If $-x$ lies on right hand side of the number line, then x is ...... integer.
  III. ...... is the additive identity of integers.
  IV. If a is a negative integer, then its absolute value is equal to ......

Codes

	I	II	III	IV		I	II	III	IV
a	viii	iv	ix	iiii	b	i	v	x	iii
c	vii	v	viii	iii	d	i	iv	x	vi

14. Pick the odd one out.

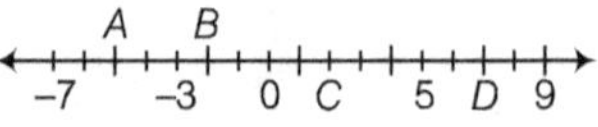

		0					4	
a	2	−1	3		b	7	39	8
		6					− 20	
		− 2					2	
c	11	5	12		d	2	− 4	7
		20					11	

A number line labelled with points: A near −5, B near −3, then 0, C near 2, 5, D near 7, 9.

15. Find the value of $D - A.$
  a 2   b −2
  c −12   d 12

16. Use the correct values of C, B, D, A and fill in the box given below.
$$C + B \;\square\; D + A$$
  a $>$
  b $<$
  c $=$
  d Can't say

17. If E represents the value $D - [4 - (-5)]$, then E is equal to
  a A b B
  c C d Zero

18. Choose the appropriate integers on the places of (i) and (ii).
$$11, -13, 8, -10, 5, -7, (i), (ii)$$
  a $2, -5$ b $-5, 3$
  c $2, -4$ d $-2, -5$

19. State 'T' for true and 'F' for false.
  I. Sum of two positive integers is a positive integer.
  II. Sum of two negative integers is always a negative integer.
  III. Difference of a positive and negative integers is always a negative integer.
  IV. 1 is the additive identity of integers.

Codes

	I	II	III	IV
a	T	T	F	T
b	T	T	F	F
c	F	T	T	F
d	T	F	F	T

 On the basis of the given information, answer the following questions.

In an atom, the number of electrons is equal to the number of protons, where electrons are negatively charged particles and protons are positively charged particles. The number of protons is referred to as the atomic number, whereas mass number = number of protons + number of neutrons (uncharged particles).

Elements	A	B	Mass number	Number of neutrons
Lithium	3	−3	7	4
Oxygen	(i)	−8	(ii)	8
Neon	(iii)	(iv)	20	10
Sodium	11	(v)	(vi)	12

20. What does A and B denote?
   a A-Number of protons, B-Atomic number
   b A-Number of neutrons, B-Number of protons
   c A-Number of protons, B-Number of electrons
   d Can't be determined

21. Match the following on the basis of table given above.

Column A		Column B	
I.		(i)	10
II.		(ii)	−11
III.		(iii)	8
IV.		(iv)	23
V.		(v)	16
VI.		(vi)	10

Codes

	I	II	III	IV	V	VI
a	(iii)	(v)	(i)	(vi)	(ii)	(iv)
b	(i)	(ii)	(iv)	(iii)	(vi)	(v)
c	(ii)	(i)	(iii)	(iv)	(vi)	(v)
d	(i)	(i)	(iv)	(iii)	(v)	(vi)

22. What number should logically replace the question mark?

5	7	6	8
6	2	5	1
?	4	9	5
3	5	2	4

   a 7   b 8
   c 5   d 3

23. Mr. Anil had a balance of ₹ 11700 in his account. He deposited amount of ₹ 1925, ₹ 3380, ₹ 4000 on different days of a month and withdraw ₹ 2500, ₹ 5850, ₹ 1000 also. What is his final balance (in ₹) at the end of the month?
   a 11700   b 11655
   c −2000   d −2050

24. If y is an integer, then which of the following must be an odd integer?
   a $2y^3 + 3$
   b $3y$
   c $y^3 + 3$
   d $3y + 2$

B Multiplication & Division of Integers and Their Properties

1. Choose the correct option for $2 \times (3 \times 2) = ?$.
   a $2 \times 3 \times 2$ b $2 \times 2 + 3$
   c $2 \times 3 + 2 \times 2$ d None of these

2. If $(-a)^n$ is positive, then n is an
   a odd number   b even number
   c Either (a) or (b)   d None of these

3. If we multiply -1 to itself 20 times, then what would be the answer?
   a 1   b −1   c 0   d Can't say

4. The value of $(-12) \times (-2) \times (+3) \times (-1)$ is equal to
   a 12   b −72
   c −24   d −18

5. Which property is satisfied by multiplication but not division of integers?
   a Closure   b Commutative
   c Both (a) and (b)   d None of these

6. Pick the odd one out.

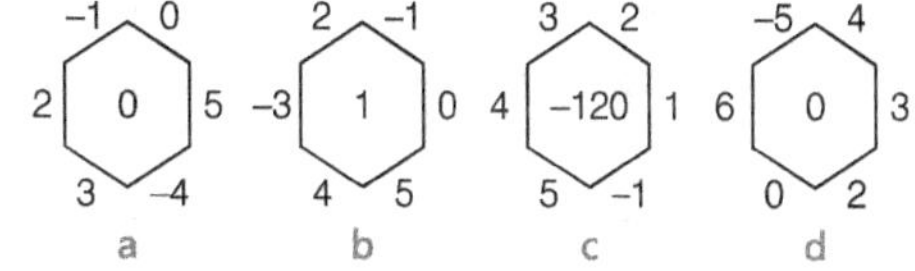

7. Choose the incorrect option.
   a $a \times b = b \times a$ b $a \div b = b \div a$
   c Both (a) and (b)   d None of these

8. The value of $3 \times (-7) \times (-8) \times 9 \times 0 \times 4 \times 2$ is equal to

   a   −12096   b 0
   c   12096   d 1

9. Fill in the box with the correct option.

$$2 \times (5 + 6) = (2 \times 5) \square (2 \times 6)$$

   a ÷   b ×
   c +   d −

10. "Product of a negative and a positive integers depends on the sign of the greater integer."

If the above statement is not correct, then choose the following statements to correct it.

   a Product of a negative and a positive integers depends on the sign of the smaller integer.
   b Product of a negative and a positive integers is always negative.
   c Product of a negative and a positive integers is always positive.
   d No change

11. If '÷' is replaced by '×', then find the correct value of the following problem.

$$(-2) \div 3 \times (-4) \div 1 = ?$$

   a 24   b −12
   c 8   d −6

12. Fill in the blanks with the help of options, given in the box.

(i) odd,	(ii) negative,	(iii) 0,
(iv) even	(v) 1,	(vi) division,
(vii) positive,	(viii) Multiplication,	(ix) operations,
(x) greater,	(xi) integers,	(xii) less

   I. …… is a commutative operation.
   II. If two negative integers are multiplied, then the result cannot be ……
   III. The multiplicative identity of integers is ……
   IV. If $(-1)^n$ is negative, then n is ……
   V. Addition, subtraction, multiplication and division are…… .
   VI. A negative number is …… than zero.

VII. Positive and negative whole numbers with zero are called…… .

VIII. −1 is between −2 and …… on the number line.

Codes

	I	II	III	IV	V	VI	VII	VIII
a	viii	ii	v	i	ix	xii	xi	iii
b	vi	ii	iii	i	x	ix	xi	v
c	vi	vii	v	iv	xi	x	ix	iii
d	viii	vii	iii	iv	xi	ix	x	v

13. Fill in the correct 'sign'.

   I. $24 \div (-3) \square 2 \times 6$
   II. $1 \times 0 \square (-2) \times 9$
   III. $(-8) \div 2 \square -2 \times (+2)$
   IV. $7 \times 8 \times (-9) \square 0$

Codes

	I	II	III	IV		I	II	III	IV
a	>	<	>	=	b	<	>	=	<
c	=	>	>	<	d	<	<	=	>

14. If $a * b = a \times b$ and $a \boxed{\bigcirc} b = a \div b$, then which of the following options is correct?

   a $2 * 3 > (-24) \boxed{\bigcirc} (-4)6$
   b $42 \boxed{\bigcirc} (-6) \boxed{<} (-7) * 8$
   c $2 * 3 \boxed{=} (-36) \boxed{\bigcirc} 6$
   d $(-7) * (-9) \boxed{>} 21 \boxed{\bigcirc} 3$

15. State 'T' for true and 'F' for false.

   I. Zero is the multiplicative identity of integers.
   II. Any number multiplied by 1 is equal to 1.
   III. Multiplication of integers is commutative.
   IV. Cube of a negative number is negative always.

Codes

	I	II	III	IV
a	F	F	T	T
b	F	T	F	T
c	T	F	F	F
d	T	F	T	T

16. **Assertion** (A) $(-2) \times (-3) \times (-1) = 6$

Reason (R) Multiplication of odd numbers of negative integers is always negative.

   a A is true and R is correct explanation of A
   b A is false and R is correct explanation of A
   c A is true and R is false
   d Both A and R are true

Simplification using Addition, Subtraction, Multiplication and Division

1. State which property is shown below.

$$7 \times (8 + 9) = 7 \times 8 + 7 \times 9$$

- a Commutative
- b Associative
- c Closure
- d Distributive

2. Simplified value of $31 \times 79 - 31 \times 76$ is

- a 93
- b 94
- c 96
- d 99

3. Which of the following will give '−2' as the simplified value?

- a $\dfrac{(-2) \times (-2) + 2 \div (-1)}{1}$
- b $\dfrac{(-2) \times 2 - 2 \div 1}{1}$
- c $\dfrac{2 \times (-2) + 2 \div (-1)}{-1}$
- d $\dfrac{2 \times 2 + 2 \div (-1)}{-1}$

4. Match the following.

	Column A		Column B
I.	$(-31) + 30 + (-31) + 30$ $+ \ldots 30$ terms	(i)	-15
II.	$(-7) \times 5 + 1 \times 0$	(ii)	$+35$
III.	$42 \times (91 - 91)$	(iii)	0
IV.	$21 \div (5 - 8)$	(iv)	-35
		(v)	$+15$
		(vi)	-7

Codes

	I	II	III	IV
a	(v)	(iv)	(iii)	(ii)
b	(v)	(iii)	(vi)	(ii)
c	(i)	(iii)	(iv)	(ii)
d	(i)	(iv)	(iii)	(vi)

5.

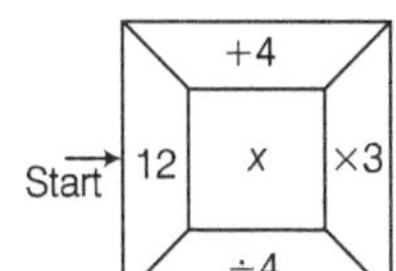

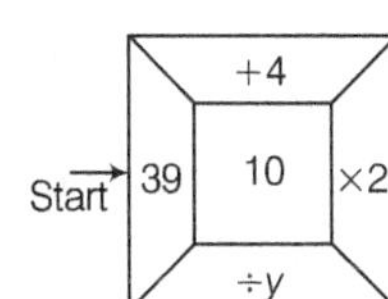

Following the order of operations, find the values of x and y.

- a 13 and 13
- b 13 and 10
- c 10 and 13
- d 10 and 10

6. Simplify and choose the correct option.

$$22 - \{(2 + \overline{3 - 4}) \times \overline{(-1) + 2}\}$$

- a 22
- b 16
- c 18
- d 21

7. If moving towards East is taken as positive and moving towards West is taken as negative and a man is walking at a speed of 1.2 km/min. If he starts from 7 km East and reaches 5 km West. How much time does he take?

- a 10 min
- b 15 min
- c 1.7 min
- d Can't be determined

8. **Assertion** (A) $17 - \{(2 + \overline{7 - 3}) - 8\} = 19$

Reason (R) In simplification, it is not necessary to follow the order of operations.

- a A is true and R is correct explanation of A
- b A is false and R is correct explanation of A
- c A is true and R is false
- d Both A and R are false

9. An elevator descends at a speed of 1 floor/s. If Mohan takes the elevator from 24th floor of a multistoreyed building to reach to the 3rd basement of parking, then how much time will he take?

- a 27 s
- b 24 s
- c 21 s
- d 18 s

Directions (Q. Nos. 10-11) Simplify the given questions.

10. $7 + \{-(2 + \overline{4 - 3} - 1) + 2 \times 10 \div 5\}$ will be equal to

- a 3
- b 6
- c 7
- d 9

11. $20 - \{(4 + \overline{7 - 8}) - 14 \div 2\}$ is equal to

- a 22
- b 26
- c 24
- d 28

12. Match the following.

	Column A		Column B
I.	$8 - 4(2 + 5^2) \div 9$	(i)	2
II.	$(6 + 2) - 15 \div 5 \times 2$	(ii)	0
III.	$3 - (5 - 6 \div 3)$	(iii)	1
IV.	$28 - 5 \times 6 + 2 + 1$	(iv)	-4

Codes

	I	II	III	IV		I	II	III	IV
a	iv	i	iii	ii	b	i	iv	iii	ii
c	iv	i	ii	iii	d	i	iv	ii	iii

13. If $a \pentagon b = a \div b$, $a \star b = a \times b$, $a \square b = a - b$ and $a \triangle b = a + b$, then determine the value of $0 \square 7 \star 8 \pentagon (2\triangle - 10)$.

   a 7   b -18 c -38 d 0

14. If '+' is replaced by $\div$,

   '$-$' is replaced by $\times$,

   '$\div$' is replaced by $-$

   and '$\times$' is replaced by $+$,

then the value of $18 + 9 \times 10 \div 3 - 2$ will be

   a 6   b 88   c 2   d 20

15. Fill in the blanks with the help of options, given in the box.

(i) absolute value,	(ii) $72 \div 8$,
(iii) addition,	(iv) BODMAS,
(v) $>$,	(vi) $(4^2 + 2)$,
(vii) simplification,	(viii) $<$,
(ix) $=$	

   I. In BODMAS, 'A' refers to ....

   II. In simplifying $6 \times 8 - (4^2 + 2) + 72 \div 8$, the part which will be simplified first is ....

   III. .... rule species the order of operations.

   IV. $3^3 + 5 \times 3 .... 2 + 8(35 \div 7)$

Codes

	I	II	III	IV
a	i	ii	viii	v
b	iii	ii	iv	v
c	i	vi	vii	viii
d	iii	vi	iv	ix

16. Using integer, write an expression and simplify to answer.

"The difference of negative thirteen and twenty four divided by the product of square of negative two and three".

   a -31 b -57

   c 57   d -24

17. Simplify and choose the correct option.

$$2550 - [510 - \{270 - (90 - \overline{80 + 70})\}]$$

   a 2730   b 2230   c 2270   d 2370

18. Which of the following gives the answer as 62?

   a $63 - [(-3)\{-2 - \overline{8 - 3}\}] \div [3\{5 + (-2)(-1)\}]$

   b $63 + (-3)\{-2 - \overline{8 - 3}\} \div 3\{5 + (-2)(-1)\}$

   c Both (a) and (b)

   d None of the above

19. Which of the following sequences of operator will satisfy the equation given below?

$$(-3) \;\square\; (-8) \;\square\; (-4) \;\square\; 2 \;\square\; (-2) = 3$$

   a $+, -, \times, \div$ b $\div, +, \times, -$

   c $+, \div, -, \times$ d $\times, \div, +, -$

20. Find the values of $\diamond$ and ∇ in the given equations.

$$100 \times \nabla = \nabla + \nabla + 98 \times 7$$

and $153 \div \diamond = 923 - 230 \times 4$

   a $\nabla = 41$, $\nabla = 7$

   b $\nabla = 7$, $\diamond = 51$

   c $\diamond = 7$, $\nabla = 41$

   d $\nabla = 51$, $\diamond = 7$

21. Dr. Christian advised her patient to take three tablets A, B and C such that the patient had to take A and B in the numbers two and one respectively in a day and to take tablet C once in every two days. How many tablets in all did she advise to take in 30 days?

   a 60   b 90   c 105   d 120

22. What is the number you started with?

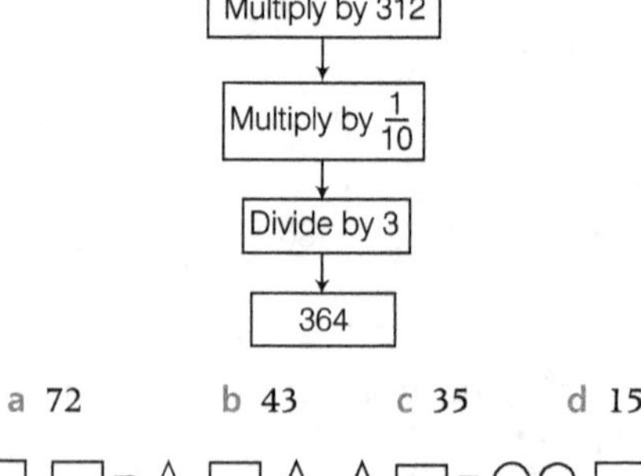

   a 72   b 43   c 35   d 15

23. 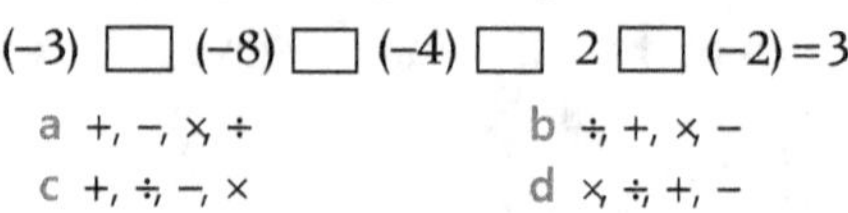

$\square \; \square = \triangle \; \square \; \triangle$, $\triangle \; \square = \bigcirc \bigcirc$, $\square = 50$

Using the diagram above, which of the following statement is true?

   a $\square < \bigcirc$ b $\square < \triangle$

   c $\triangle < \square$ d $\bigcirc < \triangle$

Chapter 2

Rational Numbers

1. If A and B represent a rational number, then $(A - B)$ is equal to

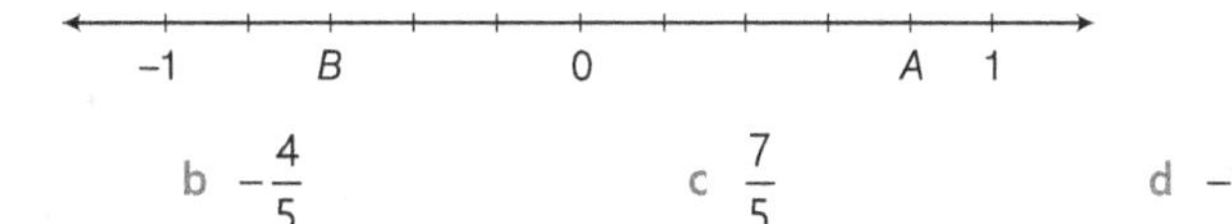

a $\dfrac{2}{5}$ b $-\dfrac{4}{5}$ c $\dfrac{7}{5}$ d -1

2. Pick the odd one out.

a $\dfrac{2}{3} \times \left(\dfrac{1}{2} - \dfrac{1}{4}\right) = \dfrac{2}{3} \times \dfrac{1}{2} - \dfrac{2}{3} \times \dfrac{1}{4}$ b $\dfrac{4}{5} \times \left(\dfrac{2}{3} - \dfrac{2}{7}\right) = \dfrac{4}{5} \times \dfrac{2}{3} + \dfrac{4}{5} \times \dfrac{-2}{7}$

c $\dfrac{7}{9} \times \left(\dfrac{-7}{11} + \dfrac{2}{11}\right) = \dfrac{7}{9} \times \dfrac{2}{11} + \dfrac{7}{9} \times \dfrac{7}{11}$ d $\dfrac{3}{5} \times \left(\dfrac{3}{7} - \dfrac{2}{5}\right) = \dfrac{3}{5} \times \dfrac{3}{7} + \dfrac{3}{5} \times \dfrac{2}{-5}$

3. If $p = -\dfrac{2}{3} + \dfrac{4}{5} + 1$ and $q = \dfrac{2}{3} - \dfrac{4}{5} + \dfrac{7}{15}$, then

a $p > q$ b $p < q$

c $p = q$ d Can't be determined

4. To represent $\dfrac{-2}{7}$ on number line, distance between which two numbers will be divided

equally and into how many parts?

a 0 and 1, 2 parts b 0 and −1, 7 parts

c −1 and −2, 5 parts d −2 and −7, 5 parts

5. Chaaru simplified the number in this manner $\dfrac{-49}{-63} = \dfrac{7}{-9}$. Did she simplify correctly?

a Yes b No

c Can't say d None of these

6. Evaluate and choose the correct option $\dfrac{2}{5} + \left(-\dfrac{5}{6}\right) + \left(-\dfrac{7}{9}\right)$.

a $-\dfrac{109}{90}$ b $\dfrac{-14}{90}$

c $\dfrac{14}{9}$ d $\dfrac{27}{20}$

7. Which of the following rational numbers doesn't lie between $\dfrac{2}{101}$ and $\dfrac{3}{71}$?

a $\dfrac{150}{7171}$ b $\dfrac{1000}{35855}$

c $\dfrac{4}{914}$ d $\dfrac{500}{21513}$

8. Which is the correct sequence of numbers in ascending order?

a $\dfrac{1}{3} < \dfrac{3}{7} < \dfrac{2}{5}$ b $\dfrac{3}{7} < \dfrac{1}{3} < \dfrac{2}{5}$

c $\dfrac{2}{5} < \dfrac{3}{7} < \dfrac{1}{3}$ d $\dfrac{1}{3} < \dfrac{2}{5} < \dfrac{3}{7}$

9. What is the reciprocal of $\left(\dfrac{3}{2} \times \dfrac{1}{3}\right) + \left(\dfrac{1}{3} \times 9\right)$?

a $\dfrac{7}{2}$ b $\dfrac{5}{3}$

c $\dfrac{3}{5}$ d $\dfrac{2}{7}$

10. Match the following.

Column A		Column B	
I.	$\dfrac{7}{9}$	(i)	$\dfrac{10}{-15}$
II.	$\dfrac{-2}{3}$	(ii)	$-\left(\dfrac{-44}{-52}\right)$
III.	$\dfrac{4}{-7}$	(iii)	$\dfrac{-24}{42}$
IV.	$\dfrac{-11}{13}$	(iv)	$\dfrac{-49}{-63}$

Codes

	I	II	III	IV
a	iv	ii	i	iii
b	i	iv	ii	iii
c	i	iv	iii	ii
d	iv	i	iii	ii

11. What should be added to $\dfrac{-1}{4}$ to obtain the nearest natural number?

a $\dfrac{2}{4}$ b $\dfrac{-1}{4}$

c $\dfrac{-5}{4}$ d $\dfrac{5}{4}$

12. **Assertion** (A) Rational numbers are always closed under subtraction.

Reason (R) Any rational number with zero as denominator is not defined.

a A is true and R is correct explanation of A
b A is false and R is correct explanation of A
c A is true and R is false
d Both A and R are false

13. The sum of two rational numbers is $\dfrac{8}{9}$. If one of them is $\dfrac{2}{18}$, then the other is

a $\dfrac{1}{18}$ b $\dfrac{3}{18}$ c $\dfrac{7}{9}$ d $\dfrac{6}{9}$

14. Which of the following rational numbers satisfies the property $(a + b) + c = a + (b + c)$?

a $a = -2,\ b = -\dfrac{2}{3},\ c = -\dfrac{3}{5}$

b $a = -10,\ b = -\dfrac{9}{11},\ c = -\dfrac{7}{12}$

c $a = -\dfrac{7}{21},\ b = -\dfrac{7}{11},\ c = \dfrac{5}{12}$

d All of the above

15. Choose the correct statement.

a Rational numbers are closed under division.
b Rational numbers are commutative under division.
c Rational numbers are associative under division.
d None of the above

16. What should be subtracted from $\left(\dfrac{2}{3} - \dfrac{3}{4}\right)$ to get $-\dfrac{1}{6}$?

a $-\dfrac{1}{2}$ b $\dfrac{1}{12}$

c $\dfrac{1}{6}$ d $-\dfrac{1}{6}$

17. Choose the correct sequence.

a $\dfrac{-7}{-6} > \dfrac{-3}{-5} > \dfrac{1}{2} > \dfrac{-1}{-4} > 0$

b $\dfrac{2}{3} > \dfrac{1}{2} > \dfrac{-4}{-5} > 1$

c $\dfrac{1}{4} > \dfrac{-4}{-9} > \dfrac{2}{3} > \dfrac{5}{7}$

d $\dfrac{7}{-18} > \dfrac{4}{-9} > \dfrac{-2}{3} > \dfrac{-5}{12}$

18. Match the following.

Column A		Column B	
I.	$\left(\dfrac{-6}{25}\right) \times \dfrac{50}{36}$	(i)	$\dfrac{-10}{9}$
II.	$\dfrac{3}{11} \times \left(\dfrac{-33}{21}\right)$	(ii)	-1
III.	$\dfrac{5}{21} \times \left(\dfrac{42}{-9}\right)$	(iii)	$\dfrac{-1}{3}$
IV.	$\left(\dfrac{-7}{11}\right) \times \dfrac{77}{49}$	(iv)	$\dfrac{3}{-7}$

Codes

	I	II	III	IV
a	iii	i	iv	ii
b	ii	i	iv	iii
c	iii	iv	i	ii
d	ii	iv	i	iii

19. Which of the following statements is true?

  a $-\dfrac{3}{5}$ lies to the right of zero on number line.

  b The rational numbers $\dfrac{-17}{-13}$ and $\dfrac{-7}{17}$ lie on the same side of zero.

  c The rational numbers $\dfrac{-4}{-5}$ and $\dfrac{-4}{5}$ lie on opposite side of number line.

  d None of the above

20. A train is moving at a speed of $\dfrac{2024}{15}$ km/h.

How much distance will it cover in $\dfrac{25}{4}$ h?

  a $\dfrac{2530}{3}$ km

  b 2560 km

  c $\dfrac{2560}{15}$ km

  d None of the above

21. Assertion (A) $\dfrac{1}{0}$ is a rational number.

  Reason (R) $\dfrac{p}{q}$ is a rational number, if $q \neq 0$.

  a A is true and R is correct explanation of A

  b A is false and R is correct explanation of A

  c A is true and R is false

  d Both A and R are false

22. Fill in the blanks with the help of options, given in the box.

(i) $\dfrac{-5}{28}$,	(ii) $\dfrac{+20}{29}$,	(iii) opposite,
(iv) $\dfrac{-79}{30}$,	(v) $\dfrac{89}{30}$,	(vi) $\dfrac{28}{5}$,
(vii) same,	(viii) $\dfrac{-20}{19}$,	(ix) greater,
(x) less,	(xi) true,	(xii) false

  I. ..... should be added to $\left(\dfrac{1}{2} + \dfrac{1}{3} + \dfrac{1}{5}\right)$ to get 4.

  II. The rational number $\dfrac{120}{-114}$ when reduced to standard form is ....

  III. ...... must be added by $\dfrac{-15}{28}$ to get $\dfrac{-5}{7}$.

  IV. The rational numbers $\left(\dfrac{-11}{-5}\right)$ and $\left(\dfrac{7}{-26}\right)$ lie on the ...... side of 0 on the number line.

  V. $\dfrac{-5}{8}$ is ...... than $\dfrac{-7}{-12}$.

  VI. The rational numbers $\dfrac{1}{3}$ and $\dfrac{-5}{2}$ are on the opposite sides of 0 on the number line. It is ....

  VII. $\dfrac{-4}{-9}$ is ...... than $\dfrac{1}{4}$.

Codes

	I	II	III	IV	V	VI	VII
a	v	iv	vi	viii	xi	x	ix
b	ii	viii	i	iii	ix	x	xi
c	ii	iv	vi	vii	x	ix	xi
d	v	viii	i	iii	x	xi	ix

23. Mr Tiwari had a piece of land which he distributed among his three children. He gave $\dfrac{1}{3}$rd to his eldest son and $\dfrac{2}{5}$ of the remaining to his daughter and the left amount of land to his youngest child. How much did his youngest child got, if Mr Tiwari had 25000 sq m of land?

  a 5000 sq m

  b 10000 sq m

  c 15000 sq m

  d 2000 sq m

24. Which of the given answers do we get, on evaluating the following equation?

$$\left(1-\dfrac{1}{2}\right)\left(1-\dfrac{1}{3}\right)\left(1-\dfrac{1}{4}\right)\left(1-\dfrac{1}{5}\right)\ldots\left(1-\dfrac{1}{100}\right)$$

  a $\dfrac{99}{100}$

  b $\dfrac{1}{100}$

  c $\dfrac{1}{99}$

  d None of the above

25. Shehnaz earns ₹ 25000 per month. She spends $\dfrac{1}{5}$ of her income on food, $\dfrac{3}{10}$ of the remainder on house rent and $\dfrac{9}{28}$ of remainder on the education of children. How much money is still left with her?

  a ₹ 10000

  b ₹ 8500

  c ₹ 10500

  d ₹ 9500

26. State 'T' for true and 'F' for false.

    I. All fractions are rational numbers.   II. The value of $\left(\dfrac{-16}{21} \div \dfrac{-4}{3}\right)$ is $\dfrac{4}{7}$.

    III. $\dfrac{9}{72}$ and $\dfrac{-3}{21}$ are equivalent rational numbers.   IV. $\dfrac{48}{-96}$ is in standard form.

    V. $\dfrac{-55}{-77}$ is equivalent to $\dfrac{25}{-35}$.

Codes

	I	II	III	IV	V			I	II	III	IV	V
a	F	F	T	T	F		b	T	T	F	F	F
c	T	F	F	T	T		d	F	T	F	F	T

27. If $a * b = \dfrac{ab}{a+b}$, then what is $\dfrac{1}{1*2} - \dfrac{1}{2*3} + \dfrac{1}{3*4} - \dfrac{1}{4*5} \cdots \dfrac{1}{2000*2001}$ equal to?

  a $\dfrac{1}{2}$ b $\dfrac{2001}{2000}$ c $\dfrac{2}{2001}$ d $\dfrac{2000}{2001}$

28. For two rational numbers that are in standard form $\dfrac{A}{B}$ and $\dfrac{C}{D}$; which of the following condition(s) is/are true?

  a If $AD > BC$, then $\dfrac{A}{B} > \dfrac{C}{D}$ b If $AD < BC$, then $\dfrac{A}{B} < \dfrac{C}{D}$

  c If $AD = BC$, then $\dfrac{A}{B} = \dfrac{C}{D}$ d All of these

29. What is the percentage of the smallest number to the greatest number, if $\dfrac{5}{6}, \dfrac{7}{12}, \dfrac{13}{18}, \dfrac{23}{24}$ are arranged in descending or ascending order?

  a $31\dfrac{2}{24}$ b $39\dfrac{3}{23}$ c $35\dfrac{3}{18}$ d None of these

30. Match the following.

	Column A		Column B
I.	$\left(-7\dfrac{1}{24}\right) + \left(-3\dfrac{1}{16}\right) = \left(-3\dfrac{1}{16}\right) + \left(-7\dfrac{1}{24}\right)$	(i)	Associative property
II.	$\left(\dfrac{3}{5} \times \dfrac{12}{13}\right) \times \dfrac{7}{18} = \dfrac{3}{5} \times \left(\dfrac{12}{13} \times \dfrac{7}{18}\right)$	(ii)	Distributive property
III.	$\left(\dfrac{-12}{5}\right) \times \left\{\dfrac{4}{15} + \left(\dfrac{-16}{25}\right)\right\} = \left(\dfrac{-12}{5}\right) \times \dfrac{4}{15} + \left(\dfrac{-12}{5}\right) \times \left(\dfrac{-16}{25}\right)$	(iii)	Commutative property

Codes

	I	II	III			I	II	III			I	II	III			I	II	III
a	i	ii	iii		b	i	iii	ii		c	iii	i	ii		d	ii	i	iii

Chapter 3

Fractions and Decimals

A Fractions

1. What fraction of the following figure is shaded?

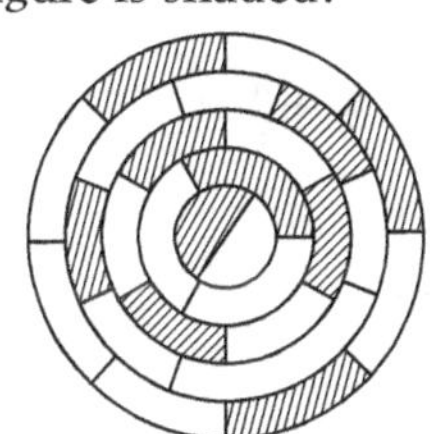

   a $\dfrac{14}{25}$ b $\dfrac{5}{13}$ c $\dfrac{9}{26}$ d $\dfrac{10}{27}$

2. Pick the odd one out.

   a $14\dfrac{2}{3}$ b $13\dfrac{2}{5}$ c $\dfrac{16}{7}$ d $\dfrac{17}{24}$

3. Choose the correct statement.

   a Fractions are in the form of $\dfrac{p}{q}$, where p, q are integers and $q \neq 0$.

   b $\dfrac{7}{9}$ is not a fraction.

   c Mixed fractions can be converted into proper fractions.

   d Improper fractions have numerator greater than denominator.

4. $\dfrac{19}{\square}$ is a fraction that lies between $\dfrac{1}{9}$ and $\dfrac{1}{11}$. What will be the correct whole number to fill the box?

   a 99   b 198   c 189   d 110

5. How many more triangles in the figure must be shaded to make the fraction of shaded squares equal to $\dfrac{4}{9}$?

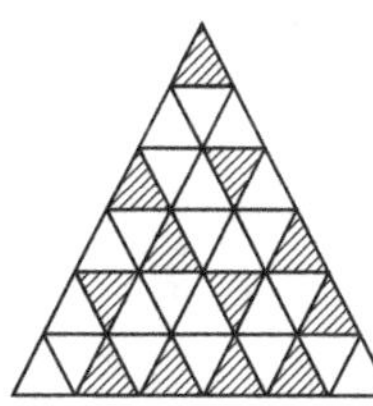

   a 3   b 4   c 5   d 6

6. Which of the following fractions is closest to zero?

   a $\dfrac{6}{13}$ b $\dfrac{3}{5}$ c $\dfrac{5}{6}$ d $\dfrac{1}{4}$

7. If $\square + 2\dfrac{37}{44} = 10\dfrac{9}{44}$, then missing fraction in the box is

   a $7\dfrac{4}{11}$ b $2\dfrac{10}{44}$ c $8\dfrac{1}{44}$ d $4\dfrac{7}{11}$

8. Given a set of fractions $\dfrac{7}{5}, \dfrac{21}{15}, 1\dfrac{22}{55}, \dfrac{147}{105}$, what type of fractions are these?

   a Proper and equivalent fractions
   b Proper and mixed fractions
   c Improper and equivalent fractions
   d Improper and mixed fractions

9. Which fraction is represented on the number line given below?

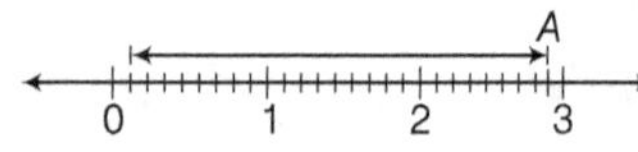

   a $A = \dfrac{2}{3}$ b $A = \dfrac{8}{9}$ c $A = \dfrac{26}{9}$ d $A = \dfrac{8}{3}$

10. If $\square \div 2\dfrac{1}{4} = \dfrac{4}{7}$, then fill in the missing box.

   a $\dfrac{4}{7}$ b $\dfrac{9}{7}$

   c $\dfrac{7}{9}$ d $\dfrac{4}{9}$

11. If $\dfrac{3}{2} \times x \times \dfrac{6}{3} = 3\dfrac{3}{4}$, then the value of x is

   a $\dfrac{3}{4}$ b $\dfrac{4}{3}$

   c $\dfrac{5}{4}$ d $\dfrac{5}{3}$

12. If $x = \dfrac{6}{25}$ and $y = \dfrac{3}{5}$, then the value of $\dfrac{x}{y}$ is

   a $\dfrac{6}{5}$ b $\dfrac{18}{125}$

   c $\dfrac{2}{5}$ d None of these

13. If $x = \dfrac{2}{3} + \dfrac{3}{4}$ and $y = \dfrac{3}{4} + \dfrac{5}{6}$, then the value of $\dfrac{1}{x} \div \dfrac{1}{y}$ is

   a $\dfrac{11}{38}$ b $\dfrac{17}{38}$

   c $\dfrac{22}{17}$ d $\dfrac{19}{17}$

14. One pack of cookies requires $3\dfrac{1}{2}$ cups of flour and $2\dfrac{1}{3}$ cups of sugar. Estimated total quantity of both ingredients used in 10 such packets of cookies will be

   a less than 50 cups
   b between 50 cups and 60 cups
   c between 60 cups and 70 cups
   d above 60 cups

15. Shreya distributed $2\dfrac{4}{7}$ kg of chocolate cake among her nine friends. How much cake does each friend receive?

   a $\dfrac{9}{7}$ b $\dfrac{1}{7}$ c $\dfrac{2}{7}$ d $\dfrac{1}{9}$

16. A cricket team won 12 games and lost 4 in a tournament. Then, the fraction of the games they lost, is

   a $\dfrac{4}{16}$ b $\dfrac{4}{12}$ c $\dfrac{12}{16}$ d $\dfrac{12}{4}$

17. What will be the reciprocal of product of improper fractions $2\dfrac{1}{4}$ and $3\dfrac{1}{2}$?

   a Proper fraction   b Equivalent fraction
   c Improper fraction   d Like fraction

18. A flower basket containing 36 flowers is $\dfrac{3}{11}$ full. How many more flowers are needed to fill it up?

   a 132   b 108   c 96   d 84

19. Match the following.

	Column A		Column B
I.	$\dfrac{3}{4}$ of $\dfrac{16}{27}$	(i)	$\dfrac{1}{8}$
II.	$2\dfrac{1}{4}$ of $\dfrac{1}{18}$	(ii)	$\dfrac{10}{3}$
III.	$1\dfrac{2}{3}$ of 2	(iii)	1
IV.	$\dfrac{4}{6}$ of $\dfrac{42}{28}$	(iv)	$\dfrac{4}{9}$

Codes

	I	II	III	IV
a	i	ii	iii	iv
b	iv	iii	ii	i
c	iv	i	ii	iii
d	i	iv	iii	ii

20. Which of the following options represents $\frac{3}{4}$ of 8 parts shaded?

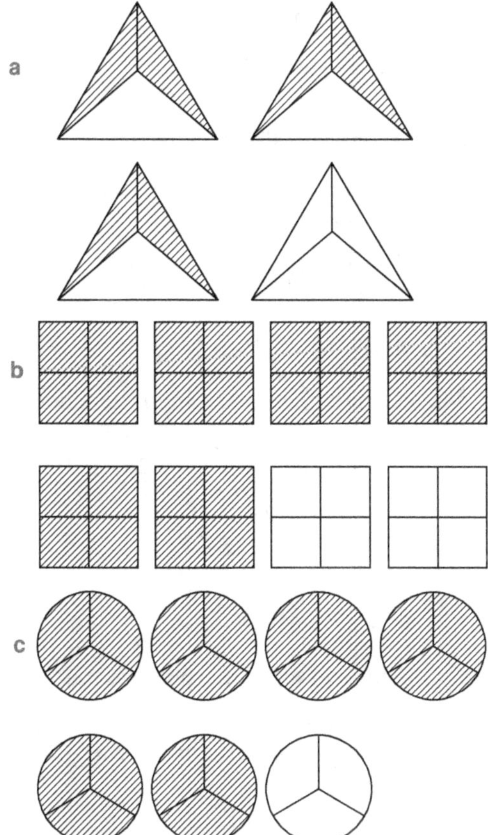

a

b

c

d None of the above

21. Evaluate and choose the correct option for
$$\left(1-\frac{2}{3}\right)\times\left(1-\frac{2}{5}\right)\times\left(1-\frac{2}{7}\right)\times\left(1-\frac{2}{9}\right)\times...\times\left(1-\frac{2}{99}\right).$$

a $\frac{2}{3}$

b $\frac{2}{99}$

c $\frac{1}{99}$

d $\frac{1}{3}$

22. If $a*b=\dfrac{a\times b}{a\div b}$, then what is the value of $21*3$?

a $\frac{21}{3}$

b $\frac{42}{7}$

c $\frac{9}{1}$

d $\frac{7}{3}$

23. Priya when asked, told her teacher that she has completed 40 questions or $\frac{2}{3}$ of the question paper. How many more questions she has to do to complete the paper?

a 60

b 40

c 20

d 10

24. Fill in the blanks with the help of options, given in the box.

> (i) proper fraction,
>
> (ii) changed,
>
> (iii) 91,
>
> (iv) $\dfrac{\text{Product of denominators}}{\text{Product of numerators}}$,
>
> (v) improper fraction,
>
> (vi) unchanged,
>
> (vii) 35,
>
> (viii) $\dfrac{\text{Product of numerators}}{\text{Product of denominators}}$

   I. Reciprocal of a proper fraction is a/an...... fraction.

   II. $\frac{7}{5}$ of 65 is ....

   III. Product of two fractions = ...

   IV. If 5 is added to numerator and 7 is added to denominator, then the fraction is ....

   Codes

	I	II	III	IV			I	II	III	IV
a	v	iii	viii	ii		b	i	iii	iv	ii
c	v	vii	viii	vi		d	i	vii	iv	vi

25. 6 yr ago, Gopal was $\frac{1}{7}$ of his father's age. If his father is 48 yr old now, then find Gopal's age 6 yr ago.

a 10 yr

b 8 yr

c 7 yr

d 6 yr

26. Mr. Ben spent $\frac{1}{6}$ of his income on food and $\frac{2}{5}$ of the remainder on transport. How much did he spent on food and transport altogether?

a $\frac{1}{5}$

b $\frac{2}{5}$

c $\frac{1}{6}$

d $\frac{1}{2}$

Directions (Q. Nos. 27-28) A three year old is seen in the pediatrician's office with fever, loose cough and wheezing. A diagnosis of bronchitis is made and following orders were prescribed for home use.

- Amoxicillin 250 mg for every 6 h.
- Tylenol 300 mg for every 4 h.
- The on-sight pharmacy supplied the following medications.
- Amoxicillin syrup 125 mg or 5 mL.
- Tylenol syrup 100 mg or 2 mL.

27. Determine the number of dosage the child need to take at once of amoxicillin syrup?

a 2

b 4

c 3

d 1

28. How many mL of tylenol syrup does the child need to take every 4 h?

    a 4 mL   b 6 mL   c 4.5 mL   d 7 mL

29. Choose the correct sign. $\dfrac{2\frac{1}{2}+\frac{1}{5}}{2\frac{1}{2}\div 5}\;\square\;\dfrac{\frac{1}{4}+\frac{1}{5}}{1-\frac{3}{8}\times\frac{3}{5}}$

    a >   b <   c =   d Can't say

Directions (Q. Nos. 30-32) In a school, 200 students participated in different sports for the sports day meet. Following is the pie chart given depicting the number of students in each sport.

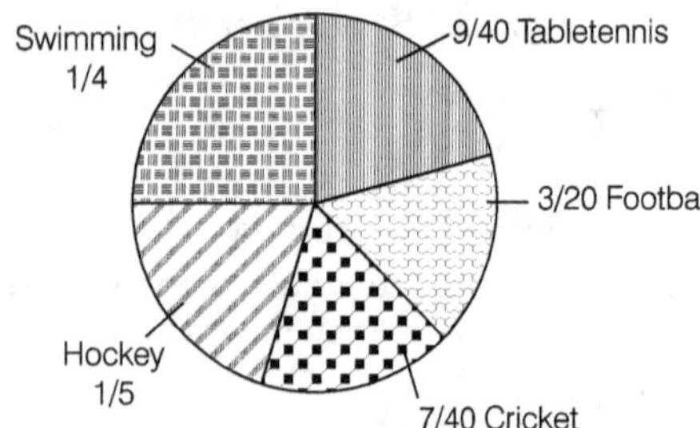

30. How many students participated in hockey?

    a 35   b 40   c 30   d 20

31. How many more students participated in swimming than in cricket?

    a 10   b 15   c 5   d 20

32. If $\frac{1}{3}$rd of the students participating in football shifts to participate in hockey, then what will be the new fraction to represent hockey?

    a $\dfrac{2}{3}$ b $\dfrac{3}{4}$ c $\dfrac{1}{4}$ d $\dfrac{1}{3}$

33. State 'T' for true and 'F' for false.

  I. A fraction acts as operator 'of '.

  II. Product of a proper and improper fraction is greater than the improper fraction.

  III. $2\frac{2}{5}\div 2\frac{1}{5}=2$.

  IV. The reciprocal of $\frac{7}{8}$ is $\frac{-7}{8}$.

  V. A mixed fraction is converted to a proper fraction.

Codes

	I	II	III	IV	V			I	II	III	IV	V
a	T	F	F	F	F		b	T	T	T	T	T
c	F	F	F	F	T		d	F	F	F	F	F

34. Evaluate the value of a in the following.

$$\cfrac{1}{1+\cfrac{1}{2+\cfrac{1}{a+\frac{1}{2}}}}=\frac{16}{23}$$

    a 2   b 3

    c 4   d 1

35. Mihir was asked to solve the fraction $\dfrac{\frac{5}{3}+1\frac{1}{2}\text{ of }\frac{7}{3}}{2+2\frac{2}{3}}$ and his answer was $\frac{1}{7}$. By how much times was his answer wrong?

    a $\dfrac{7}{10}$ b $\dfrac{29}{3}$

    c $\dfrac{31}{4}$ d None of these

B Decimals

1. The decimal expression 0.321 can be expressed as

    a $\dfrac{107}{999}$ b $\dfrac{329}{900}$ c $\dfrac{321}{1000}$ d $\dfrac{329}{1000}$

2. The quotient when 0.00441 is divided by 0.21 is

    a 0.21   b 0.0021   c 0.021   d 2.1

3. Which of the following arrangements is correct?

    a 0.723 < 0.462 < 0.572 < 0.213
    b 0.512 < 0.758 < 0.831 < 0.913
    c 0.713 < 0.721 < 0.658 < 0.412
    d 0.412 < 0.712 < 0.799 < 0.099

4. Match the following.

	Column A		Column B
I.	2 ÷ 0.5	(i)	20
II.	5 ÷ 0.25	(ii)	0.25
III.	0.75 ÷ 3	(iii)	0.1
IV.	0.5 ÷ 5	(iv)	4

Codes

	I	II	III	IV
a	ii	iii	iv	i
b	iv	i	iii	ii
c	i	iv	ii	iii
d	iv	i	ii	iii

5. The value of $14.63 - \dfrac{1}{6} \times 0.6$ is

   a 14.52   b 14.63
   c 14.62   d 14.53

6. If 0.645×10 has same value as $6450 \div \square$, then the missing value in the box is

   a 100   b 1000   c 10000   d 10

7. If $73.47 \times 100 = 92 \times 73.47 + 8 \times \square$, then what will be the missing number in the box?

   a 100   b 734.7
   c 73.47   d 7.347

8. Fill in the blanks.

	Column A		Column B
I.	0.007×700	(i)	$\square$
II.	0.009×3000	(ii)	$\square$
III.	$213.163 \times \square$	(iii)	21316.3
IV.	$\square \times 1000$	(iv)	17034

   a 49, 2.7, 100, 17.034   b 4.9, 2.7, 1000, 170.34
   c 49, 27, 100, 170.34   d 4.9, 27, 100, 17.034

9. The perimeter of a regular octagon is 33.6 cm. What is the length of each of its sides?

   a 4.7 cm   b 4.2 cm
   c 3.2 cm   d 3.7 cm

10. Choose the correct statement.

   a To multiply a decimal by 10, we move the decimal point in the number to the left by one place.
   b To multiply a decimal by 100, we move the decimal point in the number to the right by two places.
   c Both (a) and (b)
   d None of the above

11. To find the distance around a circular shape, multiply the diameter of the disc by 3.14. Then, what will be the distance covered by Sonakshi, if she runs around a circular park of radius 1.5 km?

   a 4.71 km   b 6.20 km
   c 9.42 km   d 10.12 km

12. On a map with a scale of 1 inch = 11 miles, the distance between two towns is 4.5 inch. What is the actual distance between the two towns?

   a 49.5 miles   b 45.5 miles
   c 45 miles   d 40.5 miles

13. On Tuesday, Marshall put 12 L of fuel in his car for ₹ 616.8. The following Friday, he put 15 gallons in and paid ₹ 817.5. On which day, he gets the better price?

   a Tuesday
   b Friday
   c Same on Tuesday and Friday
   d Can't say

14. The singing band is raising funds by selling chocolate bars for ₹ 1.00 each. The band can buy boxes A of 40 candy bars for ₹ 23.20 or boxes B of 250 for ₹ 152.50. Which of candy bars will given them a larger profit?

   a A
   b B
   c Both A and B
   d None of the above

15. In a Mathematics class, a teacher asked Aman, Navnidh and Jaskaran to determine the decimal by giving the following clues.

Clue 1 : between $\dfrac{2}{5}$ and $\dfrac{3}{5}$

Clue 2 : greater than $\dfrac{1}{2}$

Clue 3 : multiple of 0.11

Determine who gave the correct answer.

   a Aman $\rightarrow$ 0.55   b Navnidh $\rightarrow$ 0.66
   c Jaskaran $\rightarrow$ 0.45   d None of these

Directions (Q. Nos.16-17) One measure of average global temperature shows how each city varies from a base measure. The table shows results for different places.

City	London	Southhall	Bristol	Liverpool	Manchester
Difference from base	0.20°C	−0.27°C	−0.20°C	$\left(\dfrac{1}{20}\right)^{\circ}C$	0.74°C

16. What is the correct order of places from coldest to warmest?

   a Southhall, Bristol, Liverpool, Manchester, London
   b Southhall, Bristol, London, Liverpool, Manchester
   c Manchester, Liverpool, London, Bristol, Southhall
   d Manchester, Bristol, Southhall, London, Liverpool

17. If the city Newry, has the average temperature varied by -0.06°C from the base measure. Between which two places should Newry fall when the places ordered from warmest to coldest?

   a Southhall and Liverpool
   b Bristol and London
   c London and Manchester
   d Southhall and Manchester

18. Fill in the blanks with the help of options, given in the box.

(i) 10,	(ii) 100,
(iii) multiplying,	(iv) 16.92,
(v) 0.07,	(vi) Dividing,
(vii) 0.25,	(viii) 172.4

   I. $64.008 \times \square = 6400.8$
   II. .... by 10 shifts the decimal place to left side.
   III. $16.92 \times 100 = 16.92 \times 93 + \square \times 7$
   IV. $(0.4) \times (0.4) - (0.3) \times (0.3)$ is ....

Codes

	I	II	III	IV			I	II	III	IV
a	ii	iii	v	viii		b	i	iii	iv	vi
c	ii	vi	iv	v		d	i	vii	v	viii

19. State 'T' for true and 'F' for false.

   I. To multiply a number by 1000, we move the decimal point to the right by one place.
   II. $4.7 \div 10 = 47$
   III. $4.06 \times 100 = 406$
   IV. If cost of 5 apples is ₹ 2.15, then 40 apples can be bought for ₹ 20.

Codes

	I	II	III	IV			I	II	III	IV
a	F	F	F	F		b	T	T	T	T
c	F	F	T	F		d	T	F	F	T

 Directions (Q. Nos. 20-22) Barack and Ben go shopping to a mall. They each planning on buying one pair of jeans and 2 shirts. They each brought ₹ 1000.

Store A	Store B	Store C
Jeans A ₹ 399.7	Jeans B ₹ 449.9	Jeans C ₹ 499.5
2 shirts A ₹ 444.8	1 shirt B ₹ 224.8	1 shirt C ₹ 204.6

20. At which store should Barack and Ben shop to spend the least amount of money?

   a A   b B
   c C   d Can't say

21. Ben really likes the jeans from store C, a shirt from store A and another shirt from store B. Does he has enough money to buy these clothes? If so, how much money would he get back?

   a No
   b Yes, ₹ 50.32
   c Yes, ₹ 53.3
   d Can't say

22. Ben decides that he really wants to get 2 pairs of jeans and 1 shirt. Is it possible for him to do this, if he shops at different stores? If so, how much more money is required?

   a Yes
   b No, ₹ 4
   c No, ₹ 50
   d Can't say

Chapter 4

Simple Equations

1. If there are m number of boys and n number of girls in a class, then how many students are there in the class?

   a $m+n$ b $m-n$ c $m \div n$ d $m \times n$

2. Pick the odd one out.

   a $3m+2=14$ b $m+7=2m+3$ c $\dfrac{m}{2}+1=3$ d $5m+7=2$

3. Choose the correct statement which justifies the following equation.

   $$\frac{x}{3}=x-10$$

   a One-third of a number is ten more than the number itself.
   b One-third of a number is ten less than the number itself.
   c Difference between one-third of a number and the number itself is less than 10.
   d All the statements are correct.

4. Match the following.

	Column A		Column B
I.	Twice a number is three less than thrice of it.	(i)	$x=12$
II.	Three subtracted from two-third of a number is 5.	(ii)	$x=9$
III.	Eight times a number subtracted from 72 is zero.	(iii)	$x=3$

   Codes

	I	II	III			I	II	III			I	II	III			I	II	III
a	i	ii	iii		b	i	iii	ii		c	ii	i	iii		d	iii	i	ii

5. Nine exceeds two-third of a number by 10, is represented by

   a 2   b 3   c –2   d None of these

6. If 30% of 70% of a number is 63, then the number is

   a 400   b 700   c 210   d None of these

7. Pick the odd one out.

   a $9x-5x-19=21,\ x=10$ b $\dfrac{1}{2}x-7=-4,\ x=6$ c $\dfrac{x}{4}-6=3,\ x=24$ d $\dfrac{3}{4}x-1=8,\ x=12$

8. The equation which can be solved in integers is

   a $5y+3=12$ b $\dfrac{4}{5}x-2=2$ c $7x+4=x+8$ d None of these

9. The average of 5 numbers is 43. What is the correct expression for the new average when two numbers y and $3y$ are added to it?

   a $\dfrac{215+4y}{7}$ b $\dfrac{215}{7}$ c $\dfrac{215+3y}{7}$ d None of these

10. If $4 * a \, \Delta 10 \, \square 2$ defines an equation, then which of the following sequences of operation will satisfy the above giving an integer value?

   a $\times, -, =$ b $-, \times, =$ c $\times, =, \div$ d $+, \times, =$

11. In any triangle, the sum of the measures of the angles is $180°$. In ΔABC, if $\angle A$ is three times as large as $\angle B$. $\angle C$ measures $20°$ less than $\angle B$. Then, the measure of angle $\angle B$ is

   a $30°$ b $40°$ c $50°$ d $60°$

12. The ratio between two numbers is $3 : 5$. If each number is increased by 4, the ratio becomes $2 : 3$, then the numbers are

   a 12 and 20   b 18 and 30
   c 24 and 40   d 15 and 25

13. A number of apples are distributed among A, B and C in the ratio $5 : 7 : 8$, respectively. If A gets 45 apples, then total number of apples are

   a 180   b 300
   c 200   d None of these

14. The selling price of a certain TV is ₹ 1700 more than the price the store paid. If the selling price is ₹ 24000, then price the store paid, is

   a ₹ 22500 b ₹ 21300 c ₹ 25700 d ₹ 22300

✎ **Directions** (Q. Nos.15-16) Your TV cable operator charges ₹ 4.95 per month for the first 3 h, plus ₹ 2.50 for each additional hour. Your total charges last month were ₹ 21.83. Let x represents the number of hours you used the service.

15. Which equation models the situation?

   a $4.95x + 2.5x - 3 = 21.83$
   b $4.95 + 2.5x - 3 = 21.83$
   c $4.95 + 2.5(x - 3) = 21.83$
   d None of the above

16. Solving the correct equation in Q.No.15. What will be the value of x?

   a 8   b 10
   c 11   d 12

✎ **Directions** (Q. Nos.17-18) Cup A has t mL of milk, cup B has 40 mL less milk than cup A and cup C has twice as much milk as cup B and cup D has thrice as much milk as cup A. Milk from the 4 cups was poured into an empty container.

17. How much milk was in the container?

   a $7t - 120$ b $7t + 120$
   c $9t + 120$ d $9t - 120$

18. If $t = 40$, then what is the exact volume of milk in the container?

   a 80 mL   b 100 mL c 120 mL d 160 mL

19. Fill in the blanks with the help of options, given in the box.

(i) commutativity,	(ii) 4,
(iii) root,	(iv) Transposition,
(v) $x + 1$,	(vi) solution,
(vii) 5,	(viii) $2x + 3 = 1$

  I. .... is the method of shifting one term from one side of an equation to another side with a change of sign.

  II. .... is the solution of $4x + 2 = 18$.

  III. The value of the variable for which the equation is satisfied is called .... of the equation.

  IV. -1 is the solution of ....

Codes

	I	II	III	IV		I	II	III	IV
a	iv	ii	iii	v	b	i	vii	vi	viii
c	iv	ii	vi	viii	d	Both (a) and (c)			

20. Choose the incorrect statement.

   a Adding the same number from both sides of the equation doesn't change the equation.
   b Subtracting the same number from both sides of the equation doesn't change the equation.
   c Multiplying both sides of the equation by the same non-zero number is not allowed.
   d None of the above

21. Mrs. John bought some boxes of chocolates at ₹ 150 per box. She gave the cashier ₹ x and received ₹ 50 in change. The number of boxes of chocolates Mrs. John bought in terms of x is

   a $\dfrac{x + 50}{150}$ b $1.50x + 50$

   c $\dfrac{x - 50}{150}$ d $50x - 150$

22. To solve $7x + 3 + 9x - 5 = 18x - 3$ following steps are involved:

Step I $16x + 3 - 5 = 18x - 3$

Step II $16x - 2 = 18x - 3$

Step III $16x - 2 + 2 = 18x - 3 + 2$

Step IV $16x = 18x - 1$

Step V $\dfrac{16x}{16} = \dfrac{18x - 1}{16}$

Step VI $x = \dfrac{1}{2}$

Which of the step(s) is/are wrong?

  a Step III   b Step IV
  c Step V   d All are correct.

23. State 'T' for true and 'F' for false.

   I. If $5x - 6 = 8x - 4$, then $x = -\dfrac{2}{3}$.

  II. One-fifth of a number is 5 more than one-tenth of the number, then the number is -10.

 III. An equation remains the same, if the LHS and RHS are interchanged.

 IV. Any term of an equation may be transposed from one side of the equation to the other side of the equation by changing the sign of the term.

Codes

	I	II	III	IV			I	II	III	IV
a	T	T	F	F		b	T	F	F	T
c	T	F	T	F		d	T	F	T	T

24. If the following sets of equations define the position of letters, then determine the word so formed.

$$1\ 2\ 3\ 4\ 5\ 6\ 7\ 8\ 9$$

  I. $\dfrac{4}{3}I + 2 = 10$ II. $2E + 9 = 11$

 III. $\dfrac{3}{4}N = 3N - 18$ IV. $7U + 9 = 30$

  V. $\dfrac{5}{2}Q + 2 = 7$ VI. $2A + 14 = 22$

 VII. $10 + T - \dfrac{3T}{5} = 12$ VIII. $\dfrac{7}{9}S + 4 = 11$

 IX. $O + 42 = 49$

  a *ADDITION*   b *EQUATIONS*
  c *QUOTIENTS*   d None of these

25. In a Science quiz, 40 prizes consisting of 1st and 2nd prizes, only are to be given. 1st and 2nd prizes are worth ₹ 3000 and ₹ 2000, respectively. If the total prize money is ₹ 90000, then match the following.

	Column A		Column B
I.	If 1st prize are x in numbers. Then, the numbers of 2nd prize are	(i)	$3000x + 2000(40 - x)$
II.	The total value of prizes in terms of x is	(ii)	$1000x + 80000 = 90000$
III.	The equation formed is	(iii)	$40 - x$

Codes

	I	II	III			I	II	III
a	iii	ii	i		b	i	ii	iii
c	iii	i	ii		d	ii	iii	i

26. There are some toys to be distributed to a group of children. Let one toy will be given to one child, then one child will be left. If two children will be given a toy to share, then one toy will be left extra, then the numbers of toys and children are, respectively

  a 3 and 4   b 4 and 3
  c 2 and 3   d 3 and 2

27. The amount including the compound interest for a certain sum of money P at an interest r for t years is given by $A = P\left(1 + \dfrac{r}{100}\right)^{n}$, solve for r and write the correct equation when $n = 1$.

  a $\left(\dfrac{A}{P} - 1\right) = r$ b $\left(\dfrac{A}{P} + 1\right)100 = r$

  c $\left(\dfrac{A}{P} - 1\right)100 = r$ d None of these

28. The formula, $h = \dfrac{2A}{b_1 + b_2}$ relates the dimensions of a trapezoid. Which way can you rewrite this relationship?

  a $A = \dfrac{1}{2}hb_1 + b_2$ b $A = \dfrac{1}{2}h(b_1 + b_2)$

  c $h = \dfrac{A}{b_1 + b_2}$ d $b_1 = 2A - b_2h$

29. Which of the following is/are not solved correctly?

  a $2(x - 3) = 5$
      $2x - 3 = 5$
        $2x = 8$
          $x = 4$
  b $5 - 3x = 10$
        $2x = 10$
          $x = 5$
  c $\dfrac{1}{4}x - 2 = 7$
      $x - 2 = 28$
        $x = 30$
  d All of the above

30. The temperature within Earth's crust increases about 30°C for each kilometre of depth beneath the surface. If the temperature at Earth's surface is 20°C, at what depth would you expect the temperature to be 110°C? Write the correct equation to solve the above.

  a $110°C = 20°C + 30°C\,d$, $d = 3$
  b $110°C = 20°Cd + 30°$, $d = 4$
  c Both (a) and (b)
  d None of the above

Chapter 5

Lines and Angles

1. For two parallel lines intersected by a straight line, which of the following statements is not true?

   a Corresponding angles are equal.
   b Alternate angles are equal.
   c Sum of interior angles is 180°.
   d Sum of interior angles is 90°.

2. Pick the odd one out.

   a 30°, 60°
   b 40°, 50°
   c 55°, 35°
   d 60°, 60°

3. The fixed end point of $\overleftrightarrow{PQ}$ is

   a point P
   b point Q
   c Both P and Q
   d None of these

4. Match the following.

	Column A		Column B
I.	P•————————•Q	(i)	$\overrightarrow{PQ}$
II.	P•————————→Q	(ii)	$\overleftrightarrow{PQ}$
III.	P←————————→Q	(iii)	$\overline{PQ}$

   Codes

	I	II	III
a	iii	i	ii
b	i	ii	iii
c	ii	iii	i
d	i	iii	ii

5. Choose the correct statement.

   a Sum of the measure of two complementary angles is 180°.
   b Sum of the measure of two supplementary angles is 90°.
   c Sum of linear pair is 360°.
   d None of the above.

6. Write the pair of parallel lines in the given figure.

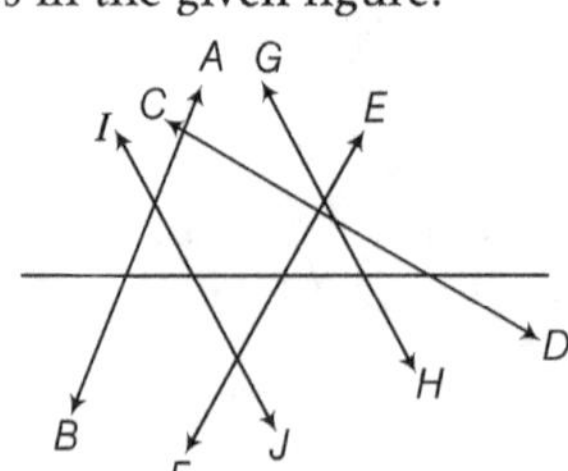

   a AB and GH
   b IJ and CD
   c AB and EF
   d IJ and GH

7. At 6 O'clock, the angle formed between the two hands of a clock is

   a right
   b straight
   c obtuse
   d acute

8. What is the value of *S* in the given figure?

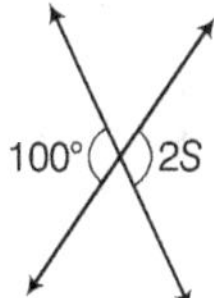

   a 100°   b 80°   c 50°   d 30°

9. In the given figure, if *PQ* and *RS* are parallel lines. Then, the value of $\angle x$ is

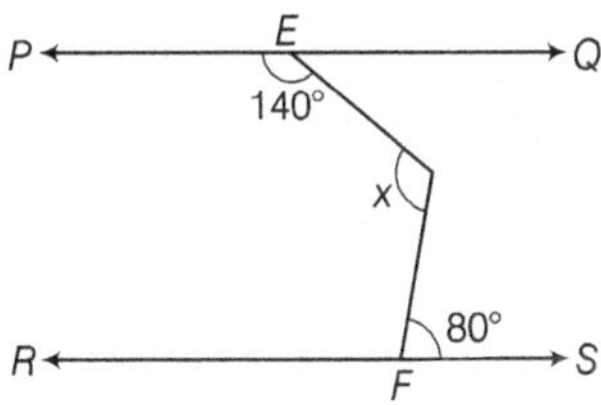

   a 120°
   b 140°
   c 160°
   d None of these

10. A line *CD* is parallel to line *EF*. This is symbolically written as

   a $\overleftrightarrow{CD} = \overleftrightarrow{EF}$
   b $\overleftrightarrow{CD} \perp \overleftrightarrow{EF}$
   c $\overleftrightarrow{CD} \parallel \overleftrightarrow{EF}$
   d $\overleftrightarrow{CD} \neq \overleftrightarrow{EF}$

11. In the given figure, find the value of $\angle y$.

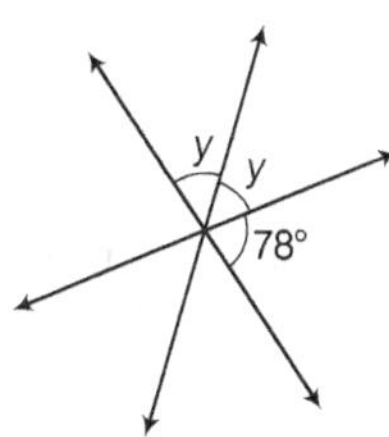

   a 102°   b 78°   c 51°   d 144°

12. Which of the following statements is true?

   a A ray has a definite length.
   b A line has a definite length.
   c A line segment has a definite length.
   d None of the above.

13. If two parallel lines are cut by a transversal, then the number of pairs of corresponding angles formed is

   a 12
   b 8
   c 2
   d 4

14. **Assertion** (A) In the given figure, $\angle 1 = \angle 2$ and $\angle 5 = \angle 8$

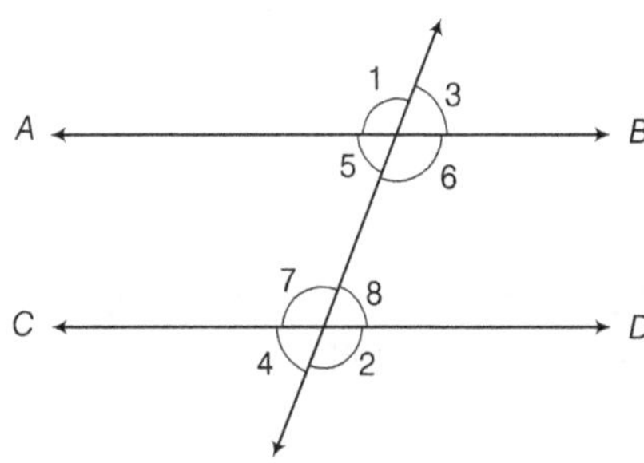

Reason (R) If two parallel lines are cut by a transversal, then each pair of corresponding angles are equal.

   a A and R are true and R is the correct explanation of A
   b A and R are true but R is not the correct explanation of A
   c A is true and R is false
   d Both A and R are false

15. What are the values of *x* and *y* in the given figure?

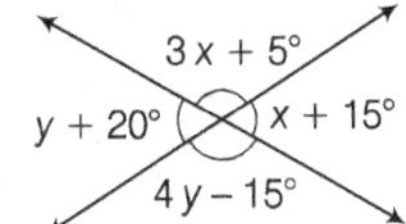

   a $x = 40°, y = 75°$
   b $x = 20°, y = 35°$
   c $x = 40°, y = 35°$
   d None of these

16. Match the following.

	Column A	Column B
I.		(i) 55°
II.		(ii) 90°
III.		(iii) 30°

Codes

	I	II	III		I	II	III
a	i	ii	iii	b	ii	iii	i
c	iii	i	ii	d	i	iii	ii

17.

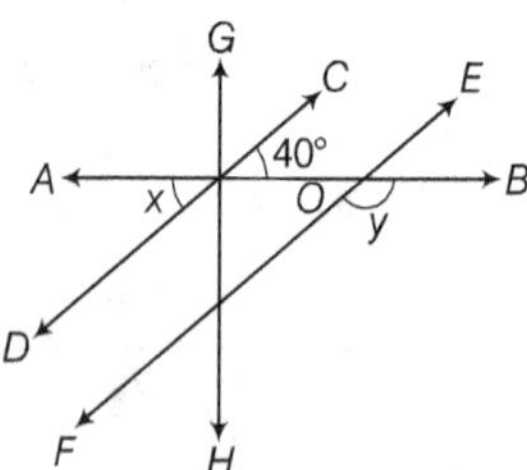

Which of the following options gives the correct values of *x* and *y*?

 a $x = 120°$, $y = 140°$
 b $x = 140°$, $y = 40°$
 c $x = 40°$, $y = 140°$
 d $x = 140°$, $y = 120°$

18. An angle exceeds 3 times its supplement by 40°. The measure of the angle is

 a 100°   b 125°
 c 145°   d 160°

19. In the given figure, if *RS* is parallel to *UT*. *CD* is a straight line, then find the value of $\angle RTC$.

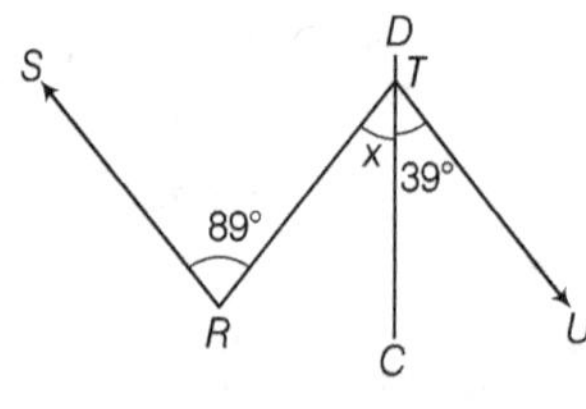

 a 89°   b 39°
 c 50°   d 49°

20. On the basis of given figure, which of the following is true?

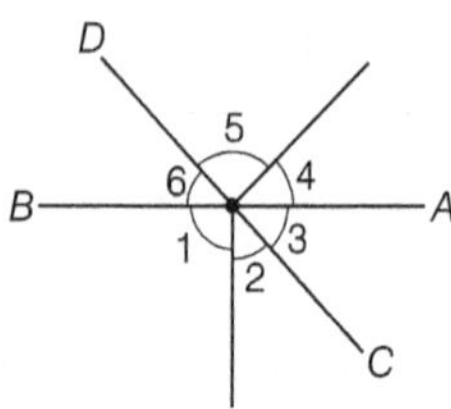

 a $\angle 4 = \angle 5$
 b $\angle 6 + \angle 5 = \angle 1 + \angle 2$
 c $\angle 5 + \angle 4 = \angle 1 + \angle 2$
 d $\angle 5 = \angle 2$

21. If two lines are perpendicular to the third line, then those lines are

 a perpendicular to each other
 b parallel to each other
 c Either (a) or (b)
 d Neither (a) nor (b)

22. The given figure shows the direction of Sun rays on Earth in the months of June and December. From the given figure, find the values of *x* and *y*.

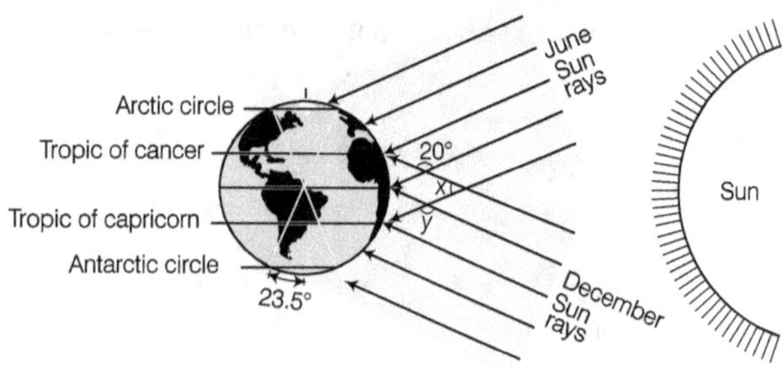

 a $x = 20°$, $y = 160°$
 b $x = 40°$, $y = 140°$
 c $x = 80°$, $y = 100°$
 d $x = 160°$, $y = 20°$

23. If an angle is its own supplementary angle, then its measure will be

 a 45°   b 90°
 c 100°   d 180°

24. Fill in the blanks with the help of options, given in the box.

(i) 79,	(ii) complementary,
(iii) alternate,	(iv) 99°,
(v) vertically opposite,	(vi) supplementary,
(vii) 100°,	(viii) 80°
(ix) parallel,	(x) intersecting,
(xi) transversal	

 I. Out of a pair of supplementary angles, one is four-fifth of the other. Then, the measure of smaller angle is ....

 II. The angle made by the direction North-East and East and South-West and West are .... angles.

 III. The angles $(x - 30°)$ and $(120° - x)$ are .... angles.

 IV. The angle which is a linear pair of 81° is ....

 V.

A ←————————→ B
C ←————————→ D

 Pair of .... lines is shown here.

 VI. If $\angle x = 79°$ and $\angle y = 101°$, then $\angle x$ and $\angle y$ are .... angles.

 VII. A line cutting two parallel lines making pairs of corresponding and alternate angles is called ....

25. In the given figure, *AOB* is a line. If $\angle a = 40°$, then measure of $\angle FOE$ is

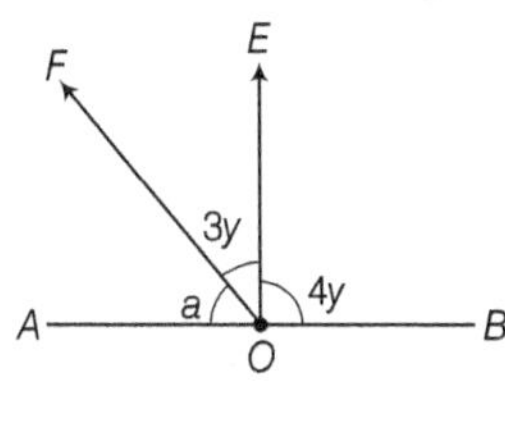

  a 60°   b 80°
  c 120°   d 160°

26. In the given figure, lines *XY* and *WZ* intersect at *O*. If $\angle XOV = 90°$ and $c : b = 7 : 3$, then the measure of $\angle a$ is

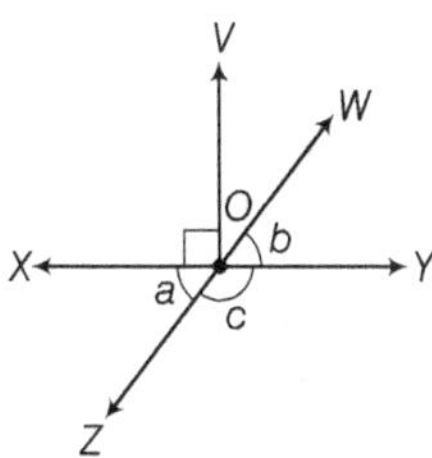

  a 46°
  b 54°
  c 64°
  d 66°

27. In pair of adjacent angles (i) vertex is not common (ii) one arm is always common and (iii) uncommon are always parallel rays, then
  a all (i), (ii) and (iii) are true.
  b only (ii) is true.
  c only (i) is true.
  d only (iii) is true.

28. In the given figure, if $AC \parallel OD$ and $AO \parallel EF$. Then, measure of angles *x* and *y* is

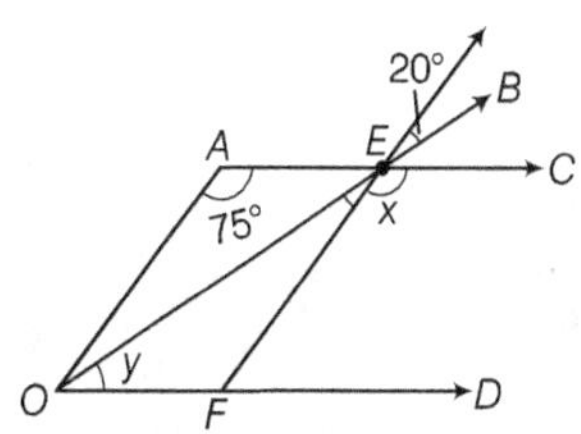

  a $x = 75°$, $y = 85°$ b $x = 95°$, $y = 85°$
  c $x = 75°$, $y = 85°$ d $x = 95°$, $y = 75°$

29. In the given figure, if $AB \parallel CD \parallel XY$ and $OC \parallel EB$, $\angle ABE = 46°$ and $\angle EDC = 33°$, then $\angle e$ and $\angle OCD$ are equal to

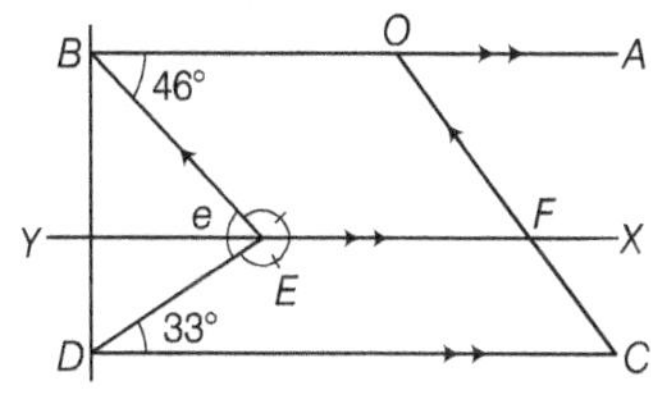

  a $\angle e = 79°$, $\angle OCD = 46°$
  b $\angle e = 101°$, $\angle OCD = 33°$
  c $\angle e = 89°$, $\angle OCD = 46°$
  d $\angle e = 99°$, $\angle OCD = 33°$

30. State 'T' for true and 'F' for false.
    I. If two parallel lines are intersected by a transversal, then each pair of interior angles on the same side of the transversal are complementary.
   II. A linear pair is a pair of adjacent angles whose non-common sides are opposite rays.
  III. The angles between North and East and North and West are supplementary.
  IV. If the transversal is perpendicular to the parallel lines, then all of the angles formed are congruent to 90° angles.

Codes

	I	II	III	IV			I	II	III	IV
a	F	T	T	T		b	T	T	T	T
c	F	F	T	T		d	F	F	F	F

Triangle : Properties and Congruence

 **A** **Triangle and Its Properties**

1. Pick the odd one out.
   a Median
   c Angle bisector
   b Altitude
   d Orthocentre

2. The total measure of three angles of a triangle is
   a $90°$
   c $360°$
   b $180°$
   d None of these

3. An equilateral triangle always has
   a exactly one acute angle
   c exactly one obtuse angle
   b exactly two acute angles
   d None of these

4. If one angle of a triangle is $90°$, then sum of the other two angles is
   a complementary
   c supplementary
   b obtuse
   d None of these

5. Choose the correct statement.
   a A median connects a vertex of a triangle to the mid-point of the opposite side.
   b An altitude has one end point at a vertex of the triangle and other on the line containing the opposite side.
   c Exterior angle is equal to the sum of interior opposite angles.
   d All of the above

6. If ΔABC is an isosceles triangle with $AB = AC$, DAB and EAC are straight lines, then what is the value of x?

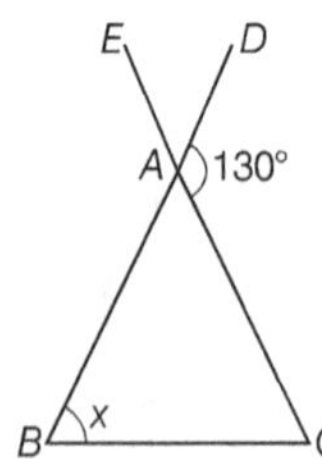

   a $130°$
   c $65°$
   b $70°$
   d Can't be determined

7. Match the following.

Column A		Column B	
I.	$AB = 6\,cm$, $BC = 7\,cm$, $AC = 6.5\,cm$	(i)	Equilateral triangle
II.	$AC = 13\,cm$, $BC = 12\,cm$, $AB = 5\,cm$	(ii)	Isosceles triangle
III.	$AB = 10\,cm$, $BC = 12\,cm$, $AC = 10\,cm$	(iii)	Scalene triangle
IV.	$AB = 2.5\,cm$, $BC = 2.5\,cm$, $AC = 2.5\,cm$	(iv)	Right angled triangle

Codes

	I	II	III	IV
a	iii	iv	ii	i
b	i	ii	iv	iii
c	ii	iii	i	iv
d	iv	i	iii	ii

8. $\angle a$ and $\angle b$ are exterior angles of a ΔPQR, at the points Q and R, respectively. Also $\angle Q > \angle R$, then relation between $\angle a$ and $\angle b$ is

  a $\angle a > \angle b$
  b $\angle a < \angle b$
  c $\angle a = \angle b$
  d None of the above

9. In an isosceles triangle PQR, if $PQ = PR$ and $\angle P = 3\angle Q$, then $\angle R$ is equal to

  a 36°　　　　　b 32°
  c 28°　　　　　d 40°

10. In the given figure, not drawn to scale, $PQ = PR$ and $\angle PRS = 136°$. What is the value of x?

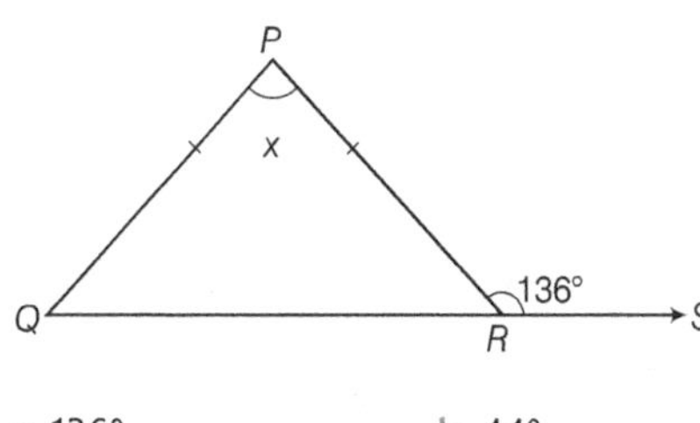

  a 136°　　　　　b 44°
  c 72°　　　　　d 92°

11. In a ΔPQR, if $2\angle P = \angle Q + \angle R$, then $\angle P$ is equal to

  a 30°
  b 60°
  c 90°
  d 120°

12. The three angles of a triangle are in the ratio 1:2:1. What is the measure of the greatest angle?

  a 45°　　　　　b 60°
  c 90°　　　　　d 120°

13. If two sides of an isosceles triangle are 2 cm and 7 cm, then the length of third side is

  a 2 cm　　　　　b 7 cm
  c 2 cm or 7 cm　　　　　d None of these

14. If the sides of a triangle are produced in an order, then the sum of the exterior angles so formed is equal to

  a 90°　　　　　b 180°
  c 360°　　　　　d None of these

15. If the angles of a triangle are in the ratio $2 : 3 : 5$, then the triangle is

  a acute angled
  b obtuse angled
  c right angled
  d right angled isosceles

16. In the given figure, find the value of $\angle ABC$.

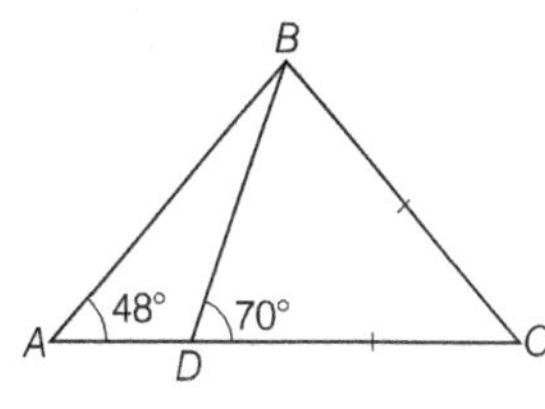

  a 92°　　　　　b 70°
  c 118°　　　　　d 42°

17. From the given figure, find the values of $\angle a$, $\angle b$ and $\angle c$.

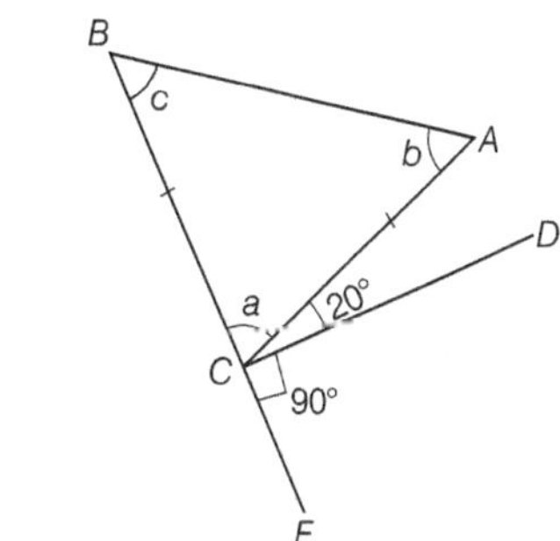

  a $a = 55°$, $b = 70°$, $c = 70°$
  b $a = 55°$, $b = 70°$, $c = 55°$
  c $a = 70°$, $b = 55°$, $c = 55°$
  d $a = 70°$, $b = 55°$, $c = 70°$

18. Fill in the blanks with the help of options, given in the box.

(i) <,	(ii) circumcentre,
(iii) centroid,	(iv) altitudes,
(v) medians,	(vi) >,
(vii) perimeter,	(viii) hypotenuse,
(ix) AB,	(x) AC,
(xi) obtuse,	(xii) acute,
(xiii) one,	(xiv) equilateral

    I. If a, b and c are the sides of a triangle, then $a + b$......c.

    II. The point equidistant from the vertices of a triangle is called...... .

    III. The centroid of a triangle is the point of concurrence of its....... .

    IV. In a right triangle, the circumradius is half the....... .

    V. In a $\triangle ABC$, if $\angle B$ is an obtuse angle, then the longest side is....... .

    VI. The angles in a right angled triangle other than the right angle are....... .

    VII. The incentre of a triangle coincides with the circumcentre, orthocentre and centroid in case of ......triangle.

VIII. A triangle can have......obtuse angle/s.

Codes

	I	II	III	IV	V	VI	VII	VIII
a	i	ii	v	vii	x	xiii	xii	xiv
b	vi	ii	v	viii	x	xii	xiv	xiii
c	vi	iii	iv	vii	ix	xiv	xiii	xi
d	i	iii	iv	viii	ix	xiv	xii	xiii

19. From the given figure, find the value of $\angle i$.

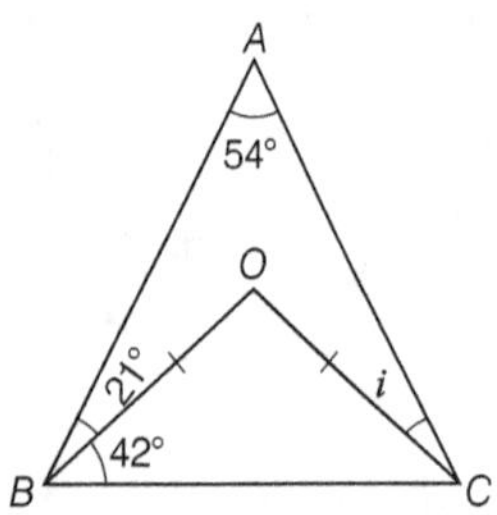

a 27°
b 23°
c 42°
d 21°

20. In the given figure,
$\angle a + \angle b + \angle c + \angle d + \angle e = \square$ right angles. What is $\square$ in box?

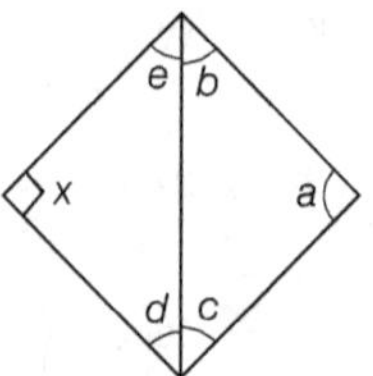

a 2   b 3
c 4   d None of these

21. A pole is made to stand with the help of the rope tied in a way shown in the figure. If the height of the pole is 15 units and length of the rope is 17 units, then what is distance between the foot of the pole and the point, where rope is tied to the ground?

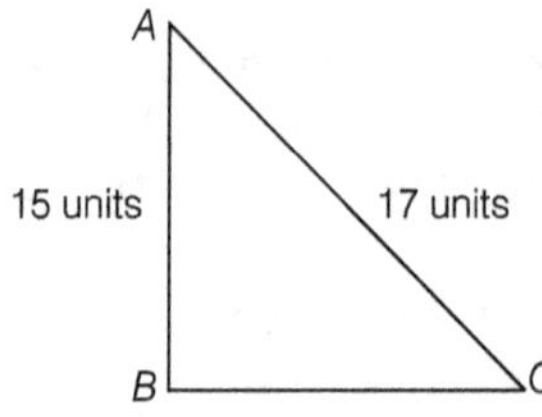

a 14 units
b 12 units
c 10 units
d 8 units

22. If thrice of each of the two angles of an isosceles triangle is 4 times the third angle, then what is the measure of the angles?
a 54°, 54°, 72°
b 36°, 36°, 48°
c 40°, 40°, 100°
d None of the above

23. Find the value of $\angle a$ in the given figure.

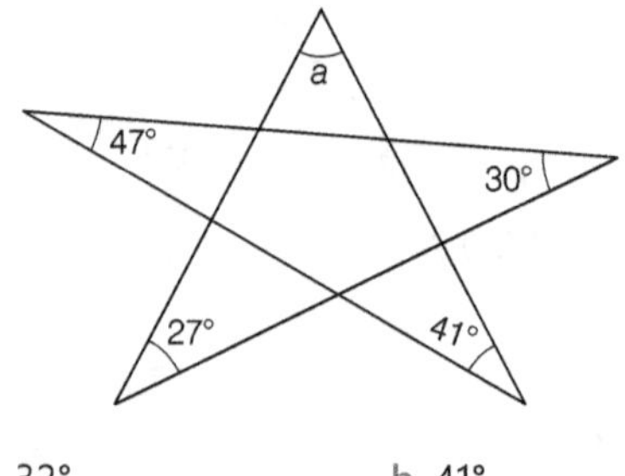

a 32°   b 41°
c 47°   d 35°

24. In a right angled triangle, other two angles are in the ratio 7 : 11, then the values of these angles are

   a 35° and 55°

   b 45° and 45°

   c 70° and 110°

   d 42° and 66°

25. In $\triangle ABC$, $\angle A = 40°$ and $\angle C = 70°$, bisectors of $\angle B$ and $\angle C$ meet at O. What is the value of $\angle BOC$?

   a 70°

   b 110°

   c 90°

   d 120°

26. Match the following.

	Column A		Column B
I.	Orthocentre	(i)	Point, where angle bisector meet
II.	Centroid	(ii)	Point, where altitude meet
III.	Circumcentre	(iii)	Point, where median meet
IV.	Incentre	(iv)	Point, where perpendicular bisector meet

Codes

	I	II	III	IV		I	II	III	IV
a	ii	iii	iv	i	b	iii	ii	i	iv
c	i	ii	iii	iv	d	iv	iii	ii	i

27. In the given figure, $AY = CY = BY$ and $XA = XB$. What are the values of $\angle CYA$ and $\angle CBX$?

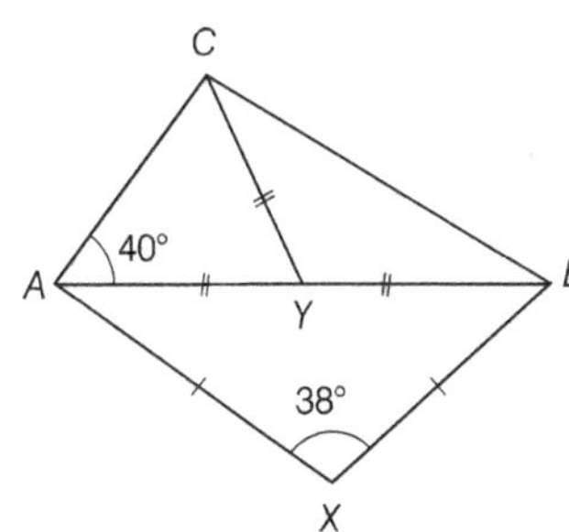

   a 109° and 100°   b 120° and 139°

   c 100° and 121°   d None of these

28. The skycrapers show below are connected by a sky walk with support beams. Find the length of each support beam.

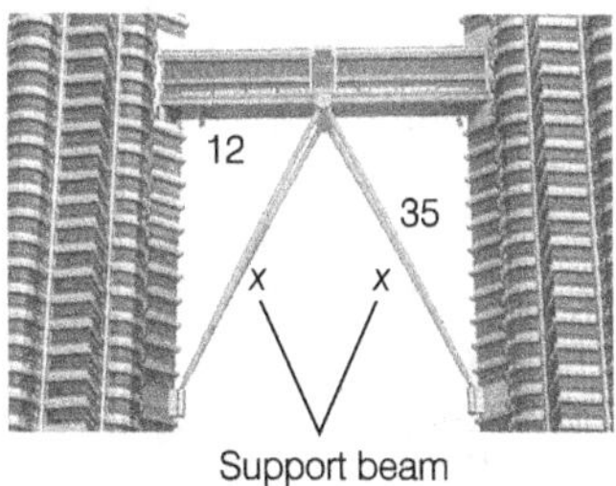

   a 40   b 39

   c 37   d 32

29. A beam of red light shines from point E reflects at point X and reaches point Y. $EX \perp ZY$. Find the value of x.

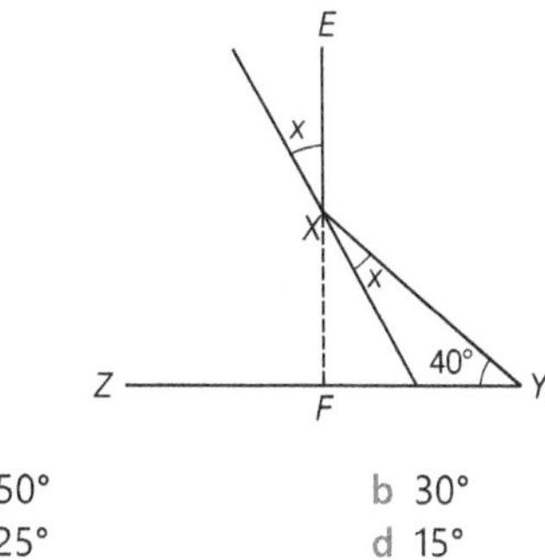

   a 50°   b 30°

   c 25°   d 15°

30. State 'T' for true and 'F' for false.

   I. In an equilateral triangle, only one angle is acute.

   II. In an right angled triangle, the side opposite to the right angle is called the hypotenuse.

   III. A triangle has infinite number of altitudes.

   IV. The orthocentre of an acute angled triangle lies in the interior of the triangle.

   V. The centroid of an acute angled triangle lies in the exterior of the triangle.

Codes

	I	II	III	IV	V
a	F	T	T	T	T
b	T	F	T	F	T
c	F	T	F	T	F
d	T	F	T	T	T

1. In $\triangle PQR$, if $PQ = PR$ and $PS \perp QR$, then by which of the following properties does $\triangle PQS \cong \triangle PRS$?
   - a SSS congruence rule
   - b RHS congruence rule
   - c SAS congruence rule
   - d ASA congruence rule

2. Pick the odd one out.

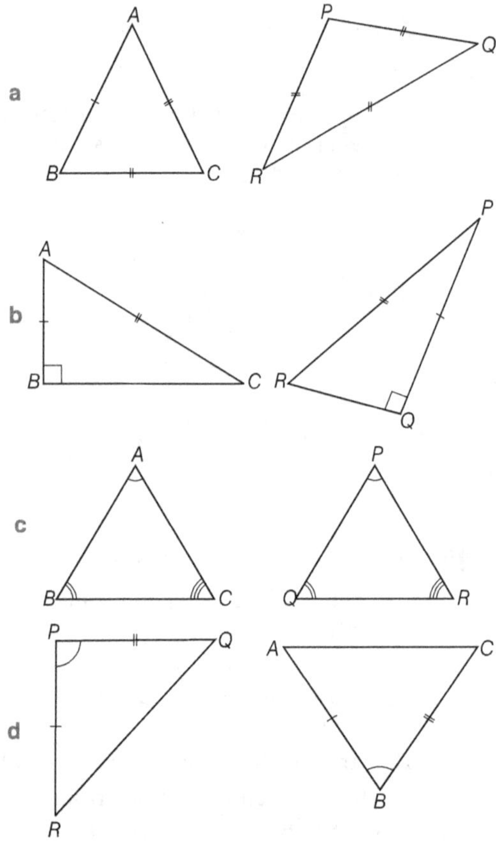

3. Choose the correct statement.
   - a All rectangles are congruent.
   - b All equilateral triangles are congruent.
   - c All right angled triangles are congruent.
   - d All of the above

4. Which of the following is not a criteria for congruency?
   - a ASA rule
   - b SAS rule
   - c SSS rule
   - d AAA rule

5. The following statements are based on congruence of triangles.

Choose the correct statement.
   - a If two triangls have their corresponding angles equal, then they are always congruent.
   - b If two triangles have their corresponding angles equal, then they are never congruent.
   - c If two triangles have their corresponding angles equal, then they can sometimes be congruent.
   - d None of the above

6. In $\triangle ABC$, $AB = AC$ and AD is a median. State by which property $\triangle ADB \cong \triangle ADC$?
   - a SAS property
   - b ASA property
   - c SSS property
   - d RHS property

7. In $\triangle PQR$ and $\triangle XYZ$, $PQ = XY$ and $QR = YZ$, where as $PR \neq XZ$. Which of the following conditions can make the two triangles congruent?
   - a $\angle P = \angle X$
   - b $\angle Q = \angle Y$
   - c $\angle R = \angle Z$
   - d None of the above

8. In $\triangle ABC$, $AB = 3$ cm, $BC = 4$ cm and $AC = 5$ cm and in $\triangle PQR$, $\angle Q = 90°$, hypotenuse and perpendicular are 5 cm and 3 cm, respectively. State whether the triangles are congruent. If yes, by which property are they congruent?
   - a No, they are not congruent.
   - b Yes, by SAS
   - c Yes, by RHS
   - d Can't be determined

9. If two triangles $\triangle ABC$ and $\triangle PQR$ are congruent to $\triangle XYZ$, then which of the following is true?
   - a $\triangle ABC \cong \triangle PQR$
   - b $\angle A = \angle P$
   - c $AB = PQ$
   - d All of these

10. In the given figure, $ABCD$ is a parallelogram, AC and BD are diagonals. What is the measure of $\angle OCD$?

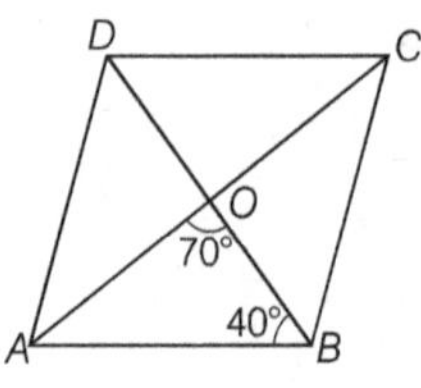

   - a 40°
   - b 70°
   - c 110°
   - d 50°

11. In the given figure, $RQ = RS$ and $\angle PRQ = \angle PRS$, then which of the following is true?

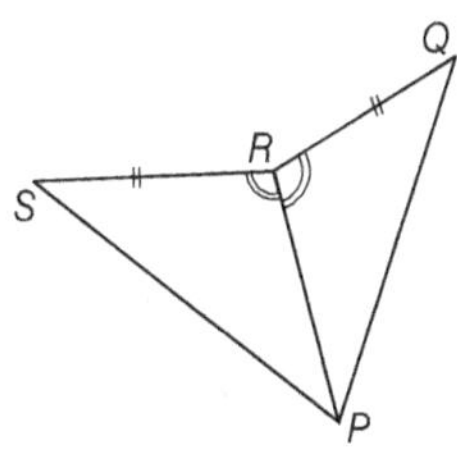

  a $PQ = PS$
  b $\triangle PRQ \cong \triangle PRS$
  c $\angle PSR = \angle PQR$
  d All of the above

12. Match the following.

Column A		Column B
I. 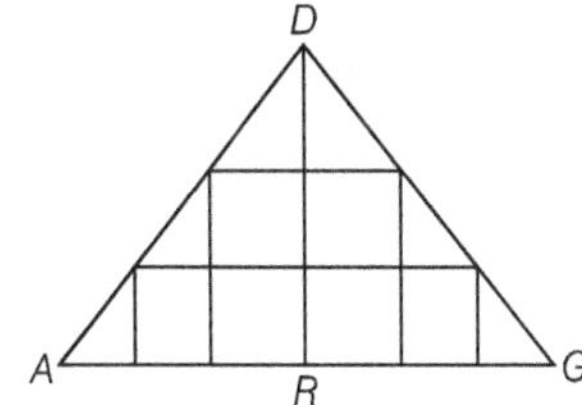	(i)	RHS rule
II.	(ii)	SAS rule
III.	(iii)	ASA rule
	(iv)	SSS rule

Codes

	I	II	III			I	II	III
a	iii	iv	i		b	i	iii	iv
c	iii	iv	ii		d	ii	i	iii

13. Amanat is designing the window shown in the photo. She wants to make $\triangle DRA$ congruent to $\triangle DRG$. She designs the window so that $DR \perp AG$. Which of the following conditions will make the two triangles congruent?

a $RA = RG$ b $DA = DG$
c Both (a) and (b)   d None of these

14. In the given figure, state whether the triangles are congruent and choose the correct order.

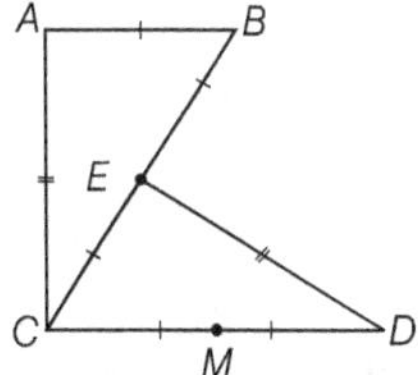

  a Yes, $\triangle ABC \cong \triangle DCE$
  b No, they are not congruent.
  c Yes, $\triangle DCE \cong \triangle CAB$
  d Yes, $\triangle DEC \cong \triangle CAB$

15. Two satellites are being launched such that their distance while moving in their respective orbits, are equal from Earth and Moon.

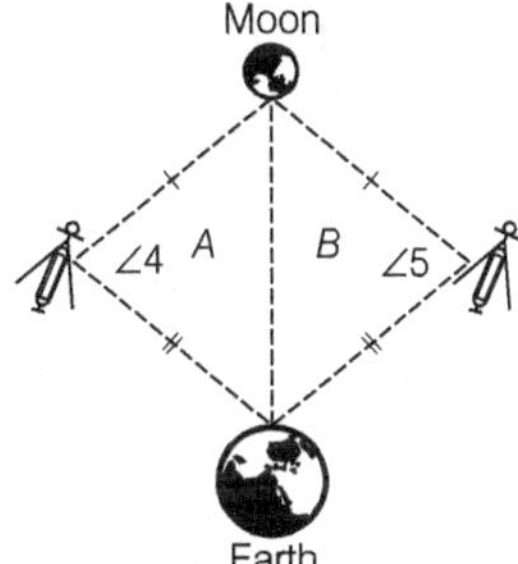

State which of the following statements is/are true.

  a Figure A is not congruent to figure B.
  b $\angle 4$ and $\angle 5$ are not congruent.
  c Both (a) and (b)
  d None of the above

16. Meera wants to know the width of the river given below. While doing so she stands on the edge of the river and look straight across to a point on the other edge without changing the inclination of the neck and head. She turns side ways until the vision is in line with a point on the side of the stream.

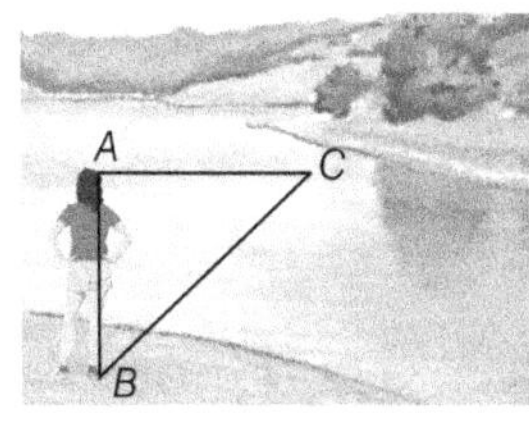

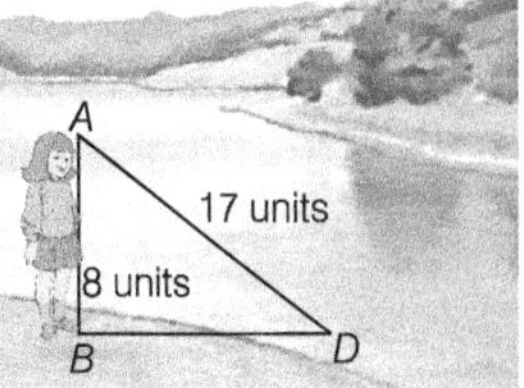

From the above description, find the value of *BC*.

a 25 units   b 12 units

c 15 units   d Can't be determined

17. Fill in the blanks with the help of options, given in the box.

(i) RHS,	(ii) SAS,
(iii) *XYZ*,	(iv) Corresponding,
(v) AAA,	(vi) opposite,
(vii) *ZXY*,	(viii) same,
(ix) congruent,	(x) four,
(xi) parts	

I. $\Delta ABC \cong$ ....

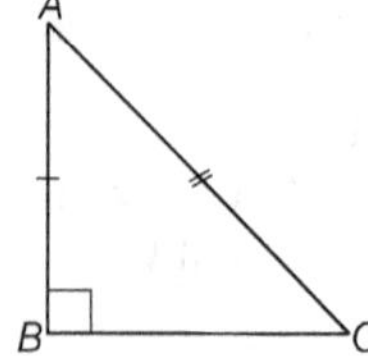 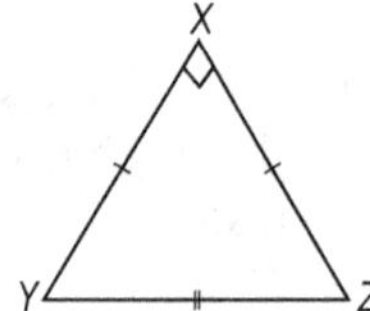

II. If two corresponding sides of two triangles are of same length and the angle between them is equal in measure, then the triangles are congruent by......... property.

III. .... parts of congruent triangles are equal.

IV. .... is not a property for congruence of triangles.

V. There are .... criterions to prove congruency of triangles.

VI. Corresponding .... of congruent triangles are equal.

VII. If the areas of two squares are same, they are ....

VIII. Two circles having .... circumference are congruent.

Codes

	I	II	III	IV	V	VI	VII	VIII
a	iii	i	vi	ii	ix	x	viii	xi
b	vii	i	vi	v	viii	xi	x	ix
c	iii	ii	iv	i	xi	x	viii	ix
d	vii	ii	iv	v	x	xi	ix	viii

18. State 'T' for true and 'F' for false.

I. By SSS property two triangles can be proved congruent but not by using ASA property.

II. Two line segments are said to be congruent, if they are of equal lengths.

III. If the areas of two rectangles are same, they are congruent always.

IV. The congruent figures coincide with each other.

Codes

	I	II	III	IV
a	T	F	T	F
b	T	T	F	F
c	F	T	F	T
d	F	F	T	T

19. **Assertion** (A) If the hypotenuse and an acute angle of one right angle is equal to the altitude and corresponding acute angle of another right triangle, then those two triangles are congruent.

Reason (R) By RHS property, the two right triangles are not congruent.

a A is true and R is correct explanation of A

b A is false and R is true

c A is true and R is false

d Both are false

Chapter 7

Comparing Quantities

A Percentage

1. Pick the odd one out.

   a 15% of 6   b 36 : 40   c 9% of 10   d 36% of 20

2. The sum of 40% of 70 and 70% of 40 is equal to

   a 28   b 36   c 48   d 56

3. What is the correct percentage form of 0.047?

   a 47%   b 0.047%   c 4.7%   d None of these

4. What per cent of 7500 is 4500?

   a 75%   b 60%   c 45%   d None of these

5. Chee Hong has 30 goats on his farm. How many goats must he buy to increase the number of goats on his farm by 20%?

   a 36   b 30   c 12   d 6

6. Mr. Brown uses 3 grey tiles for every 5 white tiles. What is the percentage of grey tiles used out of the total number of tiles, if 45 white tiles are used?

   a 37.5 %   b 45.5 %   c 56.5 %   d 60 %

7. What per cent of these shapes are circles?

   a 20%   b 25%   c 30%   d 35%

8. Fill in the blanks with the help of options, given in the box.

(i) 10,	(ii) 12%,	(iii) 200,	(iv) 2.4,	(v) 2.5%,	(vi) 5

   I. 10% of 2 km is .... m.   II. .... of 20 min is 144 s.

   III. $\dfrac{7}{5}$ of 200 cm is equal to .... % of 28 m.   IV. 25% of .... kg is 600 g.

Codes

	I	II	III	IV			I	II	III	IV
a	i	ii	iii	iv		b	iv	iii	ii	vi
c	iii	ii	i	iv		d	vi	v	ii	iv

9. Haider can quickly figure a 15% discount on a ball pen of ₹ 12 by

  a multiplying ₹ 12 × 10 by moving the decimal to the left two space to get ₹ 1.20, then adding half of that (or ₹ 0.60).

  b dividing ₹ 12 ÷ 2 to get 6, then adding 6 + 6 to get 12 again, then moving the decimal over one place to the right.

  c dividing 15 ÷ ₹ 12, then rounding up.

  d dividing ₹ 12 ÷ 15, then rounding down.

10. 1600 pupils attended a concert. 5% of the pupils were late for the concert. How many pupils were punctual for the concert?

  a 1220   b 1440   c 1520   d 80

11. If 45% of x + 30% of 90 = 30% of 210, then what is the value of x?

  a 36   b 48   c 72   d 80

12. If 25% of a number is added to 30, then the result is the number itself. Find the number.

  a 30   b 40   c 60   d 80

13. A school's population increased by 42 students. This was a 3% increase. About how many students attended before increase?

  a 2100   b 1600

  c 1400   d 1200

14. Match the following.

	Column A		Column B
I.	400% is equal to	(i)	2%
II.	$\frac{1}{4}$ is equal to	(ii)	$\frac{1}{10}$
III.	0.02 is equal to	(iii)	$\frac{25}{4}$%
IV.	$6\frac{1}{4}$% is equal to	(iv)	4
V.	10% is equal to	(v)	25%

Codes

	I	II	III	IV	V
a	v	iii	ii	iv	i
b	iv	v	i	iii	ii
c	iii	i	v	ii	iv
d	i	ii	iii	iv	v

15. The length and breadth of a rectangle are 40 cm and 30 cm. If the length is decreased by 20%, then what will be the new area of the rectangle?

  a 1200 sq cm   b 960 sq cm

  c 720 sq cm   d 1440 sq cm

16. **Assertion** (A) If there are 75 men and 60 women at a birthday party, then there are 25% more men than women in the party.

Reason (R) If $y > x$, then y is $\dfrac{y-x}{x}$% more than x.

  a A and R are true and R is correct explanation of A

  b A and R are true but R is not correct explanation of A

  c A is true and R is false

  d Both A and R are true

Directions (Q. Nos.17-19) For each of the pair of columns, choose the correct options given below.

  a The number of column A is greater.

  b The number of column B is greater.

  c The two numbers are equal.

  d The relationship cannot be determined from the given information.

17.

Column A	Column B
104% of 150	100% of 150 + 4% of 150

18.

Column A	Column B
The solution of the equation 25% of x = 400.	The solution of the equation 15% of x = 225.

19.

Column A	Column B
If 20% of a number is 60, then 45% of the same number.	The solution of the equation $\dfrac{16}{100} = \dfrac{x}{2500}$.

Directions (Q. Nos.20-22) Below given data provides the information of number of people having different blood groups. On the basis of it, answer the following questions.

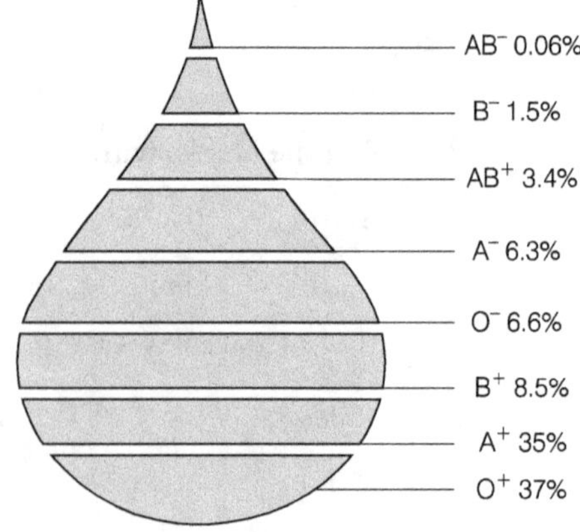

20. If person X needs O negative blood and twenty people from his family turns up, then what is the approximate number of them will have the required blood group?
 a 0
 b Less than 1
 c Less than 2
 d More than 3

21. If 200 people register to donate their blood in a blood donation camp, then what is the ratio of B negative blood group people to those having B positive blood group?
 a 3 : 19
 b 1 : 5
 c 3 : 17
 d None of the above

22. In a blood bank, the manager counted the number of bottles having AB negative blood group equal to 12. What will be the number of bottles of AB positive blood group?
 a 720   b 580
 c 420   d 680

Directions (Q. Nos. 23-24) Guideline Daily Amounts: Nutritional needs vary depending on the sex, size, age and activity levels, so the following chart in given recommending the daily amounts in a healthy, balanced diet for maintaining rather losing or gaining weight.

Guideline Daily Amounts

	Man	Woman
Energy (Kcal)	2500	2000
Protein (g)	55	45
Carbohydrates (g)	300	230
Sugar (g)	120	90
Fat (g)	95	70
Saturates (g)	30	20
Fibre (g)	24	24
Salt (g)	6	6

23. What per cent amount of energy (Kcal) in woman is less than in man?
 a 15%
 b 18%
 c 20%
 d 22%

24. What is the ratio of total requirement of sugar, fat and saturates in man to the sugar, fat and saturates in woman?
 a 49 : 36
 b 7 : 6
 c 59 : 42
 d 72 : 91

25. Ms. Chandok asked his accountant to prepare the balance sheet for reviewing the worth of his company. Part of his balance sheet showing the assets side in given here. On the basis of it answer the following questions.

Assets

Current Assets	₹
Cash in bank	42600
Inventory	4500
Prepaid expenses	2400
Total current assets	49500
Non-current assets	
Land	20000
Total non-current assets	20000
Total assets	69500

What is the percentage of non-current assets to the current assets?
 a 40.40%   b 39.2%
 c 50%   d 27.25%

26. In a dance competition, 20% of the children are below 10 yr. 22 of them were girls and the remaining $\frac{2}{3}$ were boys. How many children participated in the competition?
 a 200   b 250
 c 330   d 460

Directions (Q. Nos. 27-28) Anisha has a collection of English, French and Spanish books. 34% of them are English, 42% of them are French and there are 72 Spanish books.

27. The total number of books are
 a 300   b 600
 c 750   d 1200

28. The number of English books as a percentage of Spanish books are
 a 120.21%   b 125.72%
 c 139.21%   d 141.67%

1. The cost price of a TV set is ₹ 48000. It was sold at a profit of 15%. What is the profit earned?

   a ₹ 4800   b ₹ 3600
   c ₹ 6000   d ₹ 7200

2. Pick the odd one out.

   a CP = 750, SP = 1200
   b CP = 750, SP = 800
   c CP = 400, Profit = 200
   d CP = 250, SP = 100

3. The price of gasoline drops from ₹ 2.00 per gallon to ₹ 1.90 per gallon. What is the per cent of decrease?

   a 1%   b 3%
   c 5%   d 7%

4. Match the following.

	Column A		Column B
I.	$P = 1000$ $r = 2\%$ $t = 1$	(i)	₹ 30
II.	$P = 500$ $r = 3\%$ $t = 2$	(ii)	₹ 20
III.	$P = 250$ $r = 4\%$ $t = 4$	(iii)	₹ 40

Codes

	I	II	III		I	II	III
a	ii	i	iii	b	i	ii	iii
c	iii	i	ii	d	i	iii	ii

5. A salesman is on a commission rate of 5%. How much commission does he make on sales worth ₹ 15000?

   a ₹ 750
   b ₹ 1500
   c ₹ 250
   d None of the above

6. Meenakshi scored 97 out of 100 in Mathematics, 94 out of 100 in English and 46 out of 100 in Hindi. In order to have an aggregate of 80% in his overall marks, how much should she score in Science?

   a 93   b 73
   c 83   d 63

7. Mr. Ben bought 100 batteries at a cost of ₹ 2 each. He sold them at 4 for ₹ 10, then what is percentage of profit he made?

   a 100%   b 125%
   c 25%   d 50%

8. What simple interest will be paid on a deposit of ₹ 200 at 4% per annum after 3 yr?

   a ₹ 12   b ₹ 20
   c ₹ 24   d ₹ 8

9. If the simple interest on a sum of money at 6% per annum for 2 yr is ₹ 12. What is the sum of money?

   a ₹ 100   b ₹ 200
   c ₹ 50   d ₹ 250

10. A person buys a car for ₹ 5 lakh and sells it for ₹ 7.5 lakh. What is the profit as a percentage of the SP?

   a $6\dfrac{2}{3}\%$ b 12%
   c $33\dfrac{1}{3}\%$ d 21%

11. The usual price of a play station game pack is ₹ 7000. It is sold for ₹ 6090. What is the percentage of loss suffered?

   a 1%   b $\dfrac{1}{7}\%$
   c $1\dfrac{1}{7}\%$ d $\dfrac{2}{7}\%$

12. There are 180 apples in a basket. 40% of them are red and the rest are green. 25% of the green apples are bad in quality. How many green apples are not bad in quality?

   a 51   b 72
   c 81   d 92

13. The city of Delhi spends 15% of its annual budget on its maintenance of bus stands. If Delhi spent ₹ 30 lakh on it this year, then what was its annual budget this year?

   a ₹ 4000000
   b ₹ 50000000
   c ₹ 20000000
   d ₹ 10000000

14. Simple interest on a sum of money at 8% per annum for 4 yr is one-third of the sum invested. What is the sum of money invested?

   a 6000   b 4000
   c 2000   d Data inadequate

15. A sum of money at simple interest amounts to ₹ 840 in 2 yr and 920 in 4 yr. The sum is

   a ₹ 700
   b ₹ 640
   c ₹ 760
   d ₹ 820

16. In a club, 40% of the members are men. If 20% of the males and 30% of the females are not married, then what percentage of members are married?

   a 26%   b 20%
   c 44%   d 74%

17. If the selling price of a toy is ₹ 750 and shopkeeper sold it at a profit of 20%. Then, what is the cost price of the toy?

   a ₹ 625   b ₹ 650
   c ₹ 725   d ₹ 500

18. Sangeeta bought a VCD player at 20% discount during a sale. The price of the VCD player is ₹ 5500. After 6 months, she sold the VCD player to a friend and made a profit. What was here buying price of the VCD player? If she wants to make a profit of 10%, at what price should she sell the VCD player?

   a ₹ 5000, ₹ 4000
   b ₹ 4400, ₹ 4840
   c ₹ 3460, ₹ 3600
   d ₹ 4200, ₹ 4620

19. Mr. Ajay divided a sum of ₹ 20000 among his two sons Anish and Anuj. Anish invested the amount at the rate of 12% for 2 yr, whereas Anuj invested the amount at the rate of 8% for 2 yr. Both got same interest after 2 yr.

Find the amount each one of them got.

   a Anish = ₹ 10000
       Anuj = ₹ 10000
   b Anish = ₹ 12000
       Anuj = ₹ 8000
   c Anish = ₹ 8000
       Anuj = ₹ 12000
   d Anish = ₹ 6000
       Anuj = ₹ 14000

Directions (Q. Nos.20-21) Mr. Qureshi sold his scooter to Mr. Anand at a discount of 10%. Mr. Anand sold the same scooter to Mr. Verma at a profit of 20%.

20. If Mr. Verma paid ₹ 82440 for the scooter, then how much did Mr. Qureshi pay for the scooter?

   a ₹ 74212   b ₹ 76333
   c ₹ 72431   d ₹ 70343

21. If Mr. Anand paid the same amount as Mr. Verma to Mr. Qureshi, then what percentage profit would have been made by Mr. Qureshi?

   a 20%   b 15%
   c 10%   d None of these

22. Choose the correct option matching the result given in the columns.

Column A	Column B
Manisha has ₹ 1500. She spents 30% of the money on a watch and 10% of the remainder on a top. Find the value of money left with her.	The cost of a computer book is ₹ 1500. It was sold at loss of ₹ 15%. What is the selling price of it?

   a If value in column A is greater.
   b If value in column B is greater.
   c If values are same.
   d No relation can be established between the two columns.

Chapter 8

Algebraic Expressions

1. Which of the following is the factor of $-a^2b^3$?

    a $\ a \times b$ b $\ -a \times a \times b$ c $\ -1 \times a \times a \times b \times b \times b$ d $\ -a \times b$

2. The method of finding solution by trying out various values for the variable is known as

    a error method   b trial and error method

    c testing method   d checking method

3. Which is the correct pair of like terms in the given expressions $9a(2b-a)$ and $-6b(4a-2b)$?

    a $\ 9a, -9a^2$ b $\ 2b, 2b^2$

    c $\ 18ab, -24ab$ d None of these

4. Which of the following is equivalent to $2x^2$?

    a $\ 2(x+x)$ b $\ 2x(x)$ c $\ x^2+2$ d $\ x+x+x+2$

5. $[(2a^3b)^3][(4a^2b^2)]$ is equivalent to which of the following?

    a $\ 32a^{11}b^5$ b $\ 8a^{11}b^5$ c $\ 32a^{18}b^6$ d $\ 8a^{18}b^6$

6. The value of $\dfrac{7a-2}{5}$, when $a=3$, is

    a $\ \dfrac{21}{5}$ b $\ 4$ c $\ 5$ d $\ \dfrac{19}{5}$

7. If $3y=15$ and $2x=16$, then $3x+2y$ is equal to

    a $\ 20$ b $\ 18$ c $\ 24$ d $\ 34$

8. Which mathematical expression best describes the product of two numbers subtracted from a third number?

    a $\ (x \times y)+z$ b $\ (x-y) \times z$

    c $\ (x \times y)-z$ d $\ z-(x \times y)$

9. If $h=10$, then find the value of $3h+45-12+(3 \times 5)h$.

    a $\ 213$ b $\ 243$ c $\ 200$ d $\ 273$

10. If $C=\dfrac{5}{9}(F-32)$ gives the formula for temperature, then find the value of C, where $F=32$.

    a $\ 49$ b $\ \dfrac{5}{9}$ c $\ 1$ d $\ 0$

11. Simplify the expression by combining the like terms.

$$12a+14b-3b-11c+8.5a$$

    a $\ 4.5a+13b-11c$ b $\ 20.5a+11b-11c$

    c $\ 26a+14b-8.5c$ d None of these

12. Meera has $4q$ skirts. Tara has $12q$ skirts and Lara has $2q$ skirts. If $q = 5$, then how many more skirts does Tara have both Meera and Lara?

  a 10   b 20
  c 30   d 40

13. Find the values of the following expressions at $x = 1$ and $y = -2$.

Column A		Column B
I. $x^2 + y^2 + 3xy$	(i)	7
II. $x^2 + x^2y + xy^2 + y^2$	(ii)	-3
III. $x^2 + y^2 - 3xy$	(iii)	-1
IV. $(x^2 - y^2)$	(iv)	11

Codes

	I	II	III	IV
a	i	ii	iii	iv
b	iv	iii	i	ii
c	iii	i	iv	ii
d	ii	iv	iii	i

14. Fill in the blanks with the help of options, given in the box.

(i) Like terms,	(ii) $\dfrac{S}{t}$,
(iii) $7y - 4x$,	(iv) Unlike terms,
(v) 4,	(vi) Monomial,
(vii) St,	(viii) $4x - 7y$,
(ix) Trinomial,	(x) 5

   I. .... is an algebraic expression containing three terms.
  II. Number of terms in the expression $4x^2y - 12xy^2 + 4z^2x + 5xy$ is ....
 III. The subtraction of 4 times of x from 7 times of y is ....
 IV. The speed of train is S km/h. The distance covered by it in t hours is ....
  V. $10xy$ and $10x^2y^2$ are ....

Codes

	I	II	III	IV	V
a	ii	x	viii	vii	iv
b	vi	v	iii	ii	i
c	vi	x	viii	ii	i
d	ix	v	iii	vii	iv

15. What should be subtracted from $(-2x^3 + 5x^2 - x + 8)$ to get $5x^2 - 4x + 12$?

  a $2x^3 + 3x - 4$ b $-2x^3 - 3x + 4$
  c $-2x^3 + 3x - 4$ d $2x^3 - 3x + 4$

16. What should be added to $x + x^2 + 6$ to get $3x^2 + 2x + 1$?

  a $2x^2 + x - 5$
  b $2x^2 - 2x + 5$
  c $x^2 + 2x - 5$
  d None of these

17. Which of the following expressions is correct?

  a $\dfrac{pq + r}{q} = p + r$ b $\dfrac{p + r}{q + r} = \dfrac{q}{r}$

  c $\dfrac{pq + pr}{ps} = \dfrac{q + r}{s}$ d $\dfrac{p(q + r)}{p + s} = \dfrac{q + r}{s}$

18. Simplified value of expression $\left(\dfrac{2}{5}a^4 - 2a + 7\right) - \left(-\dfrac{3}{10}a^4 + 6a^3\right) - (2a^2 - 7)$ is

  a $\dfrac{7}{10}a^4 - 6a^3 - 2a^2 - 2a + 14$
  b $\dfrac{-5}{10}a^4 + 8a^3 - 2a^2 + 2a$
  c $\dfrac{-5}{15}a^4 + 6a^3 + 2a^2 - 2a + 7$
  d None of the above

19. The area of the given figure is

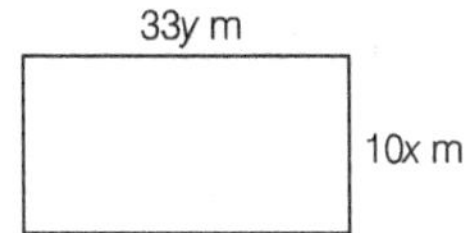

  a $33y + 10x$ b $66y + 10x$
  c $66y + 20x$ d $330xy$

20. The perimeter of the regular pentagon having sides equal to $(3x + 1)$ inch, is

  a $(15x + 1)$ inch
  b $(15x + 5)$ inch
  c $(5x + 5)$ inch
  d $(3x + 1)$ inch

21. What is the missing term in the following product?
$(2a^3 - 3)(5a^3 - 2) = 10a^6 + ... + 6$?

  a $19a^3$ b $-19a^3$
  c $16a^3$ d $-16a^3$

22. Ages of two friends are the ratio $2 : 1$. If the sum of their ages is 51, then their ages are

  a 34 yr and 20 yr
  b 34 yr and 17 yr
  c 20 yr and 10 yr
  d 30 yr and 15 yr

23. If area of a triangle is given by $A = \dfrac{1}{2} b \times h$, where $b =$ base and $h =$ height, then what is the area of given triangle?

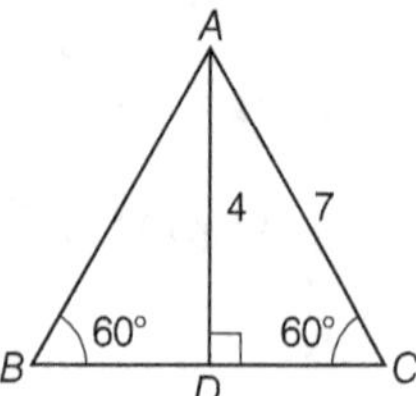

- a   20 sq units
- b   14 sq units
- c   18 sq units
- d   Can't be determined

24. If $A = 10w^3 + 20w^2 - 55w + 60$,
$B = -25w^2 + 15w - 10$ and
$C = 5w^2 - 10w + 20$,
then $A + B - C$ is equal to
- a $10w^3 + 10w^2 + 30w + 30$
- b $10w^3 + 10w^2 - 30w - 30$
- c $10w^3 - 10w^2 - 30w + 30$
- d   None of the above

25. Gargi plans to build a house that is 1.5 times as long as it is wide. She wants the land around the house to be 20 ft wider than the width of the house and twice as long as the length of the house, as shown below. Write the expression for remaining area of land and find the area of it, if $x = 30$.

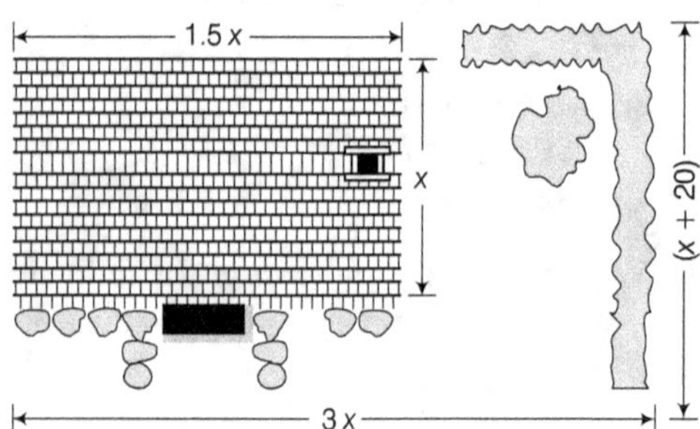

- a $2x^2 + 60x$, 3200 sq units
- b $3x^2 + 60x$, 3050 sq units
- c $3x^2 + 60x$, 3150 sq units
- d $1.5x^2 + 60x$, 3150 sq units

 Projected from 2000 to 2014, the total population P and the male population M of United Kingdom (in thousand) can be expressed by the following equations, where 't' is the number of years since 2000.

Total population, $P = 2387.74t + 155211.46$
Male population, $M = 1164.16t + 75622.43$

26. Which expression represents the female population F of the United Kingdom from 2000 to 2014?
- a $1421.21t + 7001.46$
- b $1421.46t + 72942.04t$
- c $1227.59t + 72589.03$
- d $1223.58t + 79589.03$

27. For the year 2014, the value of P is 247821.76 and the value of M is 123456.01. What will be the female population in 2014?
- a   124365.75
- b   123456.75
- c   124376.65
- d   None of these

28. Max's monthly salary was ₹ $5445\,q$. He saved 30% of it and gave $\dfrac{1}{2}$ of the remainder to his parents. If Max used $\dfrac{3}{4}$ of the amount of money, he had left to buy a guitar, then how much money would he have left, if $q = 8$?
- a   ₹ 11400.5
- b   ₹ 11434.5
- c   ₹ 11079.5
- d   None of the above

29. A vacuum cleaner set costs ₹ $154.25\,K$. Additional pipe costs ₹ $15.2\,K$.
- I. What is the total cost of 3 vacuum sets and 5 additional pipes?
  - (i) ₹ 400
  - (ii) ₹ 530.75 K
  - (iii) ₹ 538.75 K
  - (iv) ₹ 600
- II. During a sale, a vacuum cleaner set was selling at 30% less and additional pipes were selling at 75% off its usual price. If $K = 10$, then how much less Deborah pays, if she buys 3 vacuum cleaner sets and 5 additional pipes during sale?
  - (i) ₹ 1675.25
  - (ii) ₹ 2000
  - (iii) ₹ 1758.5
  - (iv) 1958.25
- a   (i), (iii)
- b   (ii), (iii)
- c   (iii), (iv)
- d   (i), (iv)

30. Kaira buys one dozen eggs worth ₹ 10, three breads where price of one bread is ₹ 5 and five bottles of juice worth ₹ 8 each. What is the total money she has to pay, if the price of the items are not given?

a $a + 3b + 5c$

b $a + b + c$

c $3a + 3b + 3c$

d Can't be determined

31. From 2007 to 2012, the amount (in crore) spent on natural gas N and electricity E by Indian residents can be described by the following expressions, where t is the number of years since 2007.

Gas spending model, $N = 1.23\,t^2 - 3.21t + 27.40$

Electricity spending model, E
$$= -0.109\,t^2 + 5.293\,t + 107.735$$

What is the total amount A spent on natural gas and electricity by Indian residents from 2007 to 2012?

a $1.467t^2 + 7.423 + 121.721$

b $1.339t^2 - 8.729\,t + 76.245$

c $1.01t^2 + 7.083 + 97.83$

d $1.121t^2 + 2.083t + 135.135$

32. State 'T' for true and 'F' for false.

I. Expression with two unlike terms is called a monomial.

II. The sum of two unlike terms is a like term with coefficient equal to the sum of coefficients of the two unlike terms.

III. The value of $3y^2 - 5y + 3$, when $y = 1$ is $+1$.

IV. The expression for the sum of angles of an 'n' sided figure is $(2n - 4) \times 90°$.

Codes

	I	II	III	IV			I	II	III	IV
a	T	T	F	F		b	T	F	T	F
c	F	T	F	T		d	F	F	T	T

33. If sum of 'n' natural numbers is given by $\dfrac{n(n + 1)}{2}$, then the value of sum of first 20 natural numbers is

a 210

b 200

c 220

d 190

34. If the volume of a rectangular prism $V = lwh$ and surface area $= 2(lw) + 2(hw) + 2(lh)$, where $l =$ length, $h =$ height and $w =$ width, then what is greater in, if length $= 8$ cm, width $= 10$ cm and height $= 6$ cm?

a Volume

b Surface area

c Both are same.

d Can't be determined

35.

$$\begin{array}{r} A \quad 4 \\ 2 \quad A \\ \hline 2\,7\,2\,6 \end{array}$$

In the product shown above, A is a digit, then find the value of A.

a 4

b 2

c 9

d 6

36. Let x be defined by $(x) = \dfrac{x - 3}{x + 1}$ for any x such that $x \neq 1$. Which of the following is equivalent to $(x) + 1$?

a $\dfrac{x + 2}{x + 1}$

b $\dfrac{2}{x - 1}$

c $\dfrac{2x - 2}{x + 1}$

d $\dfrac{x - 2}{x + 1}$

37. Monali walks at 4 km/h and she reaches the school 11 min late. If however, she walks at 5 km/h, she reaches the school 7 min before, then the distance between her house and school is

a 7 km

b 4 km

c 5 km

d 6 km

Chapter 9

Exponents and Powers

1. Which of the following is the equivalent to $\left(\dfrac{1}{x^{-4}}\right)$?

a $\dfrac{1}{x} \times \dfrac{1}{x} \times \dfrac{1}{x} \times \dfrac{1}{x}$

b $x \times x \times x \times x$

c $\dfrac{1}{x} \times \dfrac{1}{x} \times x \times x$

d None of these

2. If $x = 1$ and $y = 2$, then $x^y + y^x$ is equal to

a 3   b 4   c 5   d 6

3. Evaluate and choose the correct option for $\dfrac{(a^2 b^3 c)^2}{a^4 b^6 c^2}$.

a 0   b 1   c abc d $\dfrac{1}{abc}$

4. Match the following.

	Column A		Column B
I.	$a^2 \times b^2$	(i)	ab
II.	$a^4 \div b^4$	(ii)	$\dfrac{1}{(ab)^{-2}}$
III.	$(a^3)^{\frac{1}{3}} \times (b^2)^{\frac{1}{2}}$	(iii)	$\left(\dfrac{a^2}{b^2}\right)^2$
IV.	$(ab)^5 \div a^2 b^2$	(iv)	$a^3 b^3$

Codes

	I	II	III	IV		I	II	III	IV
a	i	iv	ii	iii	b	ii	iii	i	iv
c	iii	i	ii	iv	d	iv	ii	i	iii

5. Simplify and choose the correct option for $\left(\dfrac{169}{225}\right)^{\frac{1}{2}} \times \left(\dfrac{125}{27}\right)^{\frac{2}{3}} \times \left(\dfrac{81}{4}\right)^{\frac{1}{2}}$.

a 0   b 1   c $\dfrac{65}{6}$ d $\dfrac{75}{3}$

6. The simplified value of $\dfrac{\left(\frac{-1}{3}\right)^6}{\left(\frac{-1}{3}\right)^5} \div \dfrac{\left(\frac{-1}{27}\right)}{\left(\frac{-1}{9}\right)}$ is

a 0   b 1   c -1 d 3

7. Find the value of b, if $\left(\dfrac{4}{5}\right)^3 \times \left(\dfrac{4}{5}\right)^{b+8} = \left(\dfrac{5}{4}\right)^{-11}$.

 a 0   b 1
 c 12   d 11

8. If $\left(\dfrac{7}{9}\right)^4 \times \left(\dfrac{7}{9}\right)^{-10} = \left(\dfrac{9}{7}\right)^{-4} \times \left(\dfrac{7}{9}\right)^{2a-1}$, then the value of a is

 a 1   b $\dfrac{-5}{2}$
 c $\dfrac{-7}{4}$ d $\dfrac{-9}{2}$

9. The simplified value of $\left(4^{\frac{4}{3}} \div 8^{\frac{2}{3}}\right) \times 2^{\frac{3}{2}}$ is

 a 2   b $(2)^{\frac{1}{6}}$
 c $(2)^{\frac{4}{13}}$ d None of these

10. Which of the following is the equivalent to 9.9×10^{-6}?

 a 0.00000099   b 0.0000099
 c 0.000099   d 0.00099

11. If $2^x = 4^y = 8^z = 64$, then find the value of $x + y + z$.

 a 10   b 11
 c 13   d Can't be determined

12. The simplified value of $\dfrac{2x^2 y}{3x} \cdot \dfrac{9xy^2}{y^4}$ will be equal to

 a $\dfrac{2}{3}xy^2$ b $\dfrac{2}{3}xy$
 c $\dfrac{2x}{3y}$ d $\dfrac{6x^2}{y}$

13. The equivalent form of 0.000000748 is

 a 748×10^{-6} b 74.8×10^{-7}
 c 7.48×10^{-7} d 0.748×10^{-9}

14. Choose the correct signs.

 I. $(2^2)^3 \;\square\; 2^{2^3}$

 II. $(4^4)^{\frac{1}{2}} \;\square\; 2^4$

 III. $\left(3^{\frac{1}{3}}\right)^9 \;\square\; \left(81^{\frac{1}{4}}\right)^2$

 Codes

	I	II	III		I	II	III
a	>	<	=	b	<	=	>
c	=	<	>	d	<	>	<

15. The volume of a sphere is given by $V = \dfrac{4}{3}\pi r^3$, whereas the area of the circle having same radius is given by πr^2. What is the ratio of the area of circle to the volume of sphere?

 a $4 : 3r$
 b $3 : 4$
 c $3r : 4r$
 d $3 : 4r$

16. Simplify and choose the correct option.
$$\left(\frac{m^3 p^5}{n^7}\right)^6 \times \left(\frac{m^2 n^0 p^3}{m^4 n^2}\right)^3$$

 a $\dfrac{m^{12} p^{39}}{n^{48}}$ b $\dfrac{m^{12} p^{40}}{n^{36}}$
 c 0   d 1

17. The simplified value of $\left(\dfrac{4^{\frac{-3}{2}} x^{\frac{2}{3}} y^{\frac{-7}{4}}}{2^{\frac{3}{2}} x^{\frac{-1}{3}} y^{\frac{3}{4}}}\right)^{\frac{2}{3}}$ is

 a $8x^2 y^5$ b 1
 c $\dfrac{x^2 y^{-5}}{8}$ d $\dfrac{(x^2 y^{-5})^{\frac{1}{3}}}{8}$

18. Mr. Xen asked two of his students to solve the expression $\left(\dfrac{24a^3 b^{-8}}{6a^{-5} b^2}\right)^{\frac{-1}{2}}$ and write the answer on blackboard. Andy wrote the answer as $4a^{-4} b^5$, whereas Zuck wrote the answer as $\dfrac{4b^5}{a^4}$. Who wrote the correct answer?

 a Andy   b Zuck
 c Both of them   d None of these

19. If $5^x = 999$, then the value of 5^{x-3} is

 a $\dfrac{999}{5}$ b $\dfrac{1000}{27}$
 c $\dfrac{999}{125}$ d $\dfrac{1000}{125}$

20. A rectangular piece of land is to be sold off in smaller pieces. The total area of the land is 2^{17} sq miles. The pieces to be cut out are 16^2 sq miles in size. How many smaller pieces of the land can be sold at the given size?

 a 2^{15}
 b 16^4
 c 2^9
 d None of the above

21. The average household spends about ₹ 40000 each month. If there are about 1×10^8 households, what is the total amount of money spent by the households in one month?

    a 40×10^8 b 40000
    c 4.0×10^{14} d 4×10^{12}

22. Find the value of $(5x^7 y^3 z^{-1})^2 \times (2xy^{-5})^3 \times (2y^{-3}z^2)^3$.

    a $20x^9 y^{10} z^4$ b $400x^8 y^{-9} z^2$
    c $800x^{17} y^{18} z^4$ d $\dfrac{1600x^{17} z^4}{y^{18}}$

23. The correct value of $(-1)^{101} + (-1)^{102} + (-1)^{103} + \ldots + (-1)^{200}$ is

    a 0   b 1
    c -1 d -2

24. Match the following.

	Column A		Column B
I.	$\dfrac{6^3 \times 9^2 \times 25^2}{3^2 \times 4^2 \times 15^4}$	(i)	$5^2 \times 3^4$
II.	$\dfrac{3^8 \times 16^2 \times 7^5}{81^2 \times 2^5 \times 49^2}$	(ii)	$\dfrac{3}{2}$
III.	$\dfrac{15^4 \times 21^3}{3^3 \times 5^2 \times 7^3}$	(iii)	56

Codes

	I	II	III			I	II	III
a	i	ii	iii		b	ii	ii	i
c	ii	iii	i		d	i	iii	ii

Directions (Q. Nos.25-26) The table below shows the debt of the three most populous places and the three least populous places.

Place	Debt	Population
Tokyo	407000000000	8000000
Texas	337000000000	19000000
New York	276000000000	26000000
Brazil	4000000000	9000000
California	124000000000	40000000
Beijing	2000000000	57000000

25. What is the sum of the debts for the three most populous states? (Express in scientific notation)

    a 4.02×10^{11} b 4.02×10^{12}
    c 4.02×10^{13} d 4.02×10^{6}

26. Approximately, how many times smaller is the total population of Tokyo, Texas, New York compared to the total population of Brazil, California and Beijing?

    a $\dfrac{1}{2}$ b $\dfrac{1}{3}$
    c $\dfrac{1}{4}$ d Can't be determined

27. All the planets revolve around the Sun in elliptical orbits. Uranus's farthest distance from the Sun is approximately 3.004×10^9 km and its closest distance is approximately 2.749×10^9 km. What is the average distance of Uranus from the Sun?

    a 2.476×10^9 b 2.8765×10^9
    c 2.876×10^8 d None of these

28. Find the value of
$$7^4\left[\left(\frac{6}{7}\right)^2 + \left(\frac{6}{7}\right) - \left(\frac{6}{7}\right)^3\right] + (-7)^3\left[\left(\frac{6}{7}\right) + 1 - \left(\frac{6}{7}\right)^2\right] \times 6.$$

    a 0   b 1   c $\dfrac{7}{6}$ d $\dfrac{6}{7}$

29. Simplify and choose the correct option.
$$\left(\frac{a^{5b-3} \times a^{3-2b}}{a^{4b-6} \times a^{2b-9}}\right)^{\frac{-8}{6}}$$

    a a^{3b+15} b a^{13-3b}
    c a^{4b-20} d a^{4b+18}

30. The mass of Earth is 5.9×10^{24} kg. The mass of Pluto is 13000000000000000000000 kg. How much greater is Earth's mass?

    a 5.887×10^{24} b 5.792×10^{25}
    c 58.87×10^{24} d None of these

31. $\left(\dfrac{p^{a^4}}{p^{b^4}}\right)^{\frac{1}{a^2+b^2}} \times \left(\dfrac{p^{b^4}}{p^{c^4}}\right)^{\frac{1}{b^2+c^2}} \times \left(\dfrac{p^{c^4}}{p^{a^4}}\right)^{\frac{1}{c^2+a^2}}$ is equal to

    a 1   b 2   c 3   d 4

Chapter 10

Symmetry and Visualising Solid Shapes

1. Which of the following alphabets has a horizontal line of symmetry?

   a A   b P   c N   d H

2. A square has ....

   a one line of symmetry   b two lines of symmetry

   c three lines of symmetry   d four lines of symmetry

3. Which of the following figures is closed figure?

a    b    c    d 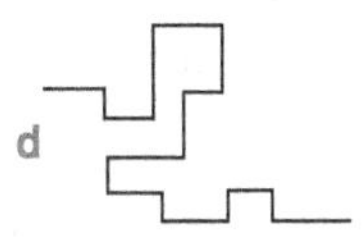

4. In the word 'MATH', which letter has vertical symmetry?

   a M, A   b T, H

   c Only H   d All of the letters

5. Which of the following is a net of the cube?

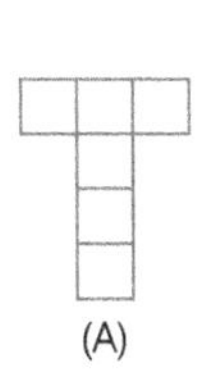

   (A)   (B)   (C)   (D)

   a A and B   b B and C   c A and D   d Only A

6. The order of a rotational symmetry of the given figure is

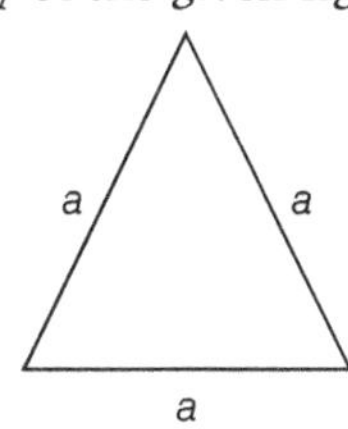

   a 1   b 2   c 3   d 4

7. Find the number of lines of symmetry of the given figure.

    a No line of symmetry
    b 2
    c 3
    d 4

8. The net shown below forms a ………. .

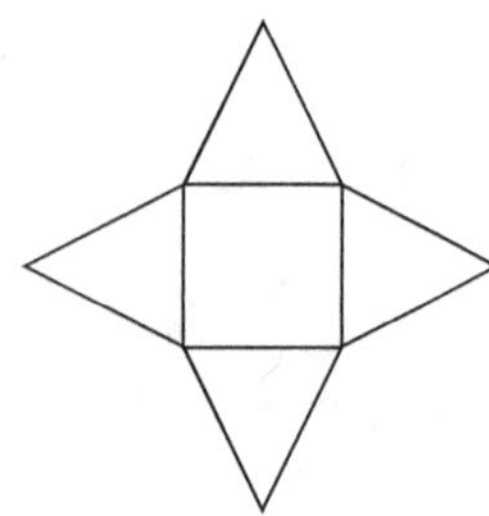

    a prism
    b cube
    c sphere
    d pyramid

9. How many corners does this shape below have?

    a 6   b 10
    c 12   d 13

10. How many faces does this solid have?

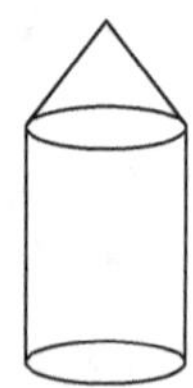

    a 1
    b 2
    c 3
    d 4

11. Match the following.

	Shape		Order of symmetry
I.		(i)	2
II.		(ii)	6
III.		(iii)	No order of symmetry

Codes

	I	II	III			I	II	III
a	i	ii	iii		b	i	iii	ii
c	ii	iii	i		d	iii	ii	i

12. What is the order of symmetry of the given figure?

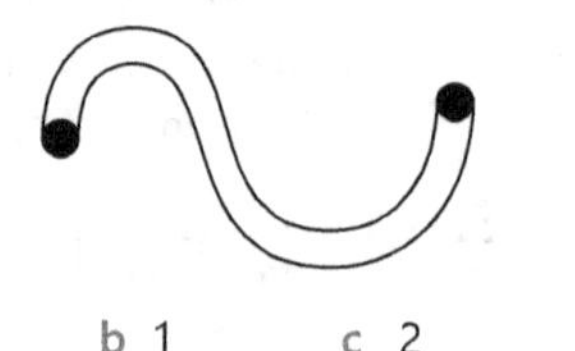

    a 0   b 1   c 2   d 3

13. How many lines of symmetry does the given figure have?

    a 0   b 1   c 2   d 3

14. Which of the following figures are formed from the given net?

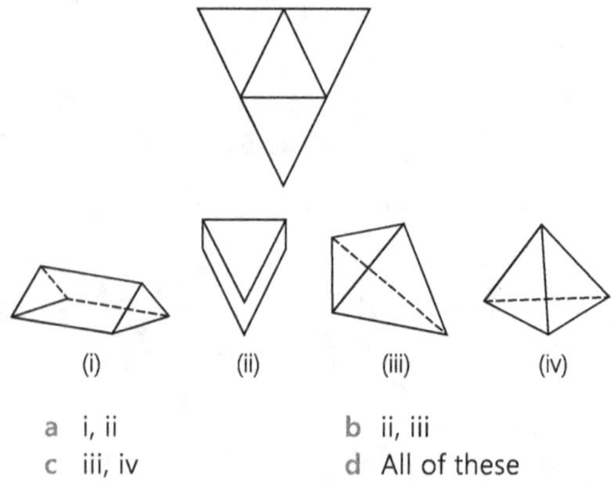

    (i)   (ii)   (iii)   (iv)

    a i, ii   b ii, iii
    c iii, iv   d All of these

15. How many faces does the given figure have?

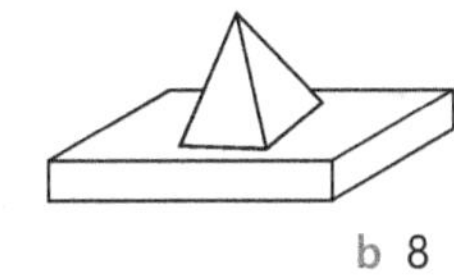

a 6
c 9
b 8
d 10

16. A cube is marked 1, 2, 3, 4, 5 and 6, which cube when unfolded does not represent the net shown below?

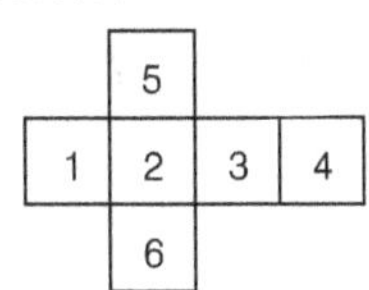

a 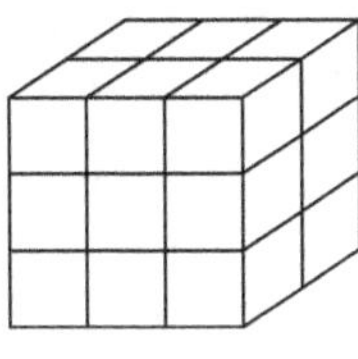
b
c 
d

17. How many cubes are needed to make the solid below?

a 9
c 18
b 12
d 21

18. The order of rotational symmetry for the given figure is

a 4
c 2
b 1
d 3

19. How many lines of symmetry does the given figure have?

a 0
c 3
b 2
d 4

20. What is the order of rotational symmetry of the given figure?

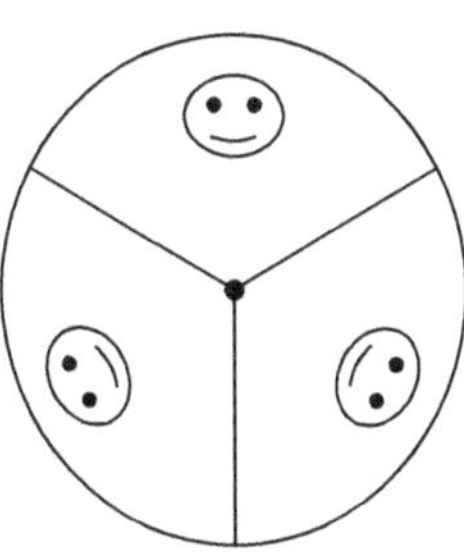

a 3
b 2
c 1
d None of the above

21. Match the following.

Figure		Line of symmetry	
I.		(i)	Four
II.		(ii)	One
III.		(iii)	Zero

Codes

	I	II	III
a	i	ii	iii
b	ii	iii	i
c	iii	i	ii
d	i	iii	ii

22. What is the order of rotational symmetry?

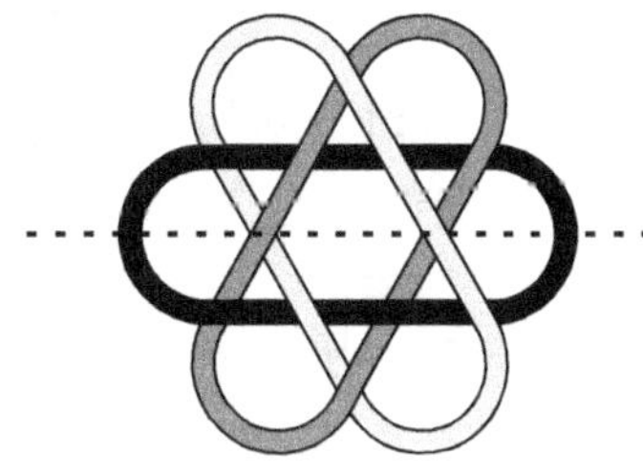

a 6
b 4
c 8
d None of the above

23. Which of the following solids can be obtained by folding the net below?

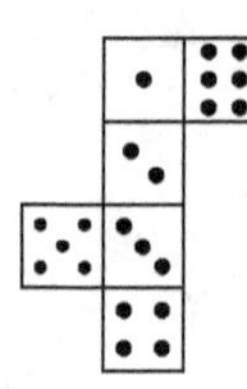

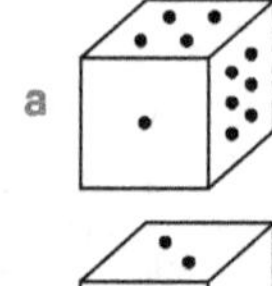

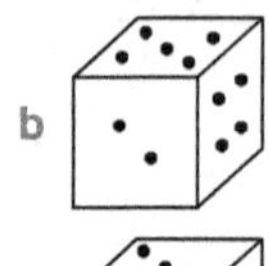

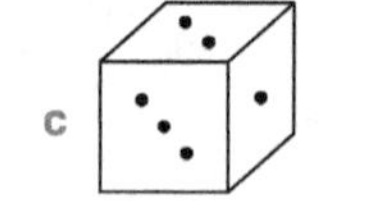

a

b

c

d

24. How many faces does this solid figure have?

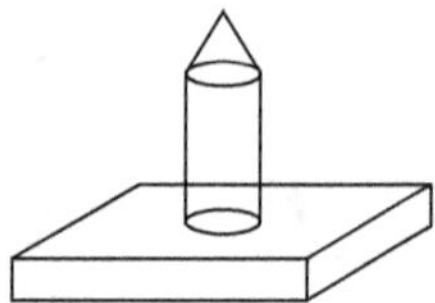

a 4
b 6
c 8
d 10

25. Which solid figure will be formed from below given net?

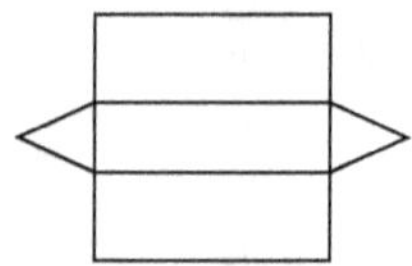

a Pyramid
b Prism
c Cone
d Frustum

26. What are the number of lines of symmetry?

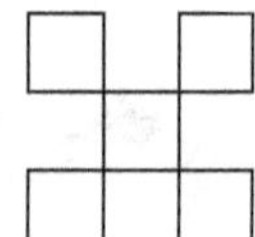

a 2
b 4
c 6
d 8

27. Which figure has only one line of symmetry?

a 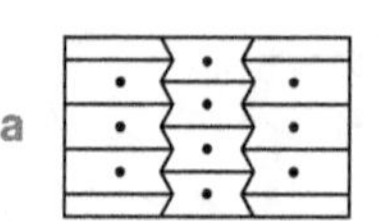   b 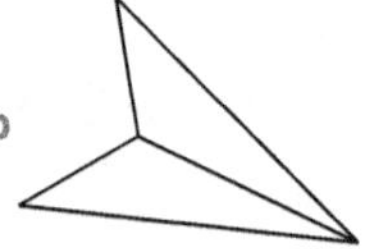

c 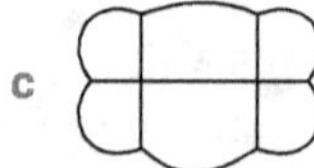   d None of these

28. Which of the following figures will be formed, if we cut the paper in below manner?

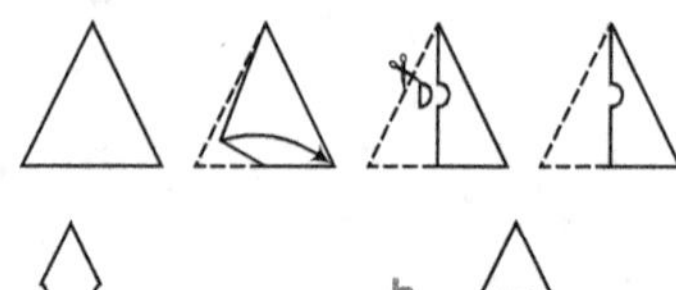

a    b 

c   d

29. Which is the resultant figure formed, if we cut the paper in below manner?

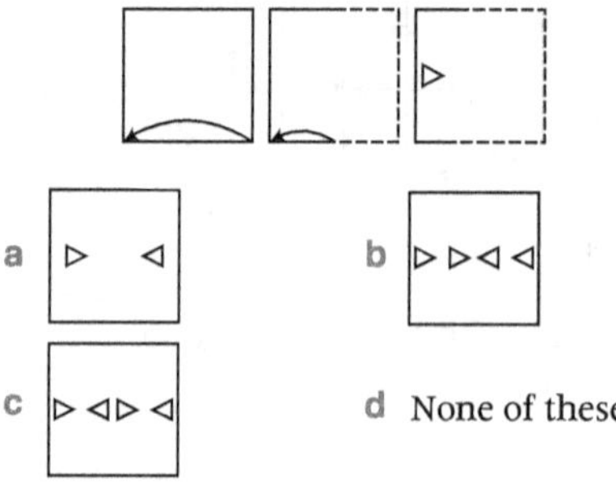

a   b

c   d None of these

30. Choose the correct figure that resembles the given figures.

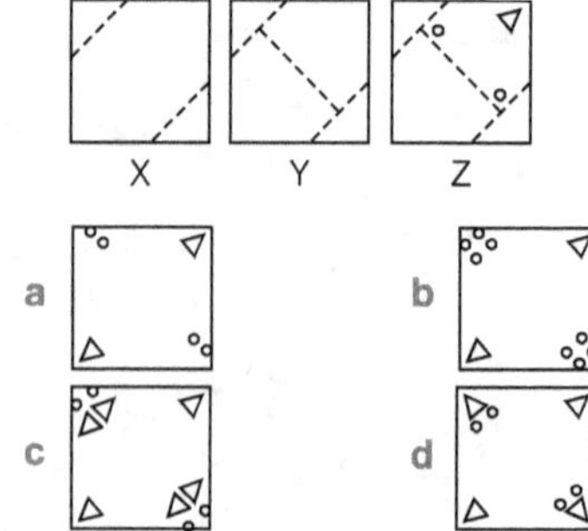

a   b

c   d

31. Fill in the blanks with the help of options, given in the box.

(i) cube,	(ii) oblique,	(iii) regular,
(iv) net,	(v) isometric,	(vi) cuboid,
(vii) irregular,	(viii) sketch	

   I. In .... sketch of the solid, the measurements are kept proportional.

  II. A .... polygon has as many lines of symmetry as it has sides.

 III. A .... is a skeleton-outline of a solid that can be folded to make the solid.

 IV. While rectangle in a 2-D figure, ... is a 3-D figure.

Codes

	I	II	III	IV		I	II	III	IV
a	v	iii	iv	vi	b	ii	vii	viii	i
c	ii	iii	iv	vi	d	v	vii	viii	i

32. Match the following with their correct view.

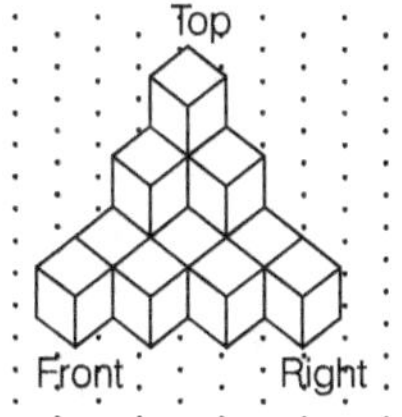

View		Figure
I.	Front	(i)
II.	Right	(ii)
III.	Top	(iii)

Codes

	I	II	III
a	i	ii	iii
b	iii	i	ii
c	ii	iii	i
d	None of the above		

Practice Sets

7

Practice Set ①

A Whole Content Based Test for Class 7th Mathematics Olympiad

1. Which of the following numbers is equal to 36?

   a $\dfrac{(-2)\times(-3)\times 3\times 4}{-2}$

   b $\dfrac{(-2)\times 6\times(-3)\times(-2)}{-3}$

   c $\dfrac{(-2)\times 9\times(-3)\times(-2)}{3}$

   d $\dfrac{(-2)\times 3\times(-3)\times(-2)}{-1}$

2. Simplify and choose the correct option.
   $$-[10\times(-2)+(-25)]\div(-5)$$
   a -9 b -5
   c -2 d 1

3. Kate bought 4 sweaters that each cost the same amount and 1 skirt that cost ₹ 20. The items she bought cost a total of ₹ 160 before tax was added. If x represents the cost of one sweater, write the correct expression to show the given problem.

   a $4x=160+20$

   b $4x+20=160$

   c $4x-20=160$

   d None of the above

4. Evaluate and choose the correct option.
   $$\left(1+\frac{1}{3}+\frac{1}{5}\right)\times\left(\frac{1}{3}+\frac{1}{5}+\frac{1}{7}\right)$$
   $$-\left(1+\frac{1}{3}+\frac{1}{5}+\frac{1}{7}\right)\times\left(\frac{1}{3}+\frac{1}{5}\right)$$
   a $\dfrac{1}{5}$ b $\dfrac{1}{3}$
   c $\dfrac{1}{7}$ d $\dfrac{1}{9}$

5. Which of the following means $5n+7=17$?

   a 7 more than 5 times a number is 17

   b 5 more than 7 times a number is 17

   c 7 less than 5 times a number is 17

   d 12 times a number is 17

6. Andrew deposited ₹ 5500 and Anamika deposited ₹ 4800 in a bank. If the bank pays a simple interest of 2% per annum, then how much more interest would Andrew get than Anamika after a year?

   a ₹ 14 b ₹ 96
   c ₹ 110 d ₹ 206

7. In the given figure, ABC is a straight line. If $EF\,\|\,AD$, $\angle BEG=104°$ and $\angle BGF=152°$, then find the values of x and y.

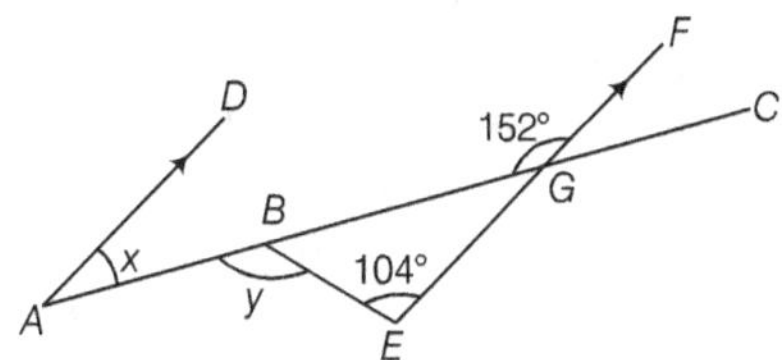

   a $x=132°, y=46°$ b $x=28°, y=132°$
   c $x=46°, y=114°$ d None of these

8. A cuboid was made using cardboard. Karishma made some changes to the size of the original cuboid. She increased the length by 10% and the breadth is $\dfrac{4}{5}$ of the original breadth. The ratio of the new height to the original height is 11 : 10. If the volume of cuboid is equal to length × breadth × height, then what is the new volume of cuboid as a percentage of its original volume?

   a 98.6% b 96.8%
   c 94.2% d 92.4%

9. Three times an angle is equal to two times its complement. What is the value of angle?

   a 180° b 120°
   c 36° d 30°

10. If the speed of light is 3.00×10^{8} m/s, then how far would a beam of light travels in 4000 s?

   a 12×10^{12} b 1.2×10^{10}
   c 1.2×10^{12} d 1200×10^{8}

11. An insurance policy pays 90% of the first ₹ 20000 of a certain patient's medical expenses, 80% of the next ₹ 40000 and 40% of the ₹ 40000 after that. If the patient's total bill is ₹ 92000, then how much will the policy pay?

   a ₹ 90000
   b ₹ 84000
   c ₹ 70000
   d ₹ 62800

12. In 2010, 3,500,000,000,000 prescription drug orders were filled in India. If the average price of each prescription was roughly ₹65, then how much did India pay for prescription drugs last year?

   a 2.275×10^{14}
   b 2.275×10^{12}
   c 2.275×10^{12}
   d None of the above

13. If $C = \dfrac{AX}{X + 15}$ is the formula for a child's dose of medicine, where A is the adult dose in grams and Y is the child's age in years, then find the dose for a child who is 10 yr old, if the adult dose is 50 g.

   a 10 g   b 20 g
   c 25 g   d 40 g

14. If $x = -2$, $y = 3$ and $z = -4$, then what is the value of $-4x + 5y + 2z$?

   a 8   b -8
   c 15   d 10

15. A travelling agent gets a commission of 4.5% on the sale of tickets. If on a certain day, he gets ₹ 31.5 as commission, then the cost of tickets sold on that day is worth

   a ₹ 700   b ₹ 400
   c ₹ 1000   d ₹ 3150

16. How many lines of symmetry does the given figure have?

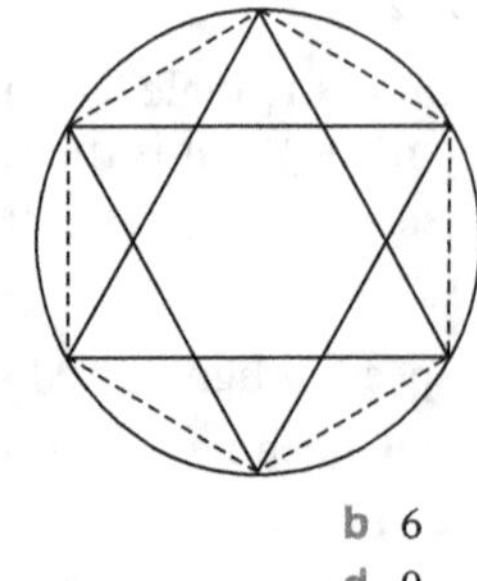

   a 4   b 6
   c 8   d 0

17. What is the front view of the given figure?

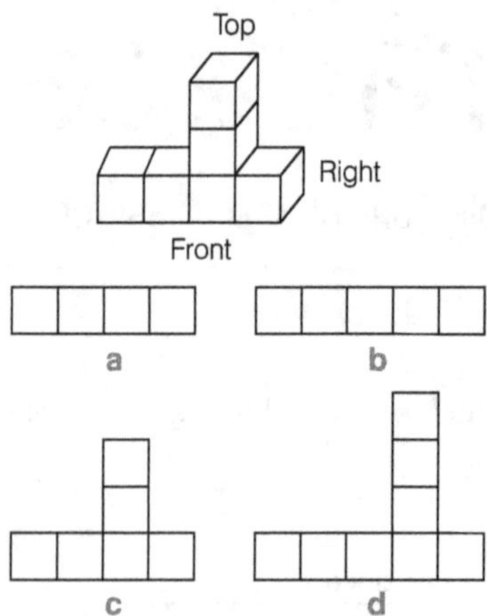

18. Simplify and choose the correct option.
$$63 - (-3)\{-3 - \overline{8 - 3}\} \div 3\{5 + (-3)(-1)\}$$

   a 62   b 52
   c 46   d 72

19. If $\angle 1 = 32°$ and $\angle 2$ and $\angle 3$ are complementary, then the measure of $\angle 4$ is

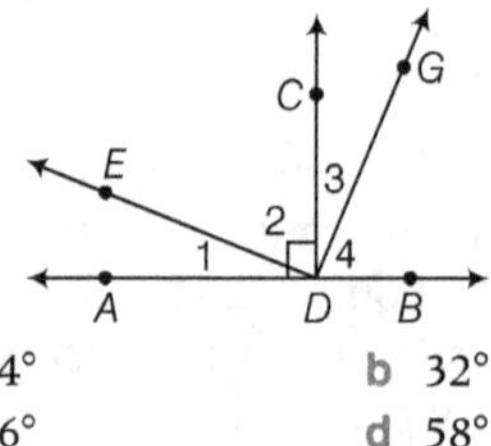

   a 54°   b 32°
   c 36°   d 58°

20. Two different brands of air conditioner were sold at the same price of ₹ 30400 each. The sale of the first set made a profit of 20% while that of the second made a loss of 25%. Find the net gain/loss on the sale of the air conditioners.

   a Gain ₹ 1520   b Loss ₹ 2000
   c Loss ₹ 5067   d Gain ₹ 2000

21. In the given figure, $ABCD$ is a parallelogram such that $AB \| CD$ and $AD \| BC$ with opposite angles equal. If $DA = DX$, then find the values of $\angle m$ and $\angle n$.

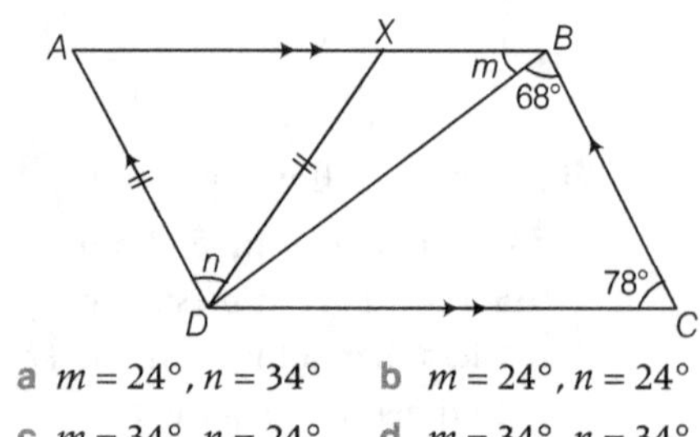

   a $m = 24°, n = 34°$ b $m = 24°, n = 24°$
   c $m = 34°, n = 24°$ d $m = 34°, n = 34°$

22. Sammy drew a rectangle that was w inches wide. The expression $2(2w) + 2(w)$ represents the perimeter of the rectangle that Sammy drew. Which statement relates the perimeter to the width of the rectangle?

   a The perimeter is 6 inch more than the width

   b The perimeter is 6 times the width.

   c The perimeter is 2 inch more than the width

   d The perimeter is 2 times the width

23. Simplify and choose the correct option.

$$\frac{(2\,hj^2k^{-2} \cdot h^4\,j^{-1}k^4)^0}{2h^{-3}\,j^{-4}\,k^{-2}}$$

   a $h^8 j^5 k^4$ b $2h^6 j^4 k^4$ c $\dfrac{h^3 j^4 k^2}{2}$ d $2h^3 j^4 k^2$

24. Which of the solid shapes shown could be made from the pattern?

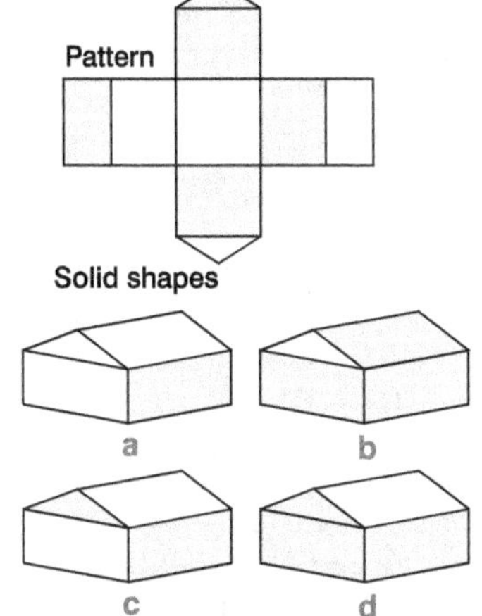

25. Simplify and choose the correct option.

$$\frac{(2m^{-1}pq^0)^{-4} \cdot 2m^{-1}p^3}{2pq^2}$$

   a $\dfrac{m^3}{16p^2q^2}$ b $16p^2q^2m^3$

   c $\dfrac{16\,m^3}{p^2q^2}$ d $\dfrac{1}{16m^3p^2q^2}$

26. In the given figure if BC is parallel to EF and $DC = DB = DA = DE = DF$. Then, what is the value of $\angle CDB$ and sum of $\angle CDF$ and $\angle ADE$?

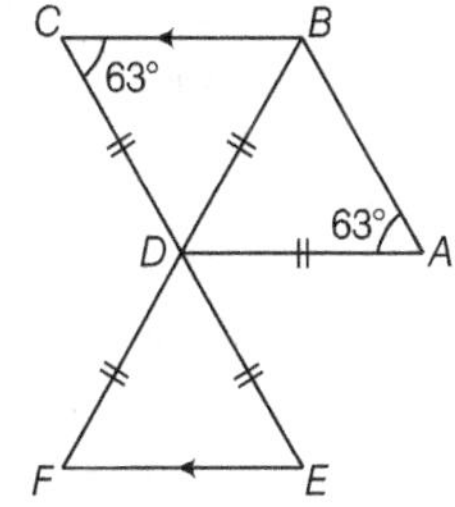

27. Choose the correct net of the given cube?

Completed cube

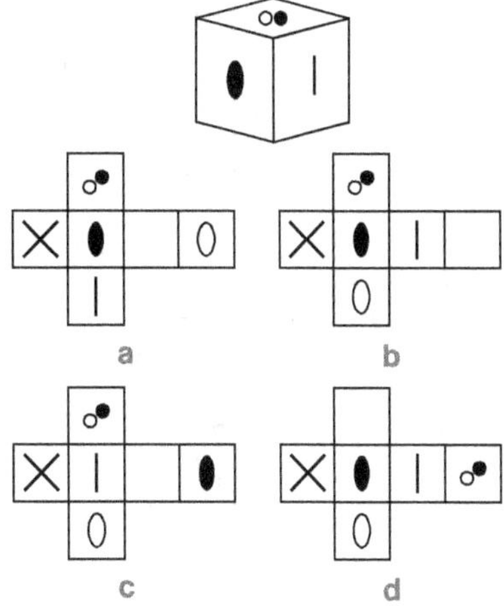

28. The formula for the sum of n terms is given by $S_n = n/2\,\{2a + (n-1)\,d\}$. If $n = 10, a = 6$ and $d = 4$, then S_n is equal to

   a 200   b 240   c 280   d 300

29. Match the following.

	Column A		Column B
I.	The supplement of 80° is	(i)	10°
II.	The complement of 80° is	(ii)	Hypotenuse
III.	The long side of a right triangle is called	(iii)	Rectangle
IV.	A parallelogram in which an angle is 90° is called a	(iv)	Altitude
		(v)	100°
		(vi)	Square

Codes

	I	II	III	IV			I	II	III	IV
a	v	i	iv	iii		b	i	v	ii	vi
c	i	v	iv	vi		d	v	i	ii	iii

Answer options for Q27:

   a 64° and 172°   b 54° and 180°

   c 64° and 184°   d 54° and 198°

30. Which of the cubes shown could be made from the pattern given?

Pattern

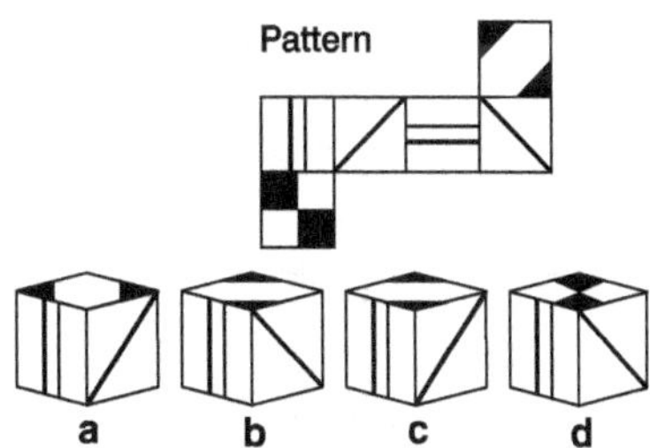

Practice Set 1

Solutions

1. (d) Consider, $\dfrac{(-2) \times 3 \times (-3) \times (-2)}{-1} = \dfrac{-36}{-1} = 36$

2. (a) Consider, $-[10 \times (-2) + (-25)] \div (-5)$
$= -[-20 - 25] \div (-5)$
$= -[-45] \div (-5)$
$= 45 \div -5 = -9$

3. (b) Given,
   Number of sweaters bought = 4
   and cost of 1 sweater = x
   $\therefore$ Cost of 4 sweaters = $4x$
   Now, number of skirts bought = 1
   Cost of 1 skirt = ₹ 20
   $\therefore$ Total cost = $4x + 20$
   According to the question,
   $$4x + 20 = 160$$

4. (c) Let $\dfrac{1}{3} + \dfrac{1}{5} = A$ and $\dfrac{1}{3} + \dfrac{1}{5} + \dfrac{1}{7} = B$

   According to the question, we have
   $(1 + A)B - (1 + B)A$
   $= B + AB - A - AB$
   $= B - A$
   $\left(= \dfrac{1}{3} + \dfrac{1}{5} + \dfrac{1}{7}\right) - \left(\dfrac{1}{3} + \dfrac{1}{5}\right) = \dfrac{1}{7}$

5. (a) 5 times a number $(n) = 5n$
   7 more than 5 times a number = $7 + 5n$
   According to the first statement,
   $$5n + 7 = 17$$

6. (a) Amount deposited by Andrew = ₹ 5500
   Rate of interest = 2%
   Time = 1 yr
   $\therefore$ Interest earned = $\dfrac{5500 \times 2 \times 1}{100} = ₹ 110$
   Amount deposited by Anamika = ₹ 4800
   Rate of interest = 2%
   Time = 1 yr
   $\therefore$ Interest earned = $\dfrac{4800 \times 1 \times 2}{100} = 96$
   $\therefore$ Difference in interests = ₹ $(110 - 96) = ₹ 14$

7. (b)

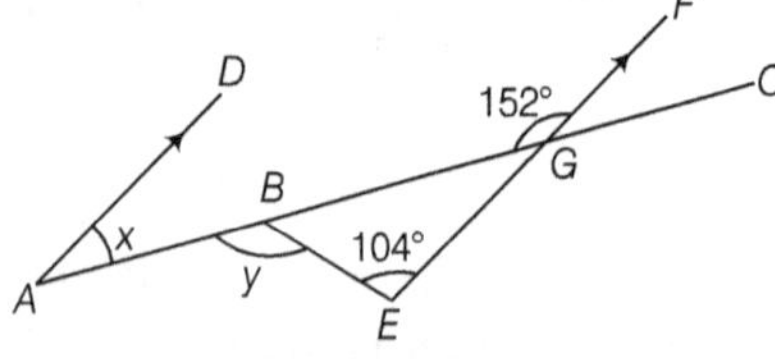

In the above figure,
$$EF \parallel AD$$
$$\angle BEG = 104°$$
$$\angle BGF = 152°$$
Now, $AD \parallel GF$
$\Rightarrow \angle x + 152° = 180°$ [interior angles on the same side of a transversal are supplementary]
$\therefore \angle x = 180° - 152° = 28°$
Also, $\angle AGF + \angle AGE = 180°$ [linear pair]

$\therefore$ $152° + \angle AGE = 180°$
$\Rightarrow$ $\angle AGE = 180° - 152° = 28°$
Now, in ΔBEG,
$\angle BEG + \angle BGE = \angle y$
[exterior angle is equal to the sum of interior opposite angles]
$\therefore$ $\angle y = 104° + 28° = 132°$

8. (b) Let original length be l, original breadth be w and original height be h.
   Original volume = lwh
   Now, new length = $\dfrac{11}{10}l$ $\left[\because \text{new length } l + \dfrac{10}{100}l\right]$
   New breadth = $\dfrac{4}{5}w$
   and new height = $\dfrac{11}{10}h$
   New volume, $\dfrac{11}{10}l \times \dfrac{4}{5}w \times \dfrac{11}{10}h = \dfrac{484}{500}lwh = 0.968\,lwh$
   $\therefore$ New volume as a percentage of original volume
   $= \dfrac{0.968\,lwh}{lwh} \times 100 = 96.8\%$

9. (c) Let the angle be x and complement be y.
   Then, $3x = 2y$
   $\Rightarrow$ $y = \dfrac{3}{2}x = 1.5\,x$
   Now, $x + y = 90°$ [complementary angles]
   $\Rightarrow$ $x + 1.5x = 90°$
   $\Rightarrow$ $2.5x = 90°$
   $\Rightarrow$ $x = 36°$

10. (c) Speed of light = 3.00×10^8 m/s
    Time to travel = 4000 s
    Distance travelled = $3 \times 10^8 \times 4000$
    $= 12000 \times 10^8 = 1.2 \times 10^{12}$

11. (d) Patient's total bill = ₹ 92000
    Money back on first ₹ 20000 = $\dfrac{90}{100} \times 20000$
    $= ₹18000$
    Money back on next ₹ 40000 = $\dfrac{40000 \times 80}{100}$
    $= ₹32000$
    Remaining amount = $92000 - 20000 - 40000$
    $= ₹ 32000$
    Money back on remaining amount = $\dfrac{32000 \times 40}{100}$
    $= ₹ 12800$
    $\therefore$ Total money received from insurance
    $= ₹ 18000 + ₹ 32000 + ₹ 12800$
    $= ₹ 62800$

12. (a) Prescription orders in India, for 2010
    $= 3,500,000,000,000$
    $= 3.5 \times 10^{12}$
    Average price of each prescription = ₹ 65
    $\therefore$ Total price = ₹ $65 \times 3.5 \times 10^{12}$
    $= 227.5 \times 10^{12} = 2.275 \times 10^{14}$

13. (b) Given, $C = \dfrac{AX}{X + 15}$

Here, $A = 50\,g$ and $X = 10\,yr$

$\therefore \quad C = \dfrac{50 \times 10}{10 + 15} = \dfrac{500}{25} = 20\,g$

14. (c) Consider, $-4x + 5y + 2z$

Given, $x = -2$, $y = 3$ and $z = -4$

$\therefore \; -4\,(-2) + 5\,(3) + 2\,(-4)$

$\Rightarrow \quad 8 + 15 - 8 = 15$

15. (a) Commission received by travelling agent at rate = 4.5%

Amount of commission received = ₹ 31.5

We have, $\dfrac{4.5}{100} \times x = ₹\,31.5$

$\therefore \qquad\qquad x = \dfrac{31.5}{4.5} \times 100 = 700$

16. (b) It has 6 lines of symmetry.

17. (c)

18. (a) Consider, $63 - (-3)\,\{-3 - \overline{8 - 3}\} \div 3\,\{5 + (-3)\,(-1)\}$

$\qquad = 63 + 3\,\{-3 - 5\} + 3\,(5 + 3)\}$

$\qquad = 63 + 3\,\{-8\} \div 3\,(8)$

$\qquad = 63 - 24 \div 24 = 63 - 1 = 62$

19. (d) Given, $\qquad\qquad \angle 1 = 32°$

and $\qquad\qquad \angle 2 + \angle 3 = 90°$

Also, $\qquad\qquad \angle 1 + \angle 2 = 90°$

$\Rightarrow \qquad\qquad \angle 1 = \angle 3 = 32°$

We know that, $\; \angle 3 + \angle 4 = 90°$

$\Rightarrow \qquad\qquad 32° + \angle 4 = 90°$

$\Rightarrow \qquad\qquad \angle 4 = 90° - 32° = 58°$

20. (c) Let the cost of air conditioner be x.

Profit on sales of first type air conditioner = 20%

Sales price of first type air conditioner = 30400

So, $\dfrac{120}{100} \times x = 30400$

$\Rightarrow \qquad x = \dfrac{30400 \times 100}{120} = 25333.33$

Loss on sales of second type air conditioner = 25%

So, $\dfrac{75}{100} \times x = 30400$

$\Rightarrow \qquad x = \dfrac{30400 \times 100}{75} = 40533.33$

Total cost price = $25333.33 + 40533.33 = 65866.66$

Total sell = $2 \times 30400 = 60800$

Gain/Loss = $60800 - 65866.66 = -5066.66 \approx -5067$

21. (c) Given, $\qquad AD \parallel BC,$

$\qquad\qquad\qquad AB \parallel CD$

and $\angle A = \angle C$, $\angle B = \angle D$

Also, given $\angle C = 78° \Rightarrow \angle A = 78°$

In $\triangle ADX$,

$\qquad\qquad\qquad AD = XD$

$\Rightarrow \qquad\qquad \angle DAX = \angle DXA$

$\qquad$ [angle opposite to equal sides are also equal]

$\therefore \qquad\qquad \angle DXA = 78°$

Also, $\angle ADX + \angle DAX + \angle DXA = 180°]$

$\qquad$ [sum of three angles of a triangle is 180°]

$\Rightarrow \; n + 78° + 78° = 180°$

$\therefore \qquad\qquad n = 24°$

Also, $\qquad\qquad AB \parallel CD$

$\therefore \; \angle ABC + \angle BCD = 180°$

$\therefore \; m + 68° + 78° = 180°$

$\qquad$ [interior angles on the same side of transversal are supplementary]

$\Rightarrow \qquad\qquad m = 34°$

22. (b) By the given statement in question,

Perimeter = $2\,(2w) + 2\,(w) = 4w + 2w = 6w$

where, w is the width of the rectangle in inches.

23. (c) Consider $\dfrac{(2hj^2k^{-2} \cdot h^4 j^{-1} k^4)^0}{2h^{-3} j^{-4} k^{-2}}$

We know that, $a^0 = 1$

$\therefore$ Numerator = 1

Denominator = $2h^{-3} j^{-4} k^{-2}$

So, we have

$\dfrac{1}{2h^{-3} j^{-4} k^{-2}} = \dfrac{h^3 j^4 k^2}{2} \qquad \left[\because a^{-m} = \dfrac{1}{a^m} \right]$

24. (d) By folding the given pattern we get this shape.

25. (a) Consider, $\dfrac{(2m^{-1} pq^0)^{-4} \cdot 2m^{-1} p^3}{2pq^2}$

$= \dfrac{(2^{-4})\,(m^{-1})^{-4}\,(p^{-4})\,(q^0)^{-4} \cdot 2m^{-1} p^3}{2pq^2} \qquad [(a^m)^n = a^{m \times n}]$

$= \dfrac{2^{-4}\,m^4\,p^{-4} \times 1 \cdot 2\,m^{-1} p^3}{2pq^2} \qquad [a^0 = 1]$

$= \dfrac{m^3}{2^4\,p^2 q^2} \qquad \left[\because a^{-m} = \dfrac{1}{a^m}, \dfrac{a^m}{a^n} = a^{m-n}, a^m \cdot a^n = a^{m+n} \right]$

$= \dfrac{m^3}{16\,p^2 q^2}$

26. (d) Consider $\triangle DCB$,

$\angle a + \angle b + \angle DCB = 180°$

$\Rightarrow \quad \angle a + \angle b + 63° = 180°$

$\Rightarrow \qquad \angle a + \angle b = 117°$

Also, $\angle b = 63°$ $[\because DC = DB]$

$\Rightarrow \quad \angle a = 54°$

In $\triangle DAB$, $\quad DB = DA$

$\Rightarrow \qquad\qquad \angle d = \angle BAD$

$\Rightarrow \qquad\qquad \angle d = 63°$

$\therefore \qquad\qquad \angle e = 54° \qquad$ [as done above]

Also, $\qquad CB \parallel FE$

$\Rightarrow \qquad\qquad \angle b = \angle g \qquad$ [alternate angles]

$\Rightarrow \qquad\qquad \angle g = 63°$

Also, $\qquad DF = DE$

$\Rightarrow \qquad\qquad \angle g = \angle h$

$\therefore \qquad\qquad \angle h = 63°$

In $\triangle DFE$,

$\qquad \angle f + \angle g + \angle h = 180°$

$\Rightarrow \quad \angle f + 63° + 63° = 180°$

$\Rightarrow \qquad\qquad \angle f = 54°$

Now, $\angle CDF + \angle CDB = 180° \qquad$ [linear pair]

$\Rightarrow \qquad \angle CDF + 54° = 180°$

$\Rightarrow \qquad\qquad \angle CDF = 126°$

Similarly,

$\angle e + \angle f + \angle ADE = 180° \qquad$ [linear pair]

$\Rightarrow 54° + 54° + \angle ADE = 180°$

$\Rightarrow \qquad\qquad \angle ADE = 72°$

$\therefore \qquad \angle CDF + \angle ADE = 126° + 72° = 198°$

27. (b) Opening the given cube we get this net.

28. (b) Given, $S_n = \dfrac{n}{2}\,\{2a + (n-1)\,d\}$

Here, $n = 10$, $a = 6$ and $d = 4$

$\therefore S_{10} = \dfrac{10}{2}\,\{2 \times 6 + (10 - 1)\,4\} = 5\,\{12 + 36\} = 240$

29. (d) I. Supplement of 80° = $180° - 80° = 100°$

II. Complement of 80° = $90° - 80° = 10°$

III. Hypotenuse

IV. Rectangle

30. (a) The given net folds to form the figure given in this cube.

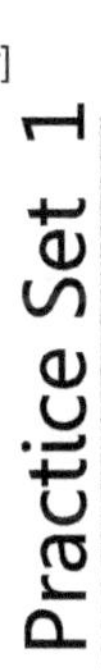

Practice Set 1

Practice Set 2

A Whole Content Based Test for Class 7th Mathematics Olympiad

1. There were fewer than 50 students in a class. Half of the students scored A^+ in a Mathematics test. $\dfrac{1}{3}$ of them scored A in the same test and another $\dfrac{1}{7}$ of them scored B^+. The rest of the students scored B. How many students scored B in the test?

   a 1
   b 3
   c 4
   d 5

2. Which of the following options is simplified value of
   $$(1 + 0.35 + 0.58) \times (0.35 + 0.58 + 0.78)$$
   $$- (1 + 0.35 + 0.58 + 0.78) \times (0.35 + 0.58)?$$

   a 0.35
   b 0.58
   c 0.78
   d 1

3. 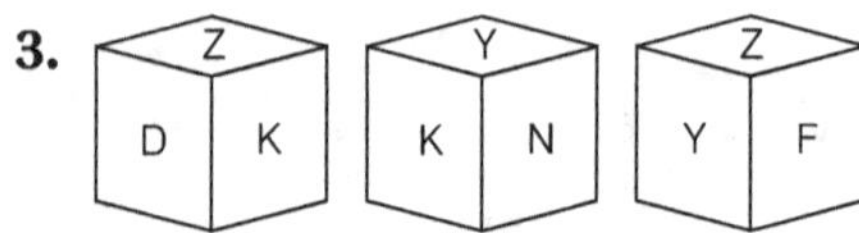

   Which letter is opposite to letter D?

   a K
   b Z
   c Y
   d F

4. Arvind went shopping with ₹ 1500. After spending 0.75 of it on 3 identical shirts, he spent the rest of the money on 2 pairs of shoes. How much did Arvind pay for a shirt and 2 pairs of shoes?

   a ₹ 750
   b ₹ 800
   c ₹ 450
   d None of the above

5. In the given figure, $XY = XZ$ and QY is parallel to PM. What is the value of $\angle QRX$?

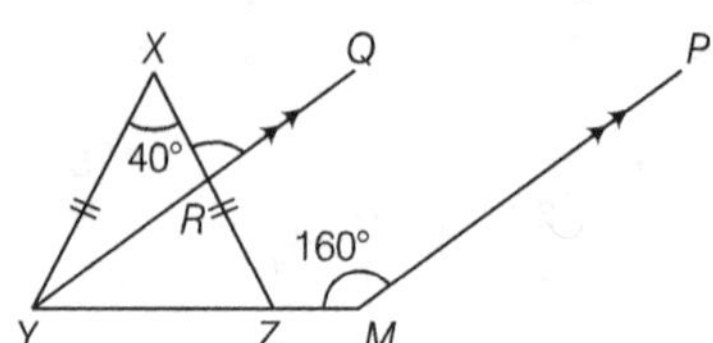

   a 80°
   b 90°
   c 75°
   d 100°

6. Find the value of $5\dfrac{1}{4} - \left(2\dfrac{1}{5} + 1\dfrac{7}{10}\right)$.

   a $1\dfrac{7}{20}$ b $1\dfrac{3}{5}$

   c $2\dfrac{7}{15}$ d $4\dfrac{3}{4}$

7. Simplify and choose the correct option.
   $$\frac{2x^2y^4 \cdot 4x^2y^4 \cdot 3x}{3x^{-3}y^2}$$

   a $10x^8y^6$ b $8x^8y^6$

   c $\dfrac{8}{3}x^4y^2$ d $\dfrac{10}{3}x^4y^2$

8. $\dfrac{2}{5}$th of the fruits at a fruit seller were oranges and the rest were bananas. When the fruit seller bought another 148 fruits, the number of oranges added to the fruit stall was $\dfrac{1}{4}$th to total number of bananas. If the number of bananas added to the fruit stall was 80, then the number of fruits at the fruit stall at first was

   a 280
   b 320
   c 360
   d 400

9. What is the value of $\dfrac{25P - 12}{3}$, when $P = 6$?

a 16
b 28
c 36
d 46

10. Johanson is 5 yr old. Joseph is n yr older than Johanson. What is their total age in 3 yr time?

a $20 + n$
b $9 + n$
c $11 + n$
d $16 + n$

11. Marya earns ₹ 30000 every month. She spends 20% of her salary on rent, 80% of the remaining amount on other expenses and saves the rest. What percentage of the salary does Marya save?

a ₹ 4800
b ₹ 3600
c ₹ 4200
d ₹ 2700

12. Evaluate and choose the correct option.
$$\dfrac{17\frac{2}{3} + 21\frac{1}{2} - 9\frac{1}{3}}{79\frac{1}{2} - 49\frac{2}{3}}$$

a $4\frac{2}{3}$
b $17\frac{2}{6}$
c 1
d None of these

13. A product is marked at 20% above CP. It is then sold at 90% of selling price. The profit is 120. Then, CP is equal to

a ₹ 1500
b ₹ 2000
c ₹ 1200
d ₹ 2500

14. The below figure is made up of a right angled triangle and an equilateral triangle. Then, value of $\angle ABC$ is

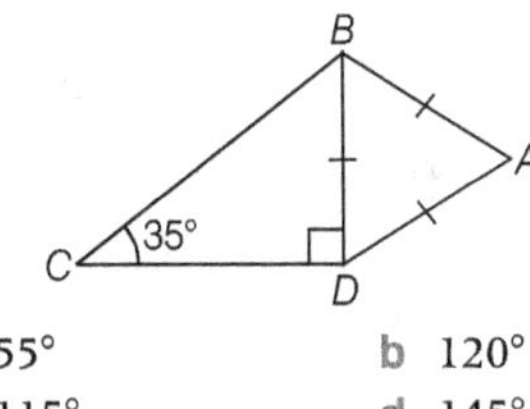

a 55°
b 120°
c 115°
d 145°

15. The following are steps involved in finding each of interior angle of 10-sided regular polygon. Arrange them in sequential order.

I. Each exterior angle $= 36°$

II. Each interior angle $= 180° - 36° = 144°$

III. Each exterior angle $= \dfrac{360°}{n} = \dfrac{360°}{10°}$

$$[\because n = 10]$$

a III, I, II
b II, I, III
c III, II, I
d II, III, I

16. Choose the net below that would make a pyramid when folded.

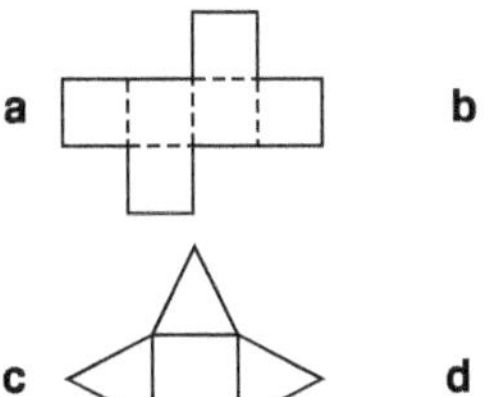

17. A laptop costs ₹ 27900 after a 10% discount. How much would the laptop cost after a further price reduction of 5% off its original undiscounted price?

a ₹ 26700
b ₹ 26350
c ₹ 24630
d ₹ 26375

18. What is the value of $\dfrac{3x - 7 + 11x + 21}{2}$, when $x = 4$?

a 35
b 42
c 32
d 70

19. In the given figure, what is the value of $\angle x + \angle y$?

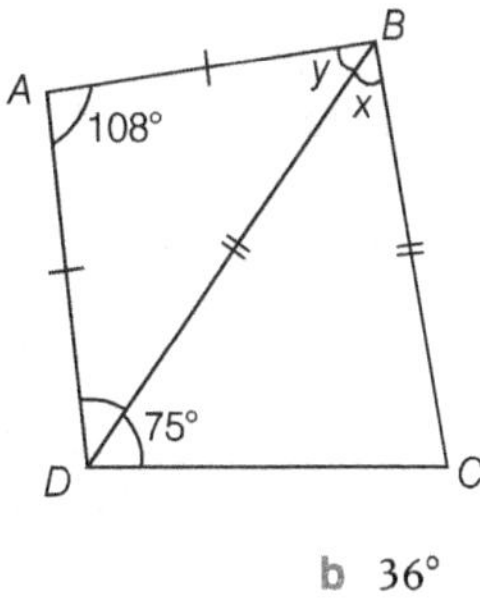

a 30°
b 36°
c 66°
d 72°

20. Mr. Puri deposits ₹ 30000 in a bank that pays an interest of 12%. If he earns an interest of ₹ 10800, then what is the time period for which he kept the money?

a 2 yr
b 3 yr
c 4 yr
d 5 yr

21. Simplify and choose the correct option.
$$\dfrac{(2x^3 z^2)^6}{8x^3 y^4 z^2 \cdot x^{-4} z^3}$$

a $\dfrac{8x^{10} z^4}{y}$
b $\dfrac{6xz^4}{y^{10}}$
c $\dfrac{8x^{10} z}{y^4}$
d None of these

22. The profit gained from the sale of a TV set is ₹ 1000. If it is sold at its selling price. If it is sold at 80% of its selling price, a loss of ₹ 600 will be incurred. What is the CP of the TV set?

    a ₹ 7000
    b ₹ 8000
    c ₹ 9000
    d ₹ 10000

23. The difference of negative twelve and four is multiplied by the square of three will be equal to

    a −144
    b −200
    c −176
    d −184

24. Observe the numbers on below given dice and find the number on the face opposite to the number 4.

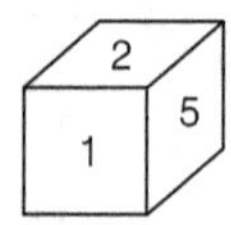 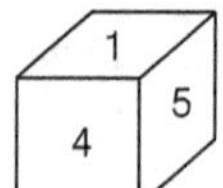

    a 1
    b 2
    c 3
    d 6

25. In the given figure, AOB is a straight line and the ray OC stand on it. If $\angle AOC = (2x-10)°$ and $\angle BOC = (3x+20)°$, then the value of $(5x+40)°$ is equal to

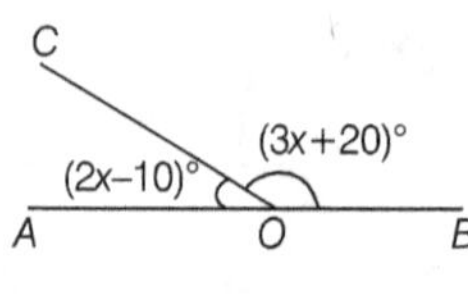

    a 110°   b 93°
    c 210°   d 195°

26. In the given figure, $AY = CY = BY$ and $XA = XB$. What is the value of $\angle CBX$?

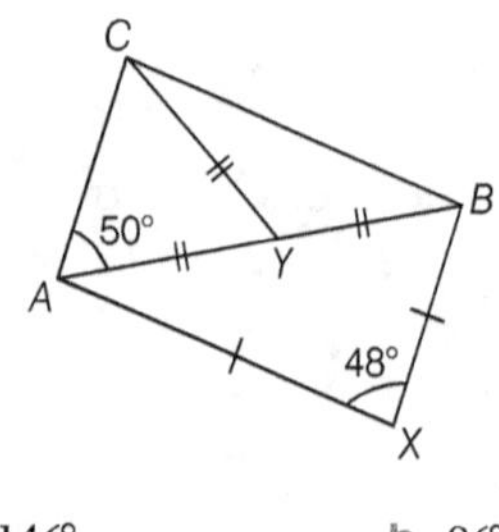

    a 146°   b 96°
    c 106°   d 126°

27. Manisha has 25% more seeds than Sangeeta. If Sangeeta gives 50 seeds to Manisha, she will have half of what Manisha has. How many seeds does Sangeeta have at first?

    a 75   b 150
    c 200   d None of these

28. Match the following.

Figure		Lines of symmetry	
I.		(i)	4
II.	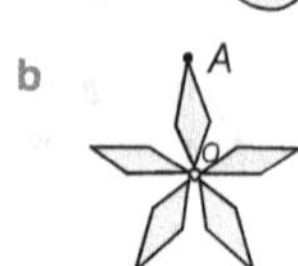	(ii)	1
III.	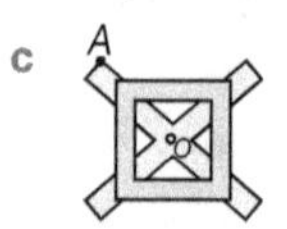	(iii)	0

Codes

	I	II	III
a	ii	i	iii
b	i	iii	ii
c	iii	i	ii
d	i	ii	iii

29. Choose the correctly matched option.

a → It has angle of rotation equal to 120°

b → It has angle of rotation equal to 72°

c → It has angle of rotation equal to 90°

d All are correct

30. The volume of a sphere is $\frac{4}{3}\pi r^3$, where r represents the radius of sphere. Zacky has a football of diameter 18 cm which got flatten. He needs to get it filled with air to play in his practice matches. How much air he needs to get filled in the ball?

    a 900 π
    b 872 π
    c 972 π
    d Can't be determined

Solutions

1. (a) Let the number of students be x.

Number of students who got grade $A^+ = \dfrac{1}{2}x$

Number of students who got grade $A = \dfrac{1}{3}x$

Number of students who got grade $B^+ = \dfrac{1}{7}x$

Total number of students = LCM of $(2, 3, 7) = 42$

$\therefore$ Number of students who got grade B

$$= 42 - 42\left(\dfrac{1}{2} + \dfrac{1}{3} + \dfrac{1}{7}\right)$$

$$= 42 - 42\left(\dfrac{21 + 14 + 6}{42}\right)$$

$$= 42 - 41 = 1$$

2. (c) Let $\quad 0.35 + 0.58 = A$

and $0.35 + 0.58 + 0.78 = B$

We have

$(1 + A)B - (1 + B)A$

$= B + AB - A - AB = B - A$

$= 0.35 + 0.58 + 0.78 - 0.35 - 0.58 = 0.78$

3. (c) Letters on the cubes = K, Z, D, Y, N, F

We have,

K is opposite to F.

Z is opposite to N.

$\therefore$ D is opposite to Y.

4. (a) Amount of money Arvind has = ₹1500

Amount spent on buying 3 identical shirts = 0.75×1500

$$= ₹1125$$

$\therefore$ Cost of 1 such shirt = $\dfrac{1125}{3} = 375$

Now, cost of 2 pairs of shoes = $1500 - 1125 = ₹375$

$\therefore$ Cost of 1 shirt + 2 pairs of shoes = $375 + 375 = ₹750$

5. (b) Given, $XY = XZ$

$\therefore \qquad \angle a = \angle b$

Also,

$\angle a + \angle b + \angle YXZ = 180°$

$\Rightarrow \quad 2\angle b + \angle 40° = 180° \qquad [\because \angle a = \angle b]$

$\Rightarrow \qquad 2\angle b = 180° - 40° = 140°$

$\Rightarrow \qquad \angle b = 70°$

Also, $QY \parallel PM$,

$\angle QYM + \angle PMY = 180°$

$\Rightarrow \qquad \angle QYM = 180° - 160°$

[interior angles on the same side of transversal are supplementary]

$$= 20°$$

In $\triangle RYZ$,

$\angle XRY$ is the exterior angle such that

$\angle XRY = \angle RYZ + \angle RZY = 20° + 70° = 90°$

So, $\angle QRX + \angle XRY = 180° \qquad$ [linear pair]

$\Rightarrow \qquad \angle QRX + 90° = 180°$

$\Rightarrow \qquad \angle QRX = 90°$

6. (a) Consider

$$5\dfrac{1}{4} - \left(2\dfrac{1}{5} + 1\dfrac{7}{10}\right) = \dfrac{21}{4} - \left(\dfrac{11}{5} + \dfrac{17}{10}\right)$$

$$= \dfrac{21}{4} - \left(\dfrac{22}{10} + \dfrac{17}{10}\right)$$

$$= \dfrac{21}{4} - \dfrac{39}{10}$$

$$= \dfrac{105 - 78}{20} = 1\dfrac{7}{20}$$

7. (b) Consider, $\dfrac{2x^2y^4 \cdot 4x^2y^4 \cdot 3x}{3x^{-3}y^2}$

$$= \dfrac{8x^{2+2+1}y^{4+4}}{x^{-3}y^2} \qquad [\because a^m \times a^n = a^{m+n}]$$

$$= \dfrac{8x^5y^8}{x^{-3}y^2}$$

$$= 8x^{5+3}y^{8-2} \qquad \left[\because \dfrac{a^m}{a^n} = a^{m-n}\right]$$

$$= 8x^8y^6$$

8. (b) Let total number of fruits be x.

$\therefore$ Number of oranges = $\dfrac{2}{5}x$

Number of bananas = $\dfrac{3}{5}x$

Number of bananas added = 80

Number of oranges added = $\dfrac{1}{4} \times \left(80 + \dfrac{3}{5}x\right)$

$$= 20 + \dfrac{3}{20}x$$

Total fruits = $\dfrac{2}{5}x + 20 + \dfrac{3}{20}x + \dfrac{3}{5}x + 80$

$\Rightarrow 148 + x = x + 100 + \dfrac{3}{20}x$

$\Rightarrow \qquad 48 = \dfrac{3}{20}x$

$\Rightarrow \qquad x = 16 \times 20$

$\therefore \qquad x = 320$

9. (d) Consider, $\dfrac{25P - 12}{3}$

Given, $\qquad\qquad P = 6$

We have,

$$\dfrac{25 \times 6 - 12}{3} = 46$$

10. (d) Age of Johanson = 5 yr

Age of Joseph = $(5 + n)$ yr

Age of Johanson, 3 yr later = $5 + 3$

$$= 8 \text{ yr}$$

and age of Joseph, 3 yr later = $8 + n$

So, their total age, after 3 yr = $8 + 8 + n$

$$= 16 + n$$

11. (a) Marya's salary = ₹ 30000

Money spent on rent = $\dfrac{20}{100} \times 30000 = $ ₹ 6000

Remaining salary = ₹ (30000 − 6000) = ₹ 24000

Money spent on other expenses = $\dfrac{80}{100} \times 24000$

$$= ₹ 19200$$

Remaining money or savings = 24000 − 19200

$$= ₹ 4800$$

12. (c) Consider, $\dfrac{17\frac{2}{3} + 21\frac{1}{2} - 9\frac{1}{3}}{79\frac{1}{2} - 49\frac{2}{3}}$

$= \dfrac{\dfrac{53}{3} + \dfrac{43}{2} - \dfrac{28}{3}}{\dfrac{159}{2} - \dfrac{149}{3}} = \dfrac{\dfrac{25}{3} + \dfrac{43}{2}}{\dfrac{159}{2} - \dfrac{149}{3}}$

$= \dfrac{\dfrac{50 + 129}{6}}{\dfrac{477 - 298}{6}} = \dfrac{\dfrac{179}{6}}{\dfrac{179}{6}} = 1$

13. (a) Let CP be x.

∴ Marked price = 20% of $x + x$

$= \dfrac{20}{100} \times x + x = \dfrac{2x}{10} + x = 1.2x$

SP of product = 90% of $1.2x = 1.08x$

Profit = 120

∴ CP = SP − Profit

$\Rightarrow \qquad\qquad x = 1.08x - 120$

$\Rightarrow \qquad\qquad 120 = 1.08x - x$

$\Rightarrow \qquad\qquad 120 = 0.08x$

$\Rightarrow \qquad\qquad x = 1500$

14. (c) In the given figure,

$\triangle ABD$ is an equilateral triangle.

∴ All angles are of measure 60°.

In $\triangle BDC$,

$\angle BDC + \angle DCB + \angle DBC = 180°$ [angle sum property]

$\Rightarrow 90° + 35° + \angle DBC = 180°$

$\Rightarrow \qquad\qquad \angle DBC = 180° - 125°$

$$= 55°$$

Now, $\angle ABC = \angle ABD + \angle DBC$

$$= 60° + 55° = 115°$$

15. (a) The correct sequence of steps :

III. Each exterior angle $= \dfrac{360°}{n} = \dfrac{360°}{10°}$ $[\because n = 10]$

I. Each exterior angle = 36°

II. Each interior angle = 180° − 36° = 144°

16. (c)

17. (b) Cost of laptop = ₹ 27900 [given]

Discount = 10%

Let actual price of laptop be x.

Then, $\qquad \dfrac{90}{100} x = 27900$

$\Rightarrow \qquad\qquad x = \dfrac{27900 \times 100}{90} = ₹ 31000$

Further, reduction of 5% = $31000 \times \dfrac{5}{100}$

$$= ₹ 1550$$

∴ Net discounted price = 27900 − 1550

$$= ₹ 26350$$

18. (a) Consider, $\dfrac{3x - 7 + 11x + 21}{2} = \dfrac{14x + 14}{2} = 7x + 7$

At $x = 4$,

$7 \times 4 + 7 = 28 + 7 = 35$

19. (c)

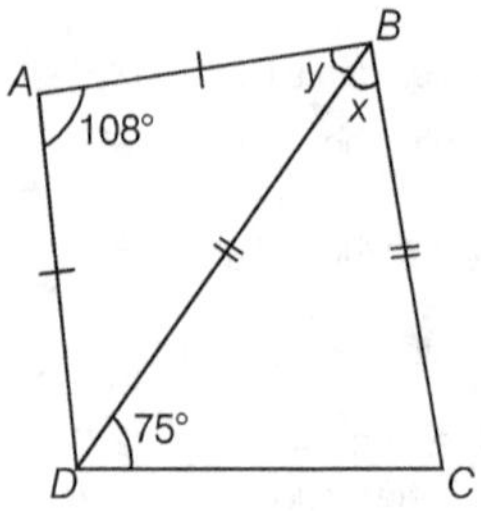

In $\triangle BDC$,

$$DB = BC$$
$$\angle BDC = \angle BCD$$

[∵ angle opposite to equal sides are also equal]

∴ $\qquad\qquad \angle BCD = \angle BDC = 75°$

Also, $\quad x + \angle BCD + \angle BDC = 180°$

[angle sum property]

$\Rightarrow x + 75° + 75° = 180°$

$\Rightarrow \qquad x + 150° = 180°$

$\Rightarrow \qquad\qquad x = 30°$

In $\triangle ABD$,

$$AB = AD$$
$$\angle ADB = \angle ABD$$

[∵ angle opposite to equal sides are also equal]

Also, $\angle ADB + \angle ABD + \angle DAB = 180°$

$\Rightarrow \qquad\qquad y + y + 108° = 180°$

$\Rightarrow \qquad\qquad\qquad 2y = 72°$

$\Rightarrow \qquad\qquad\qquad y = 36°$

∴ $\qquad\qquad \angle x + \angle y = 30° + 36° = 66°$

20. (b) Money deposited by Mr. Puri (P) = ₹ 30000

Interest paid by bank (R) = 12%

Interest earned (SI) = ₹ 10800

Let time be T.

∴ We have,

$$\text{SI} = \dfrac{P \times R \times T}{100}$$

$\Rightarrow \quad 10800 = \dfrac{30000 \times 12 \times T}{100}$

$\Rightarrow \qquad\qquad T = \dfrac{108}{3 \times 12}$

$\Rightarrow \qquad\qquad T = 3 \text{ yr}$

21. (d) Consider, $\dfrac{(2x^3z^2)^6}{8x^3y^4z^2 \cdot x^{-4}z^3}$

$= \dfrac{2^6 x^{18} z^{12}}{8x^{3-4} y^4 z^5}$ $[\because (a^m)^n = a^{m \cdot n}]$

$= \dfrac{2^6 x^{18} z^{12}}{8x^{-1} y^4 z^5} = \dfrac{2^6 x^{19} z^7}{8y^4}$

$$\left[\begin{array}{l} \because a^m \times a^n = a^{m+n}, \\[2mm] \dfrac{a^m}{a^n} = a^{m-n} \end{array} \right]$$

$= \dfrac{8x^{19} z^7}{y^4}$ $[\because 2^6 = 64]$

22. (a) Let SP be x.

$$\text{Profit} = ₹1000$$
$$\therefore \quad CP = x - 1000$$
$$\text{New} \quad SP = 80\% \text{ of } x$$
$$= \frac{8}{10}x$$
$$\text{Loss} = ₹600$$
$$\therefore \quad CP = \frac{8}{10}x + 600$$

So, we have
$$x - 1000 = \frac{8}{10}x + 600 \qquad [\because CP \text{ is same}]$$
$$\Rightarrow \quad \frac{2}{10}x = 1600$$
$$\Rightarrow \quad x = ₹\,8000$$
$$\therefore \quad CP = ₹\,(8000 - 1000) = ₹\,7000$$

23. (a) The given statement $= (-12 - 4) \times 3^2$
$$= (-16) \times 9$$
$$= -144$$

24. (b) 1 is opposite to 5.

So, 2 is opposite to 4.

25. (c) $\angle AOC + \angle COB = 180°$ [linear pair]
$$\therefore \quad \angle AOC = 2x - 10, \ \angle COB = 3x + 20$$
$$\Rightarrow \quad 2x - 10 + 3x + 20 = 180°$$
$$\Rightarrow \quad 5x + 10 = 180°$$
$$\Rightarrow \quad 5x = 170$$
$$\Rightarrow \quad x = \frac{170}{5} = 34$$

So, $(5x + 40)° = (5 \times 34 + 40)°$
$$= (170 + 40)°$$
$$= 210°$$

26. (c) Given, $AY = CY = BY$

and $\quad XA = XB$

In $\triangle CYA$ and $\triangle CYB$,
$$CY = AY \qquad [\text{given}]$$
$$\angle YCA = \angle YAC$$
and $\angle YCB = \angle YBC$ $[\because YB = YC]$

[angles opposite to equal sides are also equal]
$$\therefore \quad \angle YCA = 50°$$

Now, $\angle CYB = \angle YCA + \angle YAC$ [exterior angle property]
$$= 50° + 50° = 100°$$
$$\angle CYB + \angle YCB + \angle YBC = 180°$$
$$\Rightarrow \quad 100° + 2\angle YBC = 180°$$
$$\Rightarrow \quad 2\angle YBC = 80°$$
$$\Rightarrow \quad \angle YBC = 40° \qquad \ldots(i)$$

In $\triangle AXB$,
$$AX = BX$$
$$\Rightarrow \quad \angle XAB = \angle XBA$$

[angles opposite to equal sides are also equal]

Also,
$$\angle XAB + \angle XBA + \angle AXB = 180°$$
$$\Rightarrow \quad 2\angle XBA + 48° = 180°$$
$$\Rightarrow \quad 2\angle XBA = 132°$$
$$\Rightarrow \quad \angle XBA = 66°$$
So, $\quad \angle CBX = \angle XBA + \angle CBY$
$$= 66° + 40°$$
$$= 106°$$

27. (c) Number of seeds Sangeeta has $= x$

$\therefore$ Number of seeds Manisha has $= x + \dfrac{25x}{100}$
$$= \frac{125}{100}x$$

Number of seeds given by Sangeeta to Manisha $= 50$

We have,
$$x - 50 = \frac{1}{2}\left(\frac{125}{100}x + 50\right)$$
$$\Rightarrow \quad x - 50 = \frac{125}{200}x + 25$$
$$\Rightarrow \quad x - \frac{125}{200}x = 75$$
$$\Rightarrow \quad \frac{75}{200}x = 75$$
$$\Rightarrow \quad x = 200$$

28. (c)   I. Number of lines of symmetry $= 0$

    II. Number of lines of symmetry $= 4$

    III. Number of lines of symmetry $= 1$

29. (d) Option (a) has 3 folds of rotational i.e. $\dfrac{360}{3} = 120°$

Option (b) has 5 folds of rotational i.e. $\dfrac{360}{5} = 72°$

Option (c) has 4 folds of rotational i.e. $\dfrac{360}{4} = 90°$

30. (c) Volume of sphere $= \dfrac{4}{3}\pi r^3$ [given]

Shape of football $=$ Sphere

Radius of football $= \dfrac{\text{Diameter}}{2} = \dfrac{18}{2} = 9$ cm

Volume of air filled $=$ Volume of football
$$= \frac{4}{3} \times \pi \times 9 \times 9 \times 9$$
$$= 972\pi$$

Practice Set ③

A Whole Content Based Test for Class 7th Mathematics Olympiad

1. An angle exceeds its supplement by 20°, then the angle is
   - a 100°
   - b 55°
   - c 50°
   - d Can't say

2. If 7 # 2 * 5 is 19, 6 # 3 * 4 is 22, then 11 # 3 * 2 is equal to
   - a 30
   - b 25
   - c 17
   - d 35

3. If it is $-25°F$ in London and it is 75°F in Dubai, then what is the temperature difference between the two places?
   - a -75
   - b -50
   - c 50
   - d 100

4. A monkey sits on wall that is 24 ft above the ground. He swing up 11 ft, climbs up 6 ft more and then jumps down 13 ft. How far off the ground is the monkey now?
   - a 31 ft
   - b 25 ft
   - c 54 ft
   - d 28 ft

5. In the given figure, the measure of angle x is equal to

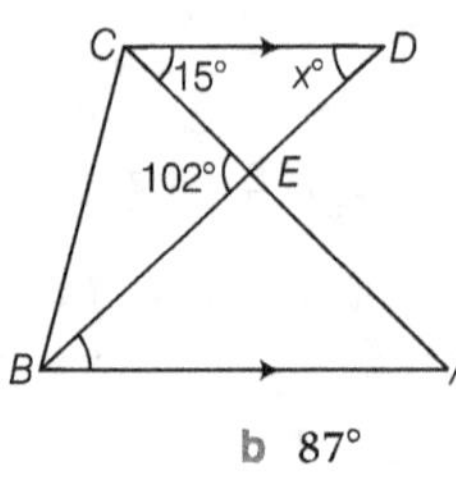

   - a 15°
   - b 87°
   - c 102°
   - d 63°

6. How many flat faces does the given figure have?

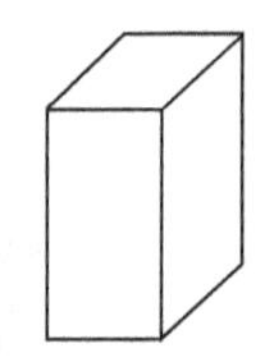

   - a 4
   - b 5
   - c 6
   - d 7

7. Find the value of $83 - \dfrac{12q}{16}$, when $q = 4$.
   - a 35
   - b 80
   - c 48
   - d 86

8. The CP of a table fan is ₹ 4000. If it is sold at ₹ 4400, then the profit per cent is
   - a 5%
   - b 10%
   - c 40%
   - d 20%

9. Lines l and m are parallel and q is a transversal meeting l at A and m at B, respectively. Then, the bisectors of a pair of corresponding angle
   - a are always parallel
   - b may be parallel
   - c cannot be parallel
   - d None of the above

10. If A's salary is 25% more than B's salary, then B's salary is less than A's salary by
    - a 15%
    - b 20%
    - c 22 %
    - d None of these

11. How many flat faces does the given figure have?

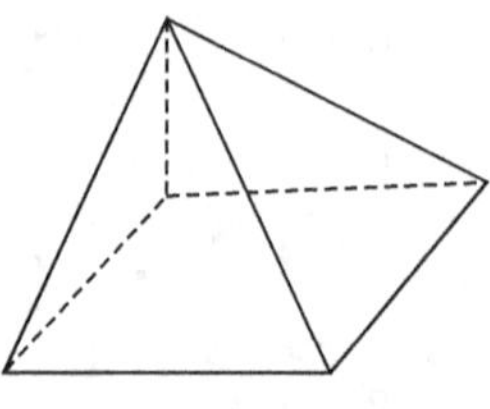

    - a 4
    - b 3
    - c 5
    - d 6

12. Jovia is very interested in cryogenics (the science of very low temperatures). With the help of her science teacher she is doing an experiment on the affect of low temperature on bacteria. She cools one sample of bacteria to a temperature of $-61°C$ and another to $-95°C$. What was the temperature difference in the two experiments?
    - a $+35$
    - b -156
    - c $+34$
    - d $+156$

13. In the given figure if $\angle f : \angle g = 3 : 2$, then what is the value of $\angle g$?

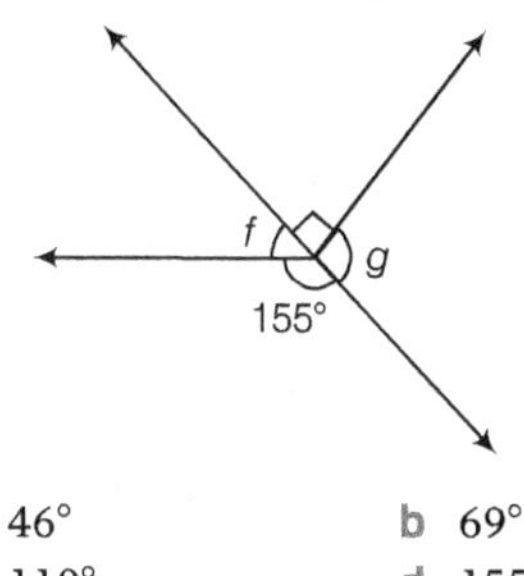

   a 46°   b 69°
   c 110°   d 155°

14. 6 yr ago, a woman was y yr old. She will be twice as old as his daughter in 2 yr's time. Expressing in terms of y, the sum of the ages of the woman and her daughter now, we get

   a $2y + 8$ b $2y + 12$
   c $y + 8$ d $\dfrac{3y + 16}{2}$

15. If $4a + 3c = 9$, then what is the value of $3 + 12a + 9c$?

   a 30   b 12
   c 27   d 18

16. There are 1500 labours in a factory. 30% of them are South Indians and 20% of the remainder are North Indians. The rest are from North-East. How many North Eastern workers are there?

   a 210
   b 840
   c 450
   d 1050

17. If $\left(\dfrac{2}{3}\right)^{x+1} \left(\dfrac{4}{9}\right)^{x+1} \left(\dfrac{8}{27}\right)^{x+2} = \left(\dfrac{3}{2}\right)^{9-x}$, then what is the value of x?

   a 2
   b 5
   c -1
   d None of the above

18. If $a = 2\dfrac{1}{2} \times 3\dfrac{1}{2}$ and $b = 3\dfrac{1}{2} \div 2\dfrac{1}{2}$, then which of the following options is correct?

   a $a > b$
   b $a < b$
   c $a = b$
   d None of the above

19. In a class of 40 students, $\dfrac{1}{5}$ of the students opted painting and $\dfrac{1}{2}$ of the students opted dance. The rest joined drama club. How many students joined drama club?

   a 10   b 12
   c 20   d 8

20. Alex is x yr old. Ibrahim is twice as old as Alex. Sridhar is 5 yr younger than Ibrahim. What is their total age?

   a $5x$ yr
   b $5x - 5$ yr
   c $2x + 5$ yr
   d $5x + 5$ yr

21. Parth has ₹ 1500. Sheen has 20% more money than Parth. Mihika has $\dfrac{4}{5}$ as much money as Sheen. How much do the three of them have altogether?

   a 4750
   b 4600
   c 4400
   d 4740

22. Four years ago, Sama was 14 yr old. Her brother was thrice her age, then what will their total age be in n years' time?

   a $(56 + 2n)$ yr   b $(64 + 2n)$ yr
   c $(60 + n)$ yr   d $(68 + n)$ yr

23. The simplified value of $\dfrac{5x^{-3}y^2}{x^5 y^{-1}} \cdot \dfrac{(2xy^3)^{-2}}{xy}$ is equal to

   a $\dfrac{5}{4}x^{11}y^{-4}$ b $\dfrac{5}{4}x^{-11}y^{-4}$
   c $20x^{-11}y^{-4}$ d $20x^{-11}y^4$

24. Evaluate $\dfrac{1.1 \times 10^{-3}}{7.7 \times 10^{-8}}$, using scientific notation and choose the correct option.

   a 0.5×10^{-3} b 0.2×10^5
   c 1×10^{-5} d None of these

25. Stephanie puts ₹ 800 in a bank that earns her a simple interest of 8% per annum. What is the amount of simple interest earned in 5 yr and when will his interest accumulate to ₹ 512?

   a ₹ 320, 4 yr   b ₹ 320, 8 yr
   c ₹ 640, 8 yr   d ₹ 640, 4 yr

26. Simplify and choose the value for $\dfrac{1+\dfrac{1}{2-\dfrac{1}{4}}}{1+\dfrac{1}{1+\dfrac{1}{3}}}$.

a $\dfrac{11}{49}$ b $\dfrac{4}{7}$

c $\dfrac{44}{49}$ d $\dfrac{7}{4}$

27. Evaluate and choose the correct option.

$$\left(1+\frac{1}{31}+\frac{1}{41}+\frac{1}{51}\right)\times\left(\frac{1}{31}+\frac{1}{41}+\frac{1}{51}+\frac{1}{61}\right)$$
$$-\left(1+\frac{1}{31}+\frac{1}{41}+\frac{1}{51}+\frac{1}{61}\right)\times\left(\frac{1}{31}+\frac{1}{41}+\frac{1}{51}\right)$$

a $\dfrac{1}{31}$ b $\dfrac{1}{41}$ c $\dfrac{1}{61}$ d $\dfrac{1}{51}$

28. The selling price of a sofa set is ₹ 12000. It is later sold at ₹ 6500 at an exhibition. The profit made is 30%. What is the percentage of profit, if the profit is ₹ 5000?

a 50%   b 75%
c 100%   d 200%

29. A shopkeeper bought 80 TV sets at ₹ 40000 each. If then sold 50 of them at a 20% profit in the first month. In the second month, the remaining TV sets were sold at 75% of the first month's SP. How much profit was made altogether?

a ₹ 500000   b ₹ 800000
c ₹ 1000000   d ₹ 1600000

30.

Planet	Distance (from Sun)	Diameter
Mercury	57, 910, 000 km 0.387 A.U.	4,800 km
Venus	108, 200,000 km 0.723 A.U.	12,100 km
Earth	149,600,000 km 1.000 A.U.	12,750 km
Mars	227,940,000 km 1.524 A.U.	6,800 km
Jupiter	778, 330, 000 km 5.203 A.U.	142,800 km
Saturn	1,424,600,000 km 9.523 A.U.	120, 660 km
Uranus	2,873, 550, 000 km 19.208 A.U.	51,800 km
Neptune	4,501,000,000 km 30.087 A.U.	49,500 km
Pluto	5,945,900,000 km 39.746 A.U.	3,300 km

Above table gives the information about the distance of planets from Sun. On the basis of it, find the difference of the distance of Pluto and Saturn from the Sun?

a 7.3705×10^{8}

b 2.5421×10^{9}

c 452.13×10^{8}

d 4.5213×10^{9}

Answers

1. *a*	2. *d*	3. *d*	4. *d*	5. *b*	6. *c*	7. *b*	8. *b*	9. *a*	10. *b*
11. *c*	12. *c*	13. *a*	14. *d*	15. *a*	16. *b*	17. *d*	18. *a*	19. *b*	20. *b*
21. *d*	22. *b*	23. *b*	24. *d*	25. *b*	26. *c*	27. *c*	28. *c*	29. *c*	30. *d*

Practice Set ④

A Whole Content Based Test for Class 7th Mathematics Olympiad

1. Which of the following solids is formed from the below net?

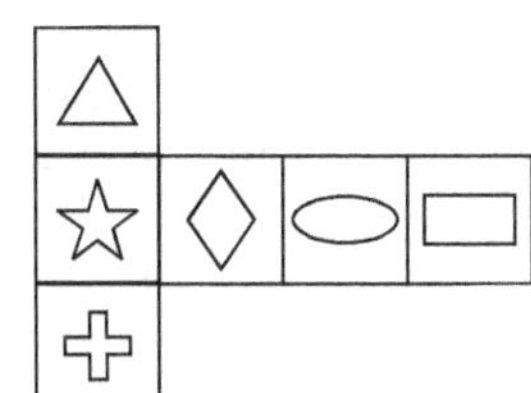

   **a**

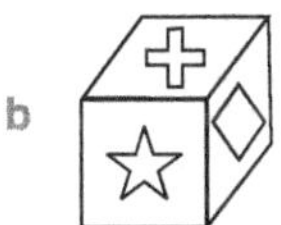   **b**

   **c**

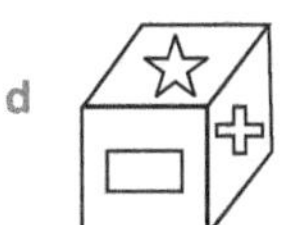   **d**

2. A pie is $\dfrac{3}{8}$ as heavy as a chocolate cake. A sponge cake is $\dfrac{2}{5}$ as heavy as the chocolate cake. If the pie is 600 g, then what is the weight of sponge cake?

   a 1600 g   **b** 1000 g
   c 640 g   **d** 240 g

3. In the given figure, the value of $\angle a$ is equal to

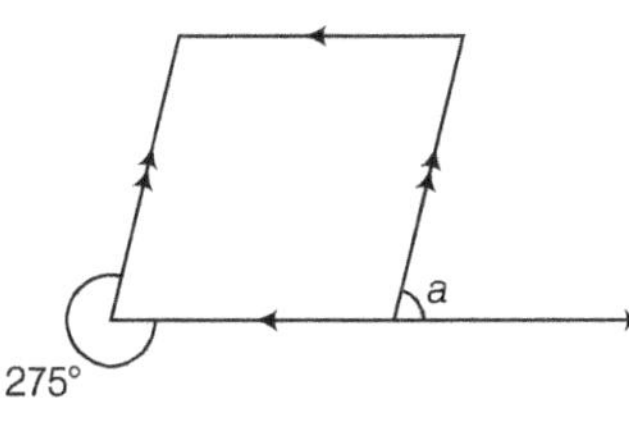

   a 190°   **b** 275°
   c 250°   **d** 95°

4. Jack withdrew 60% of his savings from the bank. He used 0.25 of it to buy a new suit and had ₹ 3960 left. How much did he withdraw?

   a ₹ 8800   **b** ₹ 3520
   c ₹ 5280   **d** None of these

5. What is the value of $4x + 2 \times 3z - (x + 3y - 2x + 4y)$, if $x = 3$, $y = 4$ and $z = 5$?

   a 30   **b** 35
   c 40   **d** 17

6. Gery bought 12 erasers and 2 pens. Each eraser's costs ₹ x and each pen's costs ₹ 20. How much did he pay altogether?

   a $12x$ **b** $14x + 20$
   c $12x + 40$ **d** $40x + 12$

7. $ABCD$ is a rectangle and CEF is an isosceles triangle. Find the values of $\angle x$ and $\angle y$.

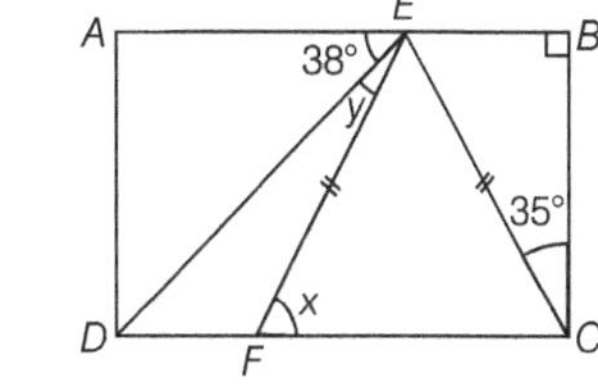

   a $x = 55°, y = 35°$ **b** $x = 35°, y = 27°$
   c $x = 55°, y = 17°$ **d** $x = 35°, y = 33°$

8. How many flat faces are there in the solid shown below?

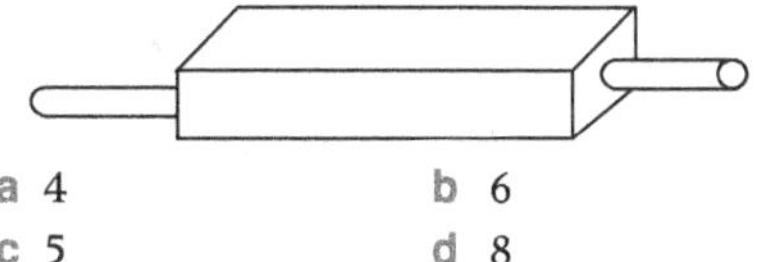

   a 4   **b** 6
   c 5   **d** 8

Direction (Q. No. 9) The pie chart below shows how Anamika spends her salary every month.

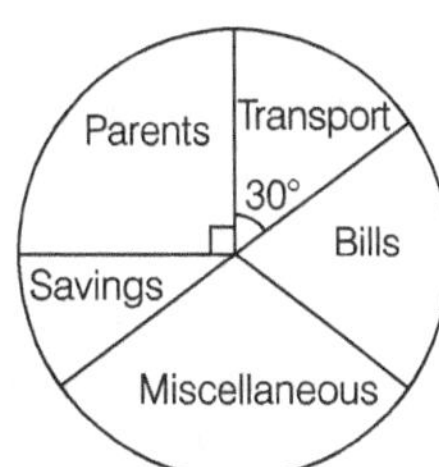

9. What percentage of her money does she save?

   a 16.67%   **b** 15%
   c 17.7%   **d** None of these

10. Anamika's monthly salary is ₹ 28000. If her parents receive an equal amount of money of her $\dfrac{1}{4}$ of monthly salary, then how much does her father receive?

   a ₹ 7000   b ₹ 5000

   c ₹ 3500   d ₹ 2500

11. Which of the following shows the correct net of the solid?

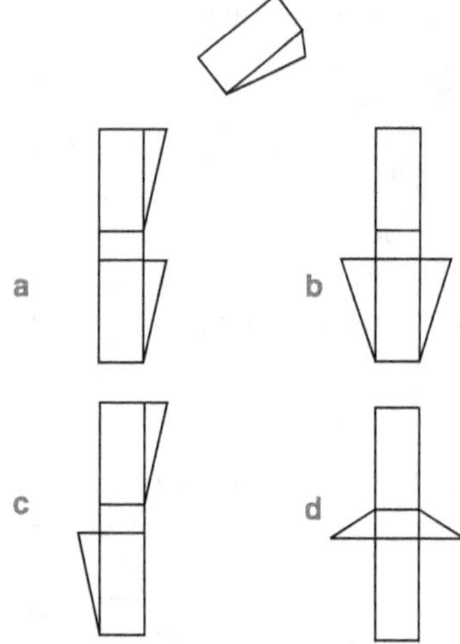

a   b

c   d

12. Ramesh bought $5\dfrac{1}{2}$ kg of sugar. He wants to make cookies for his son's Kindergarten class. The cookie recipe calls for $\dfrac{2}{3}$ kg of sugar per dozen cookies. How many dozen cookies can he make?

   a $7\dfrac{5}{4}$ b 7

   c $14\dfrac{3}{2}$ d None of these

13. Find the value of b, if

$$\cfrac{1}{3+\cfrac{1}{4+\cfrac{1}{b+\cfrac{1}{6}}}} = \dfrac{130}{421}.$$

   a 2   b 3

   c 4   d 5

14. A bank charged 8% annual interest on the money lent to its customers. Manish borrowed ₹ 20000 from the bank that was repayable within 6 yr. What is the total amount payable after 6 yr?

   a 29600   b 26900

   c 29200   d None of these

15. Evaluate and choose the correct option.

$$\frac{1}{1\times4}+\frac{1}{4\times7}+\frac{1}{7\times10}+\frac{1}{10\times13}+\ldots+\frac{1}{97\times100}$$

   a $\dfrac{40}{9799}$ b $\dfrac{33}{100}$

   c $\dfrac{45}{199}$ d $\dfrac{30}{499}$

16. 5 yr ago, a man was x yr old. He will be thrice as old as his daughter in 2 yr's time. Expressing, in terms of x, the sum of the ages of the man and his daughter now.

   a $\dfrac{4x+16}{3}$ yr   b $\dfrac{7x+15}{3}$ yr

   c $4x+25$ yr   d $3x+15$ yr

17. If $b-2a=5$, then what is the value of $\dfrac{1}{8a-4b}$?

   a $\dfrac{1}{5}$ b $-\dfrac{1}{20}$ c $\dfrac{2}{5}$ d $\dfrac{3}{10}$

18. After spending ₹ 2072 on a set of fashion jewellery, Mona spent $\dfrac{4}{7}$ of the remaining money on a dress. If Mona has 27% of the original sum of money left, then how much did she have at first?

   a ₹ 3528   b ₹ 4600

   c ₹ 3626   d ₹ 5600

19. How many lines of symmetry does the given figure have?

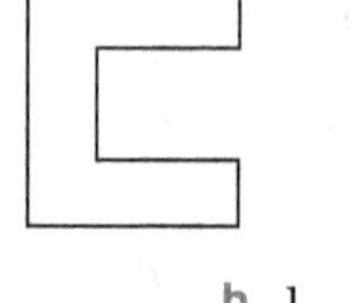

   a 0   b 1

   c 2   d Can't say

20. What is $(30+17)\times12\div3-8\times4$ equal to?

   a 146   b 132

   c 190   d None of these

21. Komal has ₹ 840, Girish has 20% less money than Komal and Boman has $\dfrac{3}{4}$ as much money as Girish. How much do the three of them have altogether?

   a ₹ 2016   b ₹ 2478

   c ₹ 2142   d ₹ 2604

Practice Set 4

22. Tarun had ₹ 200. He spent ₹ m and distributed the rest of his money equally among his 3 friends. How much money did each of his friends receive?

　　a ₹ $\dfrac{200 - m}{3}$　　　　b ₹ $3(200 - m)$

　　c ₹ $\dfrac{m}{3} - 200$　　　　d ₹ $600\,m$

23. Evaluate and choose the correct option.
$$24 \times (16 + 3) \div 6 - 28$$
　　a 30　　　　b 45

　　c 48　　　　d None of these

24. In the given figure, which of the options is correct value for $\angle x$?

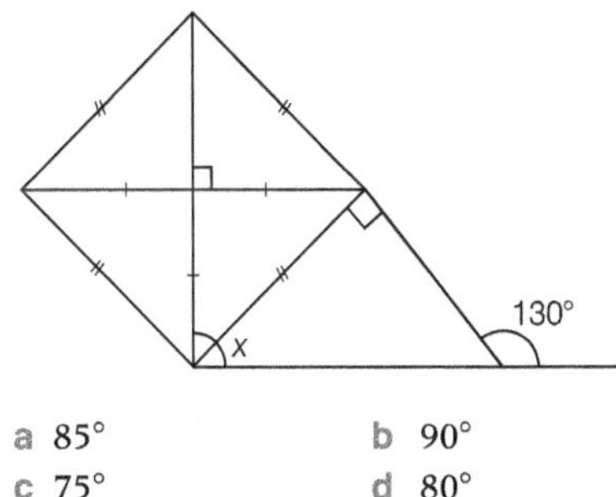

　　a 85°　　　　b 90°

　　c 75°　　　　d 80°

25. Which of the given sequences of operators satisfies the following equation?

$$3 \boxed{} 11 \boxed{} 24 \boxed{} 4 \boxed{} 16 = 43$$

　　a ×, ÷, −, +　　　　b ×, −, +, +

　　c +, ÷, −, ×　　　　d +, −, ÷, ×

26. The star Sirius in the constellation Canis Major is about 50,819,000,000,000 miles from Earth. What is correct form of scientific notation?

　　a 5.0819×10^{14}　　　　b 50.819×10^{13}

　　c 5.0819×10^{13}　　　　d 50.819×10^{12}

27. If '+' is replaced by ÷,

　　'−' is replaced by +,

　　'÷' is replaced by × and

　　'×' is replaced by −,

then what will be the correct answer for
$36 + 9 - 2 \div 5 \times 3$?

　　a 14　　　　b 11

　　c −15　　　　d None of these

28. $ABCD$ is a rhombus and CDE is an isosceles triangle. If BCE is a straight line, then what is the value of $\angle CED$?

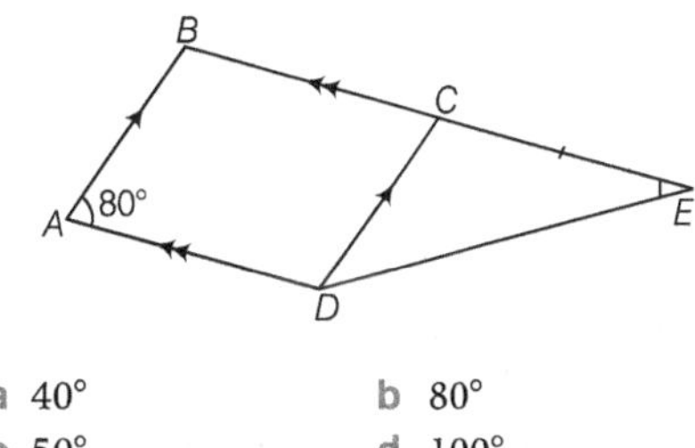

　　a 40°　　　　b 80°

　　c 50°　　　　d 100°

29. Minish has a toy in the form of hemisphere mounted by a cone. If the volume of a cone is given by $V = \dfrac{1}{3}\pi r^2 h$, whereas sphere $= \dfrac{4}{3}\pi r^3$ and radius $= 15$ units and height of cone $= 2$ units, then volume of toy is

　　a $900\,\pi$　　　　b $150\,\pi$

　　c $1050\,\pi$　　　　d $4650\,\pi$

30. Simplify and choose the correct option.
$$\left(\frac{3xy^{-2}y^4}{2x^{-1}y}\right) \cdot \left(\frac{2xy}{4x^{-1}y^{-3}}\right)^2$$

　　a $\dfrac{3}{4}x^7y^8$　　　　b $\dfrac{3}{16}x^4y^8$

　　c $\dfrac{1}{3} \cdot \dfrac{x^6}{y^9}$　　　　d $\dfrac{3}{8}x^6y^9$

Answers

1. *d*	2. *c*	3. *d*	4. *c*	5. *d*	6. *c*	7. *c*	8. *d*	9. *a*	10. *c*
11. *b*	12. *a*	13. *d*	14. *a*	15. *b*	16. *a*	17. *b*	18. *d*	19. *b*	20. *d*
21. *a*	22. *a*	23. *c*	24. *a*	25. *b*	26. *c*	27. *b*	28. *a*	29. *d*	30. *d*

Practice Set ⑤

A Whole Content Based Test for Class 7th Mathematics Olympiad

1. What is the order of rotation symmetry of the given figure?

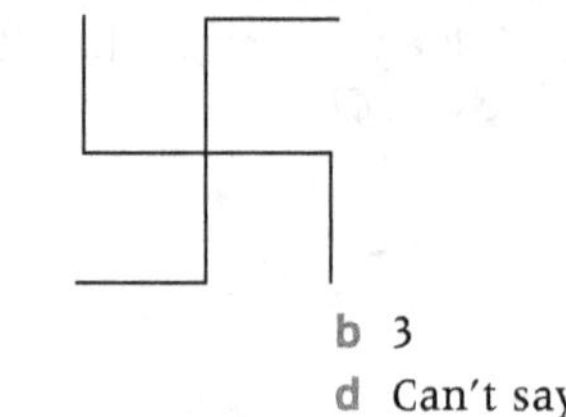

  a 1   b 3
  c 4   d Can't say

2. In the given figure, which of the options is correct measure of $\angle y$?

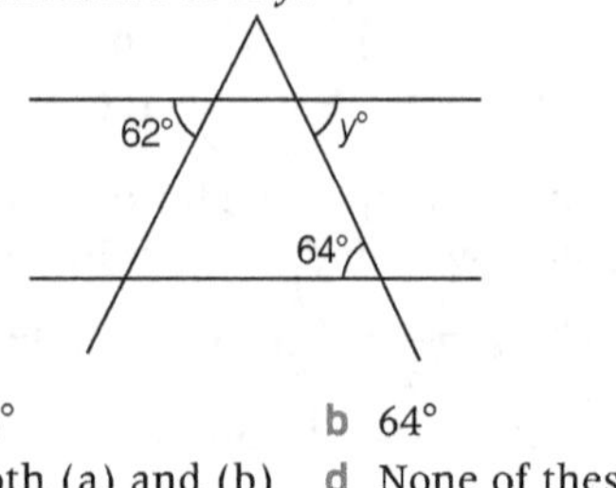

  a 62°   b 64°
  c Both (a) and (b)   d None of these

3. The oxygen hydrogen bond length in a water molecule is 0.000000001 mm. What is the equivalent form of it?

  a 1×10^{-8} b 0.1×10^{-8}
  c 1×10^{9} d 1×10^{-9}

4. A certain plant grows $2\dfrac{3}{5}$ inch every week. How long will it take the plant to grow $7\dfrac{4}{5}$ inch?

  a 3 weeks
  b 3 weeks and 2 days
  c 3 weeks and 4 days
  d 4 weeks

5. Which expression is represented by the number line and arrows shown below?

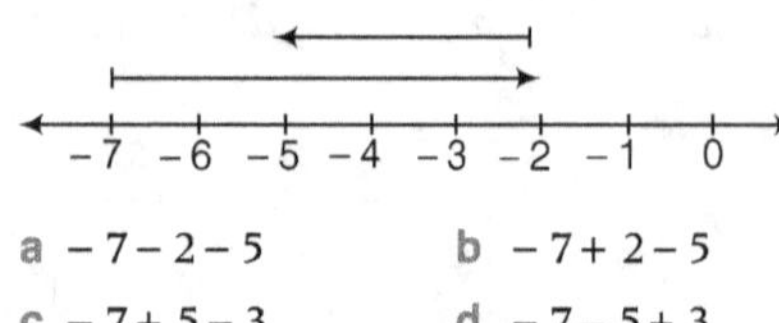

  a $-7-2-5$ b $-7+2-5$
  c $-7+5-3$ d $-7-5+3$

6. Simplify and choose the correct option.

$$\left(2cd^4\right)^2 (cd)^5$$

  a $4c^7d^{13}$ b $2c^3d^8$
  c $4c^8d^{14}$ d None of these

7. In the given figure, $ABCD$ is a parallelogram. The value of x is

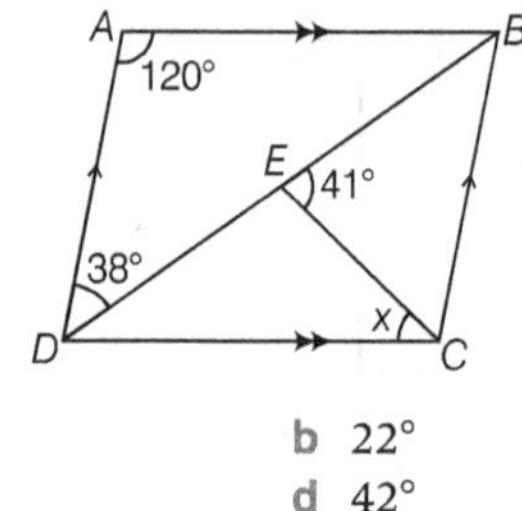

  a 19°   b 22°
  c 38°   d 42°

8. The steepest part of any walking trail in craters of the Moon National Monument rises 12 yards vertically for every 60 yards travelled horizontally. If one particular part of the trail covers a horizontal distance of 30 yards, then how much of a vertical rise is covered?

  a 6 yards   b 12 yards
  c 24 yards   d 30 yards

9. How many lines of symmetry does the given figure have?

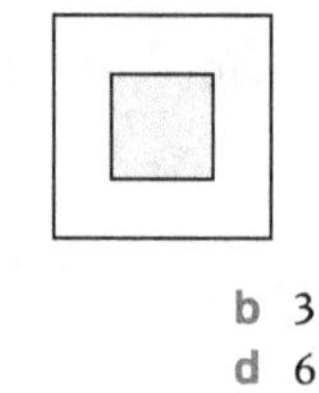

  a 2   b 3
  c 4   d 6

10. Amit bought a furniture set for ₹ 13600 and spent ₹ 400 on its transportation. He sold it for ₹ 16800. Then, his gain per cent is equal to

  a 30%   b 25%
  c 18%   d 20%

11. How much time will it take for an amount of ₹ 450 to yield ₹ 270 with simple interest 20% per annum?

  a 2 yr   b 3 yr
  c 4 yr   d None of these

12. Which of the following shapes is made from the given net?

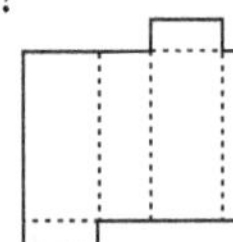

   a Cube   b Rectangular prism
   c Triangular prism   d None of these

13. If the cost of an article is ₹ P and profit on selling the article is 25%, then what is the selling price of it?

   a $5P$ b $\dfrac{4}{5}P$ c $\dfrac{5}{4}P$ d $4P$

14. The simplified value of $\left(\dfrac{-7a^2b^3c^0}{3a^3b^4c^3}\right)^{-4}$ is equal to

   a $\dfrac{21a^4b^5c^{10}}{241}$ b $\dfrac{49a^6b^6c^{14}}{289}$

   c $\dfrac{81a^4b^4c^{12}}{2401}$ d None of these

15. In the given figure, the measure of $\angle y$ is equal to

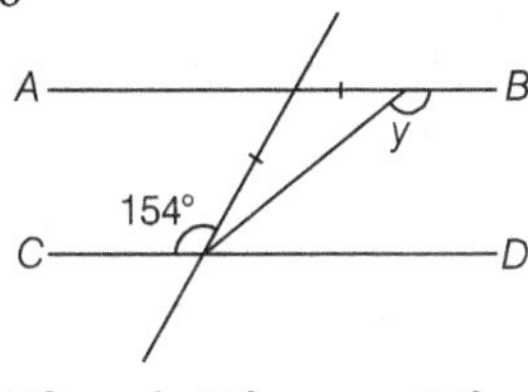

   a $154°$ b $13°$ c $26°$ d $167°$

16. What is the sum which earned interest?

  I. The total simple interest was ₹ 8000 after 8 yr.

  II. The total of sum and simple interest was double of the sum after 5 yr.

   a I alone is sufficient while II alone is not sufficient

   b II alone is sufficient while I alone is not sufficient

   c Both I and II are not sufficient to answer

   d Both I and II are necessary to answer

17. On the basis of given figure match the following Column A to Column B.

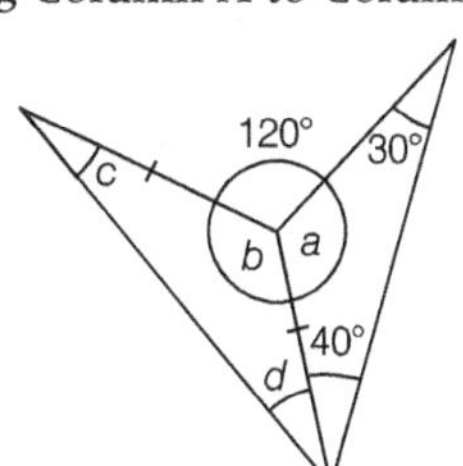

Column A		Column B	
I.	a	(i)	130°
II.	b	(ii)	25°
III.	c	(iii)	110°
IV.	d	(iv)	25°

Codes

	I	II	III	IV		I	II	III	IV
a	iii	i	ii	iv	b	i	iii	ii	iv
c	iii	i	iv	ii	d	Both (a) and (c)			

Directions (Q. Nos. 18-19) A manufacturer of electric bulbs expects 1.02% of its products to be defective. In a recent production run, 277 components were found to be defective.

18. Which form of the per cent equation would be most useful for finding the number of good components?

   a Per cent $=\dfrac{\text{Part}}{\text{Whole}}$

   b Part $=$ Per cent $\times$ Whole

   c Whole $=\dfrac{\text{Part}}{\text{Per cent}}$

   d None of the above

19. When there were 277 defective bulbs, there likely were.........good bulbs.

   a 26880   b 27190
   c 27156   d 26897

20. Which solid shape will be formed by the given net?

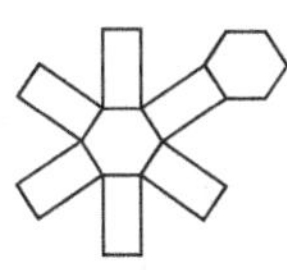

   a 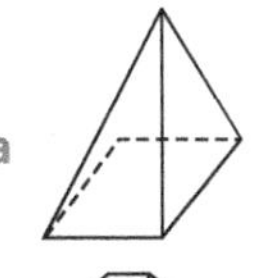   b 

   c 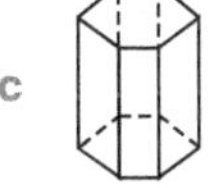   d None of these

21. Naved sells 2000 apples in a week. He recovers his total cost by selling first 1200 apples. He sells the next 300 apples for a loss of 20% and he sells the last 500 apples for a loss of 40%, what is his overall percentage of profit?

   a 45%   b 35%
   c 27%   d 12.5%

22. The expression $\dfrac{\dfrac{a}{b}-1}{\dfrac{a}{b}+1}$ is equivalent to

  a $\dfrac{a+b}{a-b}$ b $\dfrac{a-b}{a+b}$

  c $\dfrac{1}{a-b}$ d $\dfrac{1}{a+b}$

23. 1200 soldiers in a camp had enough food for 28 days. After 4 days, some soldiers were transferred to another camp and thus the food lasted for an extra 32 days. Then, the number of soldiers left the camp is equal to

  a 320   b 486   c 490   d 300

24. Alex, Browny and Kate share some marbles. Browny had 40% more marbles than Alex. Kate has $\dfrac{6}{10}$ what Browny had. If Kate had 1176 marbles, then how many marbles did they have altogether?

  a 4500   b 4526   c 4536   d 5656

25. A solid figure has 3 rectangular faces and 2 triangular bases, then the name of the solid figure is

  a triangular prism

  b triangular pyramid

  c rectangular prism

  d rectangular pyramid

26. Which of the following shows the correct solid formed when the given net is folded?

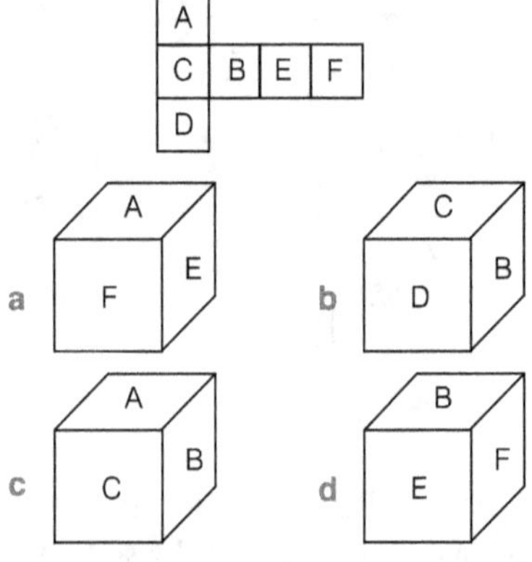

27. A retailer buys books from a wholesaler at the rate of ₹ 300 per book and marked them at ₹ 400 each. He allows some discount and gets a profit of 30% on the cost price. What per cent discount does he allows to his customers?

  a 3%   b 2.5%

  c 2%   d 1.5%

28. Simplify and choose the correct option.

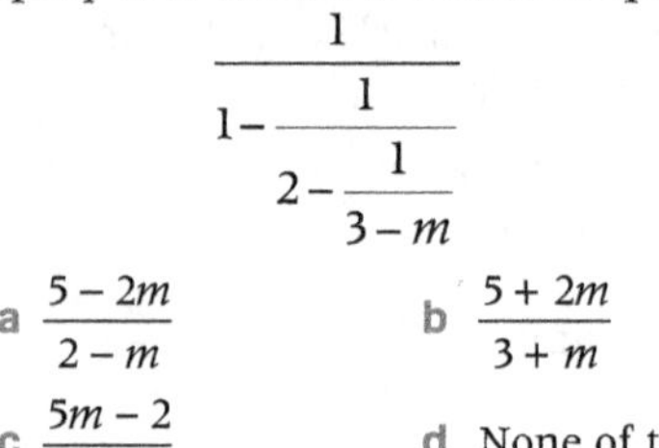

  a $\dfrac{5-2m}{2-m}$ b $\dfrac{5+2m}{3+m}$

  c $\dfrac{5m-2}{m+2}$ d None of these

29. Jaikishan bought a plot of land in the outskirts of the city for ₹ 2100000. He built a wall around it for which he spent ₹ 145000. And then he wants to sell it at ₹ 2500000 by making an advertisement in the newspaper which costs him ₹ 5000. Now, find his profit per cent.

  a 11.11%   b 12.25%

  c 15%   d 25%

30. A survey of college students found that $\dfrac{1}{2}$ of the female students had jobs and $\dfrac{2}{3}$ of the male students had jobs. It was also found that $\dfrac{1}{4}$ of the female students worked in fast-food restaurants and $\dfrac{1}{6}$ of the male students worked in fast-food restaurants. If equal numbers of male and female students were surveyed, then what fraction of the working students worked in fast-food restaurants?

  a $\dfrac{1}{14}$ b $\dfrac{5}{24}$

  c $\dfrac{3}{7}$ d $\dfrac{2}{7}$

Answers

1. *c*	2. *b*	3. *d*	4. *a*	5. *c*	6. *a*	7. *a*	8. *a*	9. *c*	10. *d*
11. *b*	12. *b*	13. *c*	14. *c*	15. *d*	16. *d*	17. *d*	18. *b*	19. *a*	20. *c*
21. *c*	22. *b*	23. *d*	24. *c*	25. *a*	26. *b*	27. *b*	28. *a*	29. *a*	30. *b*

Practice Set 5

Answer & Explanations

7

1 Integers

A. Representation of Integers on Number Line and Their Addition & Subtraction Properties

1. *c*	2. *d*	3. *c*	4. *b*	5. *c*	6. *a*	7. *b*	8. *d*	9. *b*	10. *a*
11. *d*	12. *c*	13. *c*	14. *b*	15. *d*	16. *b*	17. *b*	18. *c*	19. *b*	20. *c*
21. *a*	22. *b*	23. *b*	24. *a*						

B. Multiplication & Division of Integers and Their Properties

1. *a*	2. *b*	3. *a*	4. *b*	5. *b*	6. *b*	7. *b*	8. *b*	9. *c*	10. *b*
11. *a*	12. *a*	13. *b*	14. *d*	15. *a*	16. *b*				

C. Simplification using Addition, Subtraction, Multiplication and Division

1. *d*	2. *a*	3. *d*	4. *d*	5. *a*	6. *d*	7. *a*	8. *c*	9. *a*	10. *d*
11. *c*	12. *c*	13. *a*	14. *a*	15. *d*	16. *a*	17. *d*	18. *a*	19. *c*	20. *b*
21. *c*	22. *c*	23. *c*							

2 Rational Numbers

1. *c*	2. *c*	3. *a*	4. *b*	5. *b*	6. *a*	7. *c*	8. *d*	9. *d*	10. *d*
11. *d*	12. *c*	13. *c*	14. *d*	15. *d*	16. *b*	17. *a*	18. *c*	19. *c*	20. *a*
21. *b*	22. *d*	23. *b*	24. *b*	25. *d*	26. *b*	27. *d*	28. *d*	29. *d*	30. *c*

3 Fractions and Decimals

A. Fractions

1. *b*	2. *d*	3. *d*	4. *b*	5. *b*	6. *d*	7. *a*	8. *c*	9. *c*	10. *b*
11. *c*	12. *c*	13. *d*	14. *b*	15. *c*	16. *a*	17. *a*	18. *c*	19. *c*	20. *b*
21. *c*	22. *c*	23. *c*	24. *a*	25. *d*	26. *d*	27. *a*	28. *b*	29. *a*	30. *b*
31. *b*	32. *c*	33. *a*	34. *b*	35. *c*					

B. Decimals

1. *c*	2. *c*	3. *b*	4. *d*	5. *d*	6. *b*	7. *c*	8. *d*	9. *b*	10. *b*
11. *c*	12. *a*	13. *a*	14. *a*	15. *a*	16. *b*	17. *b*	18. *c*	19. *c*	20. *a*
21. *c*	22. *b*								

4 Simple Equations

1. *a*	2. *d*	3. *b*	4. *d*	5. *d*	6. *d*	7. *c*	8. *b*	9. *a*	10. *a*
11. *b*	12. *a*	13. *a*	14. *d*	15. *c*	16. *b*	17. *a*	18. *d*	19. *d*	20. *c*
21. *c*	22. *c*	23. *d*	24. *b*	25. *c*	26. *a*	27. *c*	28. *b*	29. *d*	30. *a*

5 Lines and Angles

1. *d*	2. *d*	3. *d*	4. *a*	5. *d*	6. *d*	7. *b*	8. *c*	9. *a*	10. *c*
11. *c*	12. *c*	13. *c*	14. *b*	15. *c*	16. *b*	17. *c*	18. *c*	19. *c*	20. *c*
21. *b*	22. *d*	23. *b*	24. *d*	25. *a*	26. *b*	27. *c*	28. *c*	29. *a*	30. *a*

6. Triangle : Properties and Congruence

A. Triangle and Its Properties

1. *d*	2. *b*	3. *d*	4. *a*	5. *d*	6. *c*	7. *a*	8. *b*	9. *a*	10. *d*
11. *b*	12. *c*	13. *b*	14. *c*	15. *c*	16. *a*	17. *c*	18. *b*	19. *d*	20. *b*
21. *d*	22. *a*	23. *d*	24. *a*	25. *b*	26. *a*	27. *c*	28. *c*	29. *c*	30. *c*

B. Congruence of Triangles

1. *b*	2. *c*	3. *d*	4. *d*	5. *c*	6. *c*	7. *b*	8. *c*	9. *d*	10. *b*
11. *d*	12. *c*	13. *c*	14. *d*	15. *d*	16. *c*	17. *d*	18. *c*	19. *b*	

7. Comparing Quantities

A. Percentage

1. *d*	2. *d*	3. *c*	4. *b*	5. *d*	6. *a*	7. *b*	8. *c*	9. *a*	10. *c*
11. *d*	12. *b*	13. *c*	14. *b*	15. *b*	16. *a*	17. *c*	18. *a*	19. *b*	20. *c*
21. *c*	22. *d*	23. *c*	24. *a*	25. *a*	26. *c*	27. *a*	28. *d*		

B. Application Based Problems on Percentage, Profit or Loss

1. *d*	2. *d*	3. *c*	4. *a*	5. *a*	6. *c*	7. *c*	8. *c*	9. *a*	10. *c*
11. *b*	12. *c*	13. *c*	14. *d*	15. *c*	16. *d*	17. *a*	18. *b*	19. *c*	20. *b*
21. *d*	22. *b*								

8. Algebraic Expressions

1. *c*	2. *b*	3. *c*	4. *b*	5. *a*	6. *d*	7. *d*	8. *d*	9. *a*	10. *d*
11. *b*	12. *c*	13. *c*	14. *d*	15. *c*	16. *a*	17. *c*	18. *a*	19. *d*	20. *b*
21. *b*	22. *b*	23. *b*	24. *c*	25. *d*	26. *d*	27. *a*	28. *b*	29. *c*	30. *a*
31. *d*	32. *d*	33. *a*	34. *a*	35. *c*	36. *c*	37. *d*			

9. Exponents and Powers

1. *b*	2. *a*	3. *b*	4. *b*	5. *c*	6. *c*	7. *a*	8. *d*	9. *d*	10. *b*
11. *b*	12. *d*	13. *c*	14. *b*	15. *d*	16. *a*	17. *d*	18. *c*	19. *c*	20. *c*
21. *d*	22. *d*	23. *a*	24. *c*	25. *a*	26. *a*	27. *b*	28. *a*	29. *c*	30. *a*
31. *a*									

10. Symmetry and Visualising Solid Shapes

1. *d*	2. *d*	3. *a*	4. *d*	5. *c*	6. *c*	7. *c*	8. *d*	9. *c*	10. *c*
11. *b*	12. *c*	13. *d*	14. *c*	15. *d*	16. *a*	17. *c*	18. *d*	19. *b*	20. *a*
21. *b*	22. *a*	23. *a*	24. *c*	25. *b*	26. *b*	27. *b*	28. *c*	29. *c*	30. *b*
31. *a*	32. *b*								

A) Representation of Integers on Number Line and Their Addition & Subtraction Properties

1. Here, $|-48| = 48$

2. All other options have the sum equal to -11.

4. Going above sea level $= +20$ km
   $\therefore$ Its opposite is going below sea level $= -20$ km

6. Consider
   $$|-28 + 12 + 42 - 63| = |12 + 42 - 28 - 63|$$
   $$= |54 - 91| = |-37| = 37$$

7. Consider, $-6 + (-24) - 48$
   $$= -6 - 24 - 48 = -30 - 48 = -78$$

8. By definition

9. Subtraction of integers is not commutative.
   e.g. Consider, $2 - 3 = -1$ and $3 - 2 = 1$
   Since, $\qquad -1 \neq 1$
   $\therefore \qquad 2 - 3 \neq 3 - 2$

10. Distance travelled towards North to Paris = 760 km
    Distance travelled towards South from Paris to Spain
    $$= 1100 \text{ km}$$
    $\therefore$ Marnold's position with respect to starting position
    $$= -1100 + 760 = -340 \text{ km} = 340 \text{ km South}$$

11. Distance travelled towards North in first go = 4 km
    Distance travelled towards North in second go = 8 km
    $\therefore$ Total distance travelled
    $$= (8 + 4) \text{ km} = 12 \text{ km}$$
    So, Shreya's starting position from her end position is 12 km South or -12 km.

12. The correct forecast from lowest to highest is
    $$-79°C, -70°C, -58°C, -53°C, -52°C, -48°C$$

13. I. Subtraction   II. negative   III. 0   IV. $+a$

14. In the other options, the rule followed is correct:
    (a) $(2 + 3) - (6 + 0) = -1$
    (b) $(7 + 8) - (-20 + 4) = 15 + 16 = \boxed{31} \neq 39$
    (c) $(11 + 12) - (20 - 2) = 23 - 18 = 5$
    (d) $(2 + 7) - (11 + 2) = 9 - 13 = -4$

15. Here, $\qquad D = 7$ and $A = -5$
    So, $\qquad D - A = 7 - (-5) = 12$

16. Here, $C = 2$ and $B = -2$
    $\therefore \qquad\qquad C + B = 0$
    and $\qquad D + A = 7 - 5 = +2$
    $\therefore \qquad\qquad C + B < D + A$

17. $D - [4 - (-5)] = D - (4 + 5) = D - 9 = 7 - 9 = -2 = B$

18. Given pattern of the series is as follows:

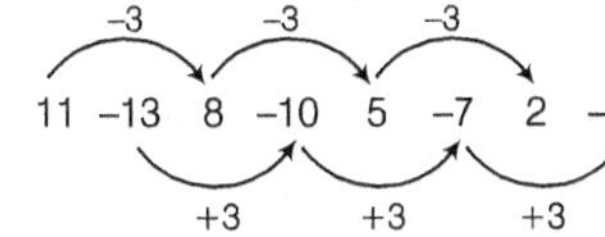

19. I. True   II. True   III. False   IV. False

20. A denotes number of protons and B denotes number of electrons.

21. I. Oxygen = Number of protons = 8
    II. Mass number = 8 + 8 = 16
    III. Neon = Number of protons = 20 − 10 = 10
    IV. Number of electrons or $B = -10$
    V. Sodium = Electrons or $B = -11$
    VI. Mass number = 11 + 12 = 23

22. The sum of the four numbers in each square block is 20.
    So, $\qquad ? = 20 - (4 + 3 + 5) = 20 - 12 = 8$

23. We know that withdrawals are represented by '−' sign and deposits are represented by '+' sign.
    $\therefore$ Final amount $= 11700 - 2500 + 1925$
    $$+ 3380 - 5850 - 1000 + 4000$$
    $$= 11700 + 1925 + 3380$$
    $$+ 4000 - 2500 - 5850 - 1000$$
    $$= ₹ 11655$$

24. If $y = 2n$, $\qquad\qquad$ [even]
    then $(2y^3 + 3)$ is odd.
    $$3y \text{ is even.}$$
    $$y^3 + 3 \text{ is odd.}$$
    $$3y + 2 \text{ is even.}$$
    If $y = 2n + 1$, $\qquad\qquad$ [odd]
    then $(2y^3 + 3)$ is odd.
    $$3y \text{ is odd.}$$
    $$y^3 + 3 \text{ is even.}$$
    $$3y + 2 \text{ is odd.}$$
    So, $2y^3 + 3$ is odd in every case.

B) Multiplication & Division of Integers and Their Properties

1. $2 \times (3 \times 2) = 2 \times 3 \times 2$

2. Given $(-a)^n$ is positive.
   $\therefore n$ is an even number by definition.

3. $(-1) \times (-1) \times (-1) \times (-1) \times \dots 20$ times
   $$= (-1)^{20} = (-1)^n, \text{ where } n \text{ is even.}$$
   $\therefore \qquad (-1)^{20} = 1$
   Since, multiplication of a negative integer to itself even number of times is always positive.

4. Consider,
   $$(-12) \times (-2) \times (+3) \times (-1) = (-12) \times (-2) \times 3 \times (-1)$$
   $$= 24 \times 3 \times (-1) = 72 \times (-1) = -72$$

5. Division of integers is not commutative.

6. Other options have the correct product.
   (a) $0 \times (-1) \times 2 \times 3 \times (-4) \times 5 = 0$
   (c) $1 \times 2 \times 3 \times 4 \times 5 \times (-1) = -120$
   (d) $0 \times 2 \times 3 \times 4 \times (-5) \times 6 = 0$
   whereas in option (b), $0 \times (-1) \times 2 \times (-3) \times 4 \times 5 = 0 \neq 1$

7. $a \div b \neq b \div a$
   Since, division is not commutative. e.g. $4 \div 2 = 2$
   whereas, $2 \div 4 = \dfrac{2}{4} = \dfrac{1}{2}$
   $\therefore \qquad\qquad 2 \neq \dfrac{1}{2}$

8. Given, $3 \times (-7) \times (-8) \times 9 \times 0 \times 4 \times 2$
$$= 0 \times 3 \times (-7) \times (-8) \times 9 \times 4 \times 2 = 0$$
∵ Any number multiplied to '0' is equal to zero.

9. By associative property

11. Given, $(-2) \div 3 \times (-4) \div 1 = (-2) \times 3 \times (-4) \times 1 = 24$

12. I. Multiplication   II. negative   III. 1
    IV. odd   V. operations   VI. less
    VII. integers   VIII. 0

13.   I. $24 \div (-3) = -8$ and $2 \times 6 = 12$
    II. $1 \times 0 = 0$ and $(-2) \times 9 = -18$
    III. $(-8) \div 2 = -4 - 2 \times (+2) = -4$
    IV. $7 \times 8 \times (-9) = -504$
    ∴ Correct sign sequence is
$$<, >, =, <.$$

14. Given, $a * b = a \times b$ and $a \boxed{\bigcirc} b = a \div b$
    So, $(-7) * (-9) = (-7) \times (-9) = 63$
    and $21 \boxed{\bigcirc} 3 = 21 \div 3 = 7$
    ∴ $(-7) * (-9) \boxed{>} 21 \boxed{\bigcirc} 3$

15. I. False   II. False   III. True   IV. True

16. **Assertion** (A) We have, $-2 \times -3 \times -1 = -6 \neq 6$
    ∴ A is false and R is correct explanation of A.

C   Simplification using Addition, Subtraction, Multiplication and Division

1. Given, $7 \times (8 + 9) = 7 \times 8 + 7 \times 9$
Here, distributive property of multiplication over addition is used.

2. Consider, $31 \times 79 - 31 \times 76 = 31 \times [79 + (-76)]$
$$[\text{distributive property}]$$
$$= 31(79 - 76) = 31 \times 3 = 93$$

3. Consider, $\dfrac{2 \times 2 + 2 + (-1)}{-1} = \dfrac{2 \times 2 - 2}{-1} = \dfrac{4 - 2}{-1} = -2$

4.   I. $(-31) + 30 + (-31) + 30 + \ldots$ 30 terms
$$= (-31 + 30) + (-31 + 30) + \ldots \text{ 15 pairs}$$
$$= -1 + -1 + -1 + \ldots \text{ 15 times}$$
$$= -15$$
    II. $(-7) \times 5 + 1 \times 0 = -35 + 0 = -35$
    III. $42 \times (91 - 91) = 42 \times 0 = 0$
    IV. $21 \div (5 - 8) = 21 \div (-3) = -7$

5. Now, $x = 12 \div 4 \times 3 + 4 = 3 \times 3 + 4 = 9 + 4 = 13$
and consider,
$$10 = 39 \div y \times 2 + 4$$
$$\Rightarrow \quad 6 = 39 \div y \times 2$$
$$\Rightarrow \quad 3 = 39 \div y$$
$$\Rightarrow \quad y = 39 \div 3$$
$$\therefore \quad y = 13$$

6. Consider, $22 - \{(2 + \overline{3 - 4}) \times \overline{(-1) + 2}\}$
$$= 22 - \{(2 - 1) \times 1\}$$
$$= 22 - \{1 \times 1\} = 21$$

7.

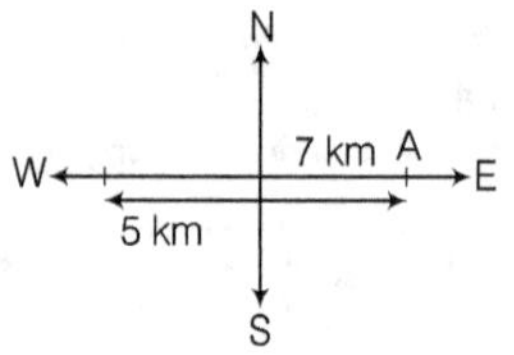

N
W
E
S
7 km A
5 km

Given, original position of man = 7 km (E) and final position of man = -5 km (W)
So, distance travelled = $7 - (-5)$ km $= 7 + 5$ km $= 12$ km
    Speed of man = 1.2 km/min
∴   Time taken $= \dfrac{12}{1.2} = 10$ min

8. **Assertion** (A) Consider,
$$17 - \{(2 + \overline{7 - 3}) - 8\} = 17 - \{(2 + 4) - 8\}$$
$$= 17 - \{6 - 8\} = 17 - (-2) = 17 + 2 = 19$$
∴ A is true and R is false.

9. Original position of Mohan = 24th floor
Final position of Mohan
$$= -3\text{rd floor [3rd basement]}$$
∴ Number of floors to be covered
$$= 24 - (-3) = 27 \text{ floors}$$
Now, speed of elevator = 1 floor/s
So, time taken $= \dfrac{27}{1} = 27$s

10. We have,
$$7 + \{-(2 + \overline{4 - 3} - 1) + 2 \times 10 \div 5\}$$
$$= 7 + \{-(2 + 1 - 1) + 2 \times 10 \div 5\}$$
$$= 7 + \{-2 + 2 \times 2\}$$
$$= 7 + \{-2 + 4\} = 7 + \{2\} = 9$$

11. We have, $= 20 - \{4 + \overline{7 - 8} - 14 \div 2\}$
$$= 20 - \{4 - 1 - 14 \div 2\}$$
$$= 20 - \{4 - 1 - 7\} = 20 - \{-4\} = 24$$

12.   I. $8 - 4(2 + 5^2) \div 9$
$$= 8 - 4(2 + 25) \div 9 = 8 - 4 \times 27 \div 9$$
$$= 8 - 4 \times 3 = 8 - 12 = -4$$
    II. $(6 + 2) - 15 \div 5 \times 2$
$$= 8 - 15 \div 5 \times 2 = 8 - 3 \times 2 = 8 - 6 = 2$$
    III. $3 - (5 - 6 + 3)$
$$= 3 - (5 - 2) = 3 - 3 = 0$$
    IV. $28 - 5 \times 6 + 2 + 1$
$$= 28 - 30 + 2 + 1 = -2 + 2 + 1 = 1$$

13. Consider,
$$0 \ \square \ 7 \ \text{✿} \ 8 \ \bigcirc \ (2\Delta - 10)$$
$$= 0 - 7 \times 8 + [2 + (-10)]$$
$$= 0 - 7 \times 8 + (-8) = 0 - 7 \times (-1) = 7$$

14. Consider, $18 + 9 \times 10 \div 3 - 2$
After replacing the given sign, we get
$$18 \div 9 + 10 - 3 \times 2 = 2 + 10 - 6 = 6$$

15. I. addition   II. $4^2 + 2$ III. BODMAS   IV. $=$

16. We have,
$$-13 - 24 \div (-2)^2 \times 3$$
$$= -13 - 24 \div 4 \times 3 = -13 - 6 \times 3$$
$$= -13 - 18 = -31$$

17. Consider, $2550 - [510 - \{270 - (90 - \overline{80 + 70})\}]$
$$= 2550 - [510 - \{270 - (90 - 150)\}]$$
$$= 2550 - [510 - \{270 + 60\}]$$
$$= 2550 - [510 - 330] = 2550 - 180 = 2370$$

18. Consider, $63 - [(-3)\{-2 - \overline{8 - 3}\}] + [3\{5 + (-2)(-1)\}]$
$$= 63 - [(-3)\{-2 - 5\}] + [3\{5 + 2\}]$$
$$= 63 - [(-3)\{-7\}] + [3(5 + 2)]$$
$$= 63 - [(-3)(-7)] + [3 \times 7] = 63 - 21 + 21$$
$$= 63 - 1 = 62$$

19. Given,

$$(-3)\,\square\,(-8)\,\square\,(-4)\,\square\,2\,\square\,(-2)=3$$

Consider the signs $+$, $+$, $-$, $\times$, we get

$(-3)+(-8)+(-4)-2\times(-2)$
$=(-3)+2-2\times(-2)=(-3)+2+4=-3+6=3$

20. Consider, $\quad 100\times\nabla=\nabla+\nabla+98\times 7$

$\Rightarrow\qquad\qquad 100\times\nabla=2\nabla+686$
$\Rightarrow\qquad\qquad 100\nabla=2\nabla+686$
$\Rightarrow\qquad\qquad 98\nabla=686$
$\Rightarrow\qquad\qquad \nabla=7$

and $\qquad 153+\diamondsuit=923-230\times 4$
$\Rightarrow\qquad 153+\diamondsuit=923-920$
$\Rightarrow\qquad 153+\diamondsuit=3\Rightarrow\diamondsuit=51$

21. Number of tables taken in a day $=2A+B$
Number of tablets taken in two days
$\qquad =2A+B+2A+B+C=7$ tablets
So, number of tablets taken in 30 days $=\dfrac{30}{2}\times 7=105$

22. Let the number be x.

Then, $\quad x=\left[\left\{(364\times 3)\div\dfrac{1}{10}\right\}\div 312\right]$

$$=\left[\left\{1092\div\dfrac{1}{10}\right\}\div 312\right]$$

$$=(1092\times 10)\div 312=10920\div 312=35$$

23. Given, $\qquad \square\,\square=\triangle\,\square\,\triangle$

$\Rightarrow\qquad\qquad 2\square=2\triangle+\square$
$\Rightarrow\qquad\qquad \square=2\triangle$
$\Rightarrow\qquad\qquad 50=2\triangle$
$\Rightarrow\qquad\qquad \triangle=25$
Also, $\qquad \triangle+\square=2\bigcirc$
$\Rightarrow\qquad 25+50=2\bigcirc$
$\Rightarrow\qquad \bigcirc=37.5$
$\therefore\qquad\qquad \triangle<\square$

2 Rational Numbers

1. Here, $\qquad A=\dfrac{4}{5}$ and $B=-\dfrac{3}{5}$

So, $\qquad A-B=\dfrac{4}{5}-\left(-\dfrac{3}{5}\right)=\dfrac{4}{5}+\dfrac{3}{5}=\dfrac{7}{5}$

3. Given, $p=-\dfrac{2}{3}+\dfrac{4}{5}+1=\dfrac{-10+12+15}{15}=\dfrac{17}{15}$

and $\quad q=\dfrac{2}{3}-\dfrac{4}{5}+\dfrac{7}{15}=\dfrac{10-12+7}{15}=\dfrac{5}{15}$

$\therefore\qquad p>q$

4. We know that, $-1<\dfrac{-2}{7}<0$

$\therefore$ It will lie between -1 and 0, where the distance is divided into 7 parts.

$$-1 \qquad\qquad -2/7 \quad 0$$

5. The correct simplification $=\dfrac{-49}{-63}=\dfrac{7}{9}$

6. Consider, $\dfrac{2}{5}+\left(-\dfrac{5}{6}\right)+\left(-\dfrac{7}{9}\right)$

$=\dfrac{2}{5}-\dfrac{5}{6}-\dfrac{7}{9}=\dfrac{36-75-70}{90}=\dfrac{36-145}{90}=-\dfrac{109}{90}$

7. Others lie between $\dfrac{2}{101}$ and $\dfrac{3}{71}$.

8. Consider, $\dfrac{1}{3},\dfrac{2}{5},\dfrac{3}{7}=\dfrac{35}{105},\dfrac{42}{105},\dfrac{45}{105}$

$\therefore$ The correct sequence of numbers in ascending order is
$\dfrac{1}{3}<\dfrac{2}{5}<\dfrac{3}{7}$.

9. Consider

$$\left(\dfrac{3}{2}\times\dfrac{1}{3}\right)+\left(\dfrac{1}{3}\times 9\right)=\left(\dfrac{1}{2}\right)+\left(\dfrac{3}{1}\right)$$

$$=\dfrac{1+6}{2}=\dfrac{7}{2}$$

$\therefore$ Reciprocal of $\dfrac{7}{2}=\dfrac{2}{7}$

10. I. $\dfrac{7}{9}\times\left(\dfrac{-7}{-7}\right)=\dfrac{-49}{-63}\qquad$ II. $\left(\dfrac{-2}{3}\right)\times\dfrac{5}{5}=\dfrac{-10}{15}=\dfrac{10}{-15}$

III. $\left(\dfrac{4}{-7}\right)\times\dfrac{6}{6}=\dfrac{24}{-42}=\dfrac{-24}{42}\qquad$ IV. $\left(\dfrac{-11}{13}\right)\times\dfrac{4}{4}=\dfrac{-44}{52}=-\dfrac{(-44)}{(-52)}$

11. Let the number to be added be x
and nearest natural number $=1$.

So, $\qquad x+\left(\dfrac{-1}{4}\right)=1$

$\Rightarrow\qquad\qquad x=1+\dfrac{1}{4}=\dfrac{5}{4}$

12. By definition and property

13. Other rational number $=\dfrac{8}{9}-\dfrac{2}{18}=\dfrac{16-2}{18}=\dfrac{14}{18}=\dfrac{7}{9}$

14. All rational numbers satisfy the property of associativity under addition.

15. By definition and property

16. Consider, $\left(\dfrac{2}{3}-\dfrac{3}{4}\right)=\dfrac{8-9}{12}=\dfrac{-1}{12}$

Let x be subtracted from $\dfrac{-1}{12}$.

$\therefore\qquad x=\dfrac{-1}{12}-\left(-\dfrac{1}{6}\right)=-\dfrac{1}{12}+\dfrac{1}{6}$

$$=\dfrac{-1+2}{12}=\dfrac{1}{12}$$

17. Consider, $\dfrac{-7}{-6},\dfrac{-3}{-5},\dfrac{1}{2},\dfrac{-1}{-4},0=\dfrac{7}{6},\dfrac{3}{5},\dfrac{1}{2},\dfrac{1}{4},0$

Converting them into equivalent fraction, we get
$$\dfrac{70}{60},\dfrac{36}{60},\dfrac{30}{60},\dfrac{15}{60},\dfrac{0}{60}$$

So, the correct sequence is
$$\dfrac{-7}{-6}>\dfrac{-3}{-5}>\dfrac{1}{2}>\dfrac{-1}{-4}>0$$

18.   I. $\left(\dfrac{-6}{25}\right) \times \dfrac{50}{36} = \dfrac{-6 \times 2}{36} = \dfrac{-1 \times 2}{6} = \dfrac{-1}{3}$

    II. $\dfrac{3}{11} \times \left(\dfrac{-33}{21}\right) = \dfrac{-3}{7} = \dfrac{3}{-7}$

    III. $\dfrac{5}{21} \times \left(\dfrac{42}{-9}\right) = \dfrac{10}{-9} = \dfrac{-10}{9}$

    IV. $\left(\dfrac{-7}{11}\right) \times \dfrac{77}{49} = -1$

19.

$$\xleftrightarrow{\qquad -4/5 \qquad\qquad 0 \qquad\qquad \frac{4}{5} \qquad}$$

We know that $\dfrac{-4}{-5} = \dfrac{4}{5}$

20. Speed of train $= \dfrac{2024}{15}$ km/h

    Time taken $= \dfrac{25}{4}$ h

    Distance $= \dfrac{2024}{15} \times \dfrac{25}{4}$

    $= \dfrac{506}{15} \times 25 = \dfrac{506 \times 5}{3} = \dfrac{2530}{3}$ km

21. **Assertion** (A) $\dfrac{1}{0}$ is not defined.

    So, A is false.

    Reason (R) It is true.

22.   I. Consider, $4 - \left(\dfrac{1}{2} + \dfrac{1}{3} + \dfrac{1}{5}\right) = 4 - \left(\dfrac{15 + 10 + 6}{30}\right)$

    $= 4 - \left(\dfrac{31}{30}\right) = \dfrac{120 - 31}{30} = \dfrac{89}{30}$

    II. $\dfrac{120}{-114} = \dfrac{40}{-38} = \dfrac{20}{-19} = \dfrac{-20}{19}$

    III. Required number $= \dfrac{-5}{7} - \left(\dfrac{-15}{28}\right) = -\dfrac{5}{7} + \dfrac{15}{28}$

    $= \dfrac{-20 + 15}{28} = \dfrac{-5}{28}$

    IV. opposite

    V. Consider, $\dfrac{-5}{8}, \dfrac{-7}{-12}, \dfrac{-15}{24}, \dfrac{-14}{-24}$

    [converting to equivalent fraction]

    $\therefore \quad \dfrac{-15}{24} < \dfrac{14}{24} \Rightarrow \dfrac{-5}{8} < \dfrac{-7}{-12}$

    VI. true

    VII. Consider, $\dfrac{-4}{-9}, \dfrac{1}{4} = \dfrac{4}{9}, \dfrac{1}{4} = \dfrac{16}{36}, \dfrac{9}{36}$

    [converting to equivalent fraction]

    $\therefore \quad \dfrac{16}{36} > \dfrac{9}{36} \Rightarrow \dfrac{-4}{-9} > \dfrac{1}{4}$

23. Share got by eldest son $= \dfrac{1}{3}$

    Remaining land $= 1 - \dfrac{1}{3} = \dfrac{2}{3}$

    Share got by the daughter $= \dfrac{2}{5} \times \dfrac{2}{3} = \dfrac{4}{15}$

    So, remaining land $= \dfrac{2}{3} - \dfrac{4}{15} = \dfrac{10 - 4}{15} = \dfrac{6}{15} = \dfrac{2}{5}$

    Hence, share of land got by youngest child

    $= 25000 \times \dfrac{2}{5} = 10000$ sq m

24. $\left(1 - \dfrac{1}{2}\right)\left(1 - \dfrac{1}{3}\right)\left(1 - \dfrac{1}{4}\right)\left(1 - \dfrac{1}{5}\right) \cdots \left(1 - \dfrac{1}{100}\right)$

    $= \left(\dfrac{1}{2}\right)\left(\dfrac{2}{3}\right)\left(\dfrac{3}{4}\right)\left(\dfrac{4}{5}\right) \cdots \left(\dfrac{99}{100}\right) = \dfrac{1}{100}$

25. Salary of Shehnaz $= ₹\ 25000$

    Amount spent on food $= \dfrac{1}{5} \times 25000 = 5000$

    Money left $= 25000 - 5000 = ₹20000$

    Amount spent on house rent $= \dfrac{3}{10} \times 20000 = ₹\ 6000$

    Money left $= ₹(20000 - 6000) = ₹14000$

    Amount spent on education of children $= 14000 \times \dfrac{9}{28}$

    $= ₹\ 4500$

    Money left $= ₹(14000 - 4500) = ₹\ 9500$

26. I. True   II. True   III. False   IV. False   V. False

27. Given, $a * b = \dfrac{ab}{a + b}$

    Consider, $1 * 2 = \dfrac{1 \times 2}{1 + 2}$

    $\therefore \quad \dfrac{1}{1 * 2} = \dfrac{1 + 2}{1 \times 2} = \dfrac{1}{2} + 1$

    Now, $2 * 3 = \dfrac{2 \times 3}{2 + 3} = \dfrac{6}{5}$

    So, $\dfrac{1}{2 * 3} = \dfrac{2 + 3}{2 \times 3} = \dfrac{1}{3} + \dfrac{1}{2}$

    Now, $3 * 4 = \dfrac{3 \times 4}{3 + 4} = \dfrac{12}{7}$

    $\therefore \quad \dfrac{1}{3 * 4} = \dfrac{3 + 4}{3 \times 4} = \dfrac{1}{4} + \dfrac{1}{3}$

    So, we have

    $= \left(1 + \dfrac{1}{2}\right) - \left(\dfrac{1}{2} + \dfrac{1}{3}\right) + \left(\dfrac{1}{3} + \dfrac{1}{4}\right) - \cdots - \left(\dfrac{1}{2000} + \dfrac{1}{2001}\right)$

    $= 1 - \dfrac{1}{2001} = \dfrac{2000}{2001}$

28. All are correct.

29. Consider, $\dfrac{5}{6}, \dfrac{7}{12}, \dfrac{13}{18}, \dfrac{23}{24}$

    Convert to equivalent fractions, $\dfrac{60}{72}, \dfrac{42}{72}, \dfrac{52}{72}, \dfrac{69}{72}$

    $\therefore$ Greatest number $= \dfrac{69}{72} = \dfrac{23}{24}$

    Smallest number $= \dfrac{42}{72} = \dfrac{7}{12}$

    So, we have $= \dfrac{\frac{7}{12}}{\frac{23}{24}} \times 100 = \dfrac{7}{12} \times \dfrac{24}{23} \times 100$

    $= \dfrac{1400}{23} = 60\dfrac{20}{23}$

30.   I. Commutative property

    II. Associative property

    III. Distributive property

$\textcircled{3}$ Fractions and Decimals

$\textcircled{A}$ Fractions

1. Number of parts = 26

Number of shaded parts = 10

$\therefore$ Required fraction $= \dfrac{10}{26} = \dfrac{5}{13}$

2. All others are improper fractions.

3. By definition

4. Consider, $\dfrac{1}{9}$ and $\dfrac{1}{11}$

Converting them into equivalent fractions, we have

$\dfrac{11}{99}$ and $\dfrac{9}{99}$

To have 19 as numerator multiply both the fractions by $\dfrac{2}{2}$,

so we get

$\dfrac{22}{198}, \dfrac{18}{198}$ i.e. $\dfrac{22}{198} > \dfrac{19}{198} > \dfrac{18}{198}$

Hence, 198 is the correct fraction.

5. Number of parts = 36

Number of shaded parts = 12

To have fraction $\dfrac{4}{9}$, we shall convert it into an equivalent fraction

having denominator equal to 36.

So, we have $\dfrac{4 \times 4}{9 \times 4} = \dfrac{16}{36}$

$\therefore$ Required number of triangles to be shaded = 16 – 12 = 4

6. $\dfrac{6}{13}, \dfrac{3}{5}, \dfrac{5}{6}, \dfrac{1}{4}$

Arranging the fractions in ascending order, we get

$\dfrac{720}{1560}, \dfrac{936}{1560}, \dfrac{1300}{1560}, \dfrac{390}{1560}$

$\Rightarrow \quad \dfrac{1}{4} < \dfrac{6}{13} < \dfrac{3}{5} < \dfrac{5}{6}$

So, $\dfrac{1}{4}$ is closest to '0'.

7. Required fraction $= 10\dfrac{9}{44} - 2\dfrac{37}{44} = \dfrac{449}{44} - \dfrac{125}{44}$

$= \dfrac{324}{44} = \dfrac{162}{22} = \dfrac{81}{11} = 7\dfrac{4}{11}$

8. Given fractions are $\dfrac{7}{5}, \dfrac{21}{15}, 1\dfrac{22}{55}, \dfrac{147}{105}$

i.e. $\dfrac{7}{5}, \dfrac{21}{15}, \dfrac{77}{55}, \dfrac{147}{105}$

All are improper and equivalent fractions.

9. $A = \dfrac{26}{9}$

10. Required number $= \dfrac{4}{7} \times 2\dfrac{1}{4} = \dfrac{4}{7} \times \dfrac{9}{4} = \dfrac{9}{7}$

11. We have, $\dfrac{3}{2} \times x \times \dfrac{6}{3} = 3\dfrac{3}{4}$

$\Rightarrow \qquad 3x = \dfrac{15}{4}$

$\therefore \qquad x = \dfrac{5}{4}$

12. Given, $x = \dfrac{6}{25}, y = \dfrac{3}{5}$

$\therefore \quad \dfrac{x}{y} = \dfrac{\frac{6}{25}}{\frac{3}{5}} = \dfrac{6}{25} \div \dfrac{3}{5} = \dfrac{6}{25} \times \dfrac{5}{3} = \dfrac{2}{5}$

13. Given, $x = \dfrac{2}{3} + \dfrac{3}{4}, y = \dfrac{3}{4} + \dfrac{5}{6}$

Consider,

$A = \dfrac{1}{\frac{2}{3} + \frac{3}{4}} = \dfrac{1}{\frac{8+9}{12}} = \dfrac{12}{17}$

and $B = \dfrac{1}{\frac{3}{4} + \frac{5}{6}} = \dfrac{1}{\frac{18+20}{24}} = \dfrac{24}{38}$

So, $A \div B$

$= \dfrac{12}{17} \div \dfrac{24}{38} = \dfrac{12}{17} \times \dfrac{38}{24} = \dfrac{19}{17}$

14. Cups of flour required for one pack $= 3\dfrac{1}{2} = \dfrac{7}{2}$

and cups of sugar required for one pack $= 2\dfrac{1}{3} = \dfrac{7}{3}$

Total cups required $= \dfrac{7}{2} + \dfrac{7}{3} = \dfrac{21+14}{6} = \dfrac{35}{6}$

Now, cups required for 10 such packets

$= 10 \times \dfrac{35}{6} = 5 \times \dfrac{35}{3}$

$= \dfrac{175}{3} = 58\dfrac{1}{3}$

So, it is between 50 and 60 cups.

15. Total amount of chocolate cake $= 2\dfrac{4}{7} = \dfrac{18}{7}$

Number of friends = 9

$\therefore$ Amount of chocolate cake each friend received

$= \dfrac{18}{7} \div 9 = \dfrac{2}{7}$

16. Total number of games = 12 + 4 = 16

Number of games won by team = 12

Number of games lost by team = 4

So, fraction of games lost by team $= \dfrac{4}{16}$

17. Product of $2\dfrac{1}{4}$ and $3\dfrac{1}{2} = \dfrac{9}{4} \times \dfrac{7}{2} = \dfrac{63}{8}$

Reciprocal of it $= \dfrac{8}{63}$ which is a proper fraction.

18. Number of flowers in the basket = 36

Fraction of basket full $= \dfrac{3}{11}$

$\therefore$ Total number of flowers that can be filled

$= 36 \times \dfrac{11}{3} = 132$

So, more number of flowers to be filled = 132 – 36 = 96

19. I. $\dfrac{3}{4}$ of $\dfrac{16}{27} = \dfrac{3}{4} \times \dfrac{16}{27} = \dfrac{4}{9}$ II. $2\dfrac{1}{4}$ of $\dfrac{1}{18} = \dfrac{9}{4} \times \dfrac{1}{18} = \dfrac{1}{8}$

III. $1\dfrac{2}{3}$ of $2 = \dfrac{5}{3} \times 2 = \dfrac{10}{3}$ IV. $\dfrac{4}{6}$ of $\dfrac{42}{28} = \dfrac{4}{6} \times \dfrac{42}{28} = 1$

20. We know that, $\dfrac{3}{4}$ of $8 = \dfrac{3}{4} \times 8 = 6$

So, option (b) has 6 parts shaded out of 8.

21. Consider, $\left(1 - \dfrac{2}{3}\right) \times \left(1 - \dfrac{2}{5}\right) \times \left(1 - \dfrac{2}{7}\right)$

$$\times \left(1 - \dfrac{2}{9}\right) \times \ldots \times \left(1 - \dfrac{2}{99}\right)$$

$$= \dfrac{1}{3} \times \dfrac{3}{5} \times \dfrac{5}{7} \times \dfrac{7}{9} \times \ldots \times \dfrac{97}{99} = \dfrac{1}{99}$$

22. Given, $\qquad a * b = \dfrac{a \times b}{a + b}$

$\therefore \qquad 21 * 3 = \dfrac{21 \times 3}{21 \div 3} = \dfrac{21 \times 3}{7} = \dfrac{9}{1}$

23. Number of questions completed by Priya = 40

Fraction of question paper = $\dfrac{2}{3}$

$\therefore$ Total number of questions = $40 \times \dfrac{3}{2} = 60$

Required questions to be done to complete the paper

$$= 60 - 40 = 20$$

24. I. improper fraction   II. 91

II. $\dfrac{\text{Product of numerators}}{\text{Product of denominators}}$ IV. changed

25. Gopal father's age at present= 48 yr

6 yr ago, Gopal father's age = 48 − 6 = 42 yr

$\therefore$ 6 yr ago, Gopal's age = $42 \times \dfrac{1}{7} = 6$ yr

26. Let total money be ₹ 1.

$\therefore$ Money spent on food = $\dfrac{1}{6}$ Remaining money = $1 - \dfrac{1}{6} = \dfrac{5}{6}$

Now, money spent on transport = $\dfrac{5}{6} \times \dfrac{2}{5} = \dfrac{1}{3}$

Money spent on food and transport altogether = $\dfrac{1}{6} + \dfrac{1}{3}$

$$= \dfrac{1+2}{6} = \dfrac{3}{6} = \dfrac{1}{2}$$

27. Amount of amoxicillin to be taken = 250 mg

Amount of amoxicillin in 1 dose = 125 mg or 5 mL

$\therefore$ Number of dosage = $\dfrac{250}{125} = 2$

28. Amount of tylenol to be taken = 300 mg

Amount of tylenol in 2 mL = 100 mg

$\therefore$ Amount of tylenol in 1 mL = 50 mg

So, quantity of syrup to be taken = $\dfrac{300}{50} = 6$ mL

29. Let I = $\dfrac{2\frac{1}{2} + \frac{1}{5}}{2\frac{1}{2} \div 5} = \dfrac{\frac{5}{2} + \frac{1}{5}}{\frac{5}{2} \times \frac{1}{5}} = \dfrac{\frac{25+2}{10}}{\frac{1}{2}} = \dfrac{27}{5}$

and II = $\dfrac{\frac{1}{4} + \frac{1}{5}}{1 - \frac{3}{8} \times \frac{3}{5}} = \dfrac{\frac{5+4}{20}}{1 - \frac{9}{40}} = \dfrac{\frac{9}{20}}{\frac{31}{40}} = \dfrac{9}{20} \times \dfrac{40}{31} = \dfrac{18}{31}$

On comparing $\dfrac{27}{5}$ and $\dfrac{18}{31}$, we get

$$\dfrac{837}{155} > \dfrac{90}{155}$$

$\Rightarrow \qquad \dfrac{27}{5} > \dfrac{18}{31}$

So, (I) > (II)

30. Number of students participated in hockey = $\dfrac{1}{5} \times 200 = 40$

31. Number of students participated in swimming = $\dfrac{1}{4} \times 200 = 50$

Number of students participated in cricket = $\dfrac{7}{40} \times 200 = 35$

$\therefore \qquad$ Difference = 50 − 35 = 15

32. Number of students participating in football = $\dfrac{3}{20} \times 200 = 30$

Number of students shifted to hockey = $\dfrac{1}{3} \times 30 = 10$

New number of students in hockey = 40 + 10 = 50

$\therefore \qquad$ Fraction = $\dfrac{50}{200} = \dfrac{1}{4}$

33. I. True   II. False   III. False   IV. False   V. False

34. Consider,

$$\cfrac{1}{1 + \cfrac{1}{2 + \cfrac{1}{a + \frac{1}{2}}}} = \dfrac{16}{23}$$

$\Rightarrow \quad \cfrac{1}{1 + \cfrac{1}{2 + \cfrac{1}{\frac{2a+1}{2}}}} = \dfrac{16}{23} \quad \Rightarrow \quad \cfrac{1}{1 + \cfrac{1}{\frac{4a+4}{2a+1}}} = \dfrac{16}{23}$

$\Rightarrow \quad \cfrac{1}{\frac{4a + 4 + 2a + 1}{4a + 4}} = \dfrac{16}{23} \quad \Rightarrow \quad \dfrac{4a + 4}{6a + 5} = \dfrac{16}{23}$

$\Rightarrow \qquad 92a + 92 = 96a + 80 \Rightarrow 12 = 4a$

$\therefore \qquad a = 3$

35. Consider,

$$\dfrac{\frac{5}{3} + 1\frac{1}{2} \text{ of } \frac{7}{3}}{2 + 2\frac{2}{3}}$$

$$= \dfrac{\frac{5}{3} + \frac{3}{2} \times \frac{7}{3}}{2 + \frac{8}{3}} = \dfrac{\frac{5}{3} + \frac{7}{2}}{\frac{2}{1} + \frac{8}{3}} = \dfrac{\frac{10+21}{6}}{\frac{6+8}{3}} = \dfrac{31}{6} \times \dfrac{3}{14} = \dfrac{31}{28}$$

But Mihir answered = $\dfrac{1}{7}$

$\therefore$ His answer is $\left(\dfrac{31}{28} \div \dfrac{1}{7}\right)$ times wrong = $\dfrac{31}{28} \times 7 = \dfrac{31}{4}$

(B) **Decimals**

1. $0.321 = \dfrac{321}{1000}$

2. Consider, $\dfrac{0.00441}{0.21} = \dfrac{00441}{21} \times \dfrac{100}{100000} = 21 \times \dfrac{1}{1000} = 0.021$

3. This option shows correct ascending order.

4. I. $2 \div 0.5 = \dfrac{2}{0.5} = \dfrac{2 \times 10}{5} = 4$

II. $5 \div 0.25 = \dfrac{5}{0.25} = \dfrac{5 \times 100}{25} = 20$

III. $0.75 \div 3 = \dfrac{0.75}{3} = \dfrac{75}{3 \times 100} = \dfrac{1}{4} = 0.25$

IV. $0.5 \div 5 = \dfrac{0.5}{5} = \dfrac{5}{5 \times 10} = \dfrac{5}{50} = \dfrac{1}{10} = 0.1$

5. We have,
$$14.63 - \frac{1}{6} \times 0.6 = 14.63 - 0.1 = 14.53$$

6. Consider, $0.645 \times 10 = 6.45$
So, we have
$$6450 \div \square = 6.45$$
$$\Rightarrow \qquad \square = 1000$$

7. We know that,
$$73.47 \times 100 = 92 \times 73.47 + 8 \times 73.47$$

8. I. $0.007 \times 700 = \dfrac{7}{1000} \times 700 = 4.9$
II. $0.009 \times 3000 = \dfrac{9}{1000} \times 3000 = 27$
III. $213.163 \times \square = 21316.3$
$$\therefore \qquad \square = 100$$
IV. 17.034

9. Number of sides in octagon = 8
Perimeter of octagon = 33.6 cm
$\therefore$ Length of each side = $\dfrac{33.6}{8}$ = 4.2 cm

11. Radius of park = 1.5 km
$\therefore$ Diameter = $2 \times 1.5 = 3$ km
Now, distance covered by Sonakshi = $3 \times 3.14 = 9.42$ km

12. We have, 1 inch = 11 miles
$\therefore \quad$ 4.5 inch = $4.5 \times 11 = 49.5$ miles

13. Price per litre on Tuesday = $\dfrac{616.8}{12}$ = 51.4
Price per litre on Friday = $\dfrac{817.5}{15}$ = ₹ 54.5
On Tuesday, Marshall gets better price.

14. Cost of a candy in box A = $\dfrac{23.20}{40}$ = ₹ 0.58
Cost of a candy in box B = $\dfrac{152.50}{250}$ = ₹ 0.61
Now, profit in buying box A is more as its price is low.

15. Let the decimal be x.
Clue 1 : It is between $\dfrac{2}{5}$ and $\dfrac{3}{5}$ or it is between 0.4 and 0.6.
Clue 2 : It is greater than $\dfrac{1}{2}$ i.e. greater than 0.5.

$\therefore$ x lies between 0.5 and 0.6.
Clue 3 : Multiple of 11
$\therefore$ It can 0.55.
$\therefore$ Aman gave the correct answer.

16. We know that,
$$-0.27°C < -0.20°C < 0.20°C < \left(\frac{1}{20}\right)^{\circ}C < 0.74°C$$

17. We know that,
$$-0.20°C < -0.06°C < 0.20°C$$
$\therefore$ It lies between Bristol and London.

18. I. 100   II. Dividing   III. 16.92   IV. 0.07

19. I. False   II. False   III. True   IV. False

20. **Store A**
Cost of 1 pair of jeans and 2 shirts = ₹ 399.7 + ₹ 444.8
$$= ₹ 844.5$$
Store B
Cost of 1 pair of jeans and 2 shirts
$$= ₹ 449.9 + ₹ 224.8 + ₹ 224.8 = ₹ 899.5$$
Store C
Cost of 1 pair of jeans and 2 shirts
$$= ₹ 499.5 + ₹ 204.6 + ₹204.6 = ₹908.7$$
$\therefore$ Store A is most economical.

21. We have, jeans C : ₹ 499.5
Shirt A : ₹ 444.8÷2 = ₹222.4
1 shirt B : ₹ 224.8
Total amount to be spend
$$= ₹499.5 + ₹222.4 + ₹224.8 = ₹ 946.7$$
Money left = ₹(1000 − 946.7) = ₹ 53.3

22. Cheapest jeans are from store A:
$\therefore$ Cost of 2 jeans from store A
$$= ₹ 399.7 \times 2 = ₹ 799.4$$
and cheapest shirt is from store C, costing ₹ 204.6.
So, total money required
$$= ₹ (799.4 + 204.6) = ₹ 1004$$
$\therefore$ Extra money required = ₹ (1004 − 1000) = ₹ 4

④ Simple Equations

1. Total number of students = $m + n$
2. All other options have positive solution.
3. Let x be the number.
Then, one-third of the number = $\dfrac{x}{3}$
We have, $\dfrac{x}{3} = x - 10$

4. I. $2x = 3x - 3 \Rightarrow x = 3$
II. $\dfrac{2}{3}x - 3 = 5 \Rightarrow \dfrac{2}{3}x = 8 \Rightarrow x = 12$
III. $72 - 8x = 0 \Rightarrow 72 = 8x \Rightarrow x = 9$

5. According to the question,
$$9 - \frac{2}{3}x = 10 \Rightarrow 9 - 10 = \frac{2}{3}x$$
$$\Rightarrow \qquad -1 = \frac{2}{3}x \Rightarrow x = -\frac{3}{2}$$

6. Let the number be x.
Then, $\dfrac{30}{100} \times \dfrac{70}{100} \times x = 63$
$$\Rightarrow \qquad \frac{21}{100}x = 63 \Rightarrow x = 300$$

7. Only in option (c), the value of x is not a solution of given linear equation.

8. $\dfrac{4}{5}x - 2 = 2 \Rightarrow \dfrac{4}{5}x = 4 \Rightarrow x = 5$

9. Old average = 43
$\therefore \qquad$ Total = $43 \times 5 = 215$
New average = $\dfrac{215 + y + 3y}{7} = \dfrac{215 + 4y}{7}$

10. Given, $4 * a \Delta 10 \square 2$

We have,
$$4 \times a - 10 = 2 \Rightarrow 4a = 12$$
$$\Rightarrow \quad a = 3 \qquad \text{[integer]}$$

11. Let $\angle B$ be x.

$\therefore \qquad \angle A = 3x$ and $\angle C = x - 20°$

We know that,
$$\angle A + \angle B + \angle C = 180°$$
$$\Rightarrow \quad x + 3x + x - 20° = 180°$$
$$\Rightarrow \quad 5x - 20° = 180°$$
$$\Rightarrow \quad 5x = 200°$$
$$\Rightarrow \quad x = 40°$$

12. Let the numbers be $3x$ and $5x$.

If each number is increased by 4, then the ratio becomes $2:3$.

So, $\qquad \dfrac{3x + 4}{5x + 4} = \dfrac{2}{3}$
$$\Rightarrow \quad 3(3x + 4) = 2(5x + 4)$$
$$\Rightarrow \quad 9x + 12 = 10x + 8$$
$$\Rightarrow \quad 9x - 10x = 8 - 12$$
$$\Rightarrow \quad -x = -4$$
$$\Rightarrow \quad x = 4$$

$\therefore$ Number are $3 \times 4 = 12$ and $5 \times 4 = 20$.

13. Let A, B and C get number of apples $5x$, $7x$ and $8x$, respectively.

$\therefore$ A have 45 apples.

So, $\qquad 5x = 45 \Rightarrow x = 9$

$\therefore$ Total number of apples
$$= 5 \times 9 + 7 \times 9 + 8 \times 9 = 45 + 63 + 72 = 180$$

14. Let the price store paid be x.

$\therefore \qquad SP = x + 1700$

Given, $\qquad SP = ₹24000$

We have,
$$24000 = x + 1700$$
$$\Rightarrow \quad x = 24000 - 1700 = ₹22300$$

15. Given, x represents the number of hours service is used.

Charges for first 3 h = ₹ 4.95

Total charges = ₹21.83

We have, $4.95 + 2.5(x - 3) = 21.83$

16. Consider, $\quad 4.95 + 2.5(x - 3) = 21.83$
$$\Rightarrow \quad 4.95 + 2.5x - 7.5 = 21.83$$
$$\Rightarrow \quad 2.5x = 21.83 + 7.5 - 4.95$$
$$\Rightarrow \quad 2.5x = 24.38$$
$$\Rightarrow \quad x = 9.752 \approx 10$$

17. Let milk in cup $A = t$ mL

Then, milk in cup $B = (t - 40)$ mL

Milk in cup $C = 2(t - 40) = (2t - 80)$ mL

and milk in cup $D = 3t$ mL

Total milk $= t + t - 40 + 2t - 80 + 3t = (7t - 120)$

18. Given, $t = 40$ mL

So, total milk $= 7 \times 40 - 120 = 280 - 120 = 160$ mL

19. I. Transposition　　　　II. 4

III. root or solution　　　IV. $x + 1$ or $2x + 3 = 1$

21. Money paid by Mrs. John $= ₹ x$

Money received back by her $= ₹ 50$

$\therefore$ Cost of chocolate boxes $= ₹(x - 50)$

Cost of 1 chocolate box $= ₹150$

$\therefore$ Total number of boxes bought $= \dfrac{x - 50}{150}$

22. Step V must be
$$16x - 18x = -1$$
$$\Rightarrow \quad -2x = -1 \Rightarrow x = \dfrac{1}{2}$$

23. I. True　　　II. False　　　III. True　　　IV. True

24. I. $\dfrac{4}{3}l + 2 = 10$
$$\Rightarrow \quad \dfrac{4}{3}l = 8 \Rightarrow l = 6$$

II. $2E + 9 = 11$

$\therefore \qquad 2E = 2 \Rightarrow E = 1$

III. $\dfrac{3}{4}N = 3N - 18$
$$\Rightarrow \quad 3N - \dfrac{3}{4}N = 18 \Rightarrow \dfrac{9N}{4} = 18 \Rightarrow N = 8$$

IV. $7U + 9 = 30 \Rightarrow U = 3$

V. $\dfrac{5}{2}Q + 2 = 7 \Rightarrow Q = 2$

VI. $2A + 14 = 22 \Rightarrow 2A = 8 \Rightarrow A = 4$

VII. $10 + T - \dfrac{3}{5}T = 12 \Rightarrow T = 5$

VIII. $\dfrac{7}{9}S + 4 = 11 \Rightarrow S = 9$

IX. $O + 42 = 49 \Rightarrow O = 7$

$\therefore$ The word formed is $EQUATIONS$.

25. I. Total number of prizes = 40

Number of Ist prizes $= x$

$\therefore$ Number of 2nd prizes $= 40 - x$

II. Total value of prizes in terms of x
$$= 3000x + 2000(40 - x)$$

III. Equation formed
$$\Rightarrow \quad 3000x + 2000(40 - x) = 90000$$
$$\Rightarrow \quad 3000x + 80000 - 2000x = 90000$$
$$\Rightarrow \quad 1000x + 80000 = 90000$$

26. Let the number of toys be x.

If one child gets one toy each, then one of the child is left with no toy.

So, number of children $= (x + 1)$

If one toy is given to two children to share, then one toy will be left extra.

Now, number of children $= (x - 1) \times 2 = 2x - 2$

We have, $\qquad x + 1 = 2x - 2$
$$\Rightarrow \quad x = 3$$

$\therefore$ Number of toys = 3

and number of children $= 2 \times 3 - 2 = 4$

27. Given, $A = P\left(1 + \dfrac{r}{100}\right)^n$

Now, $n = 1$

$\therefore \qquad A = P\left(1 + \dfrac{r}{100}\right)^1$
$$\Rightarrow \quad \dfrac{A}{P} = 1 + \dfrac{r}{100} \Rightarrow \dfrac{A}{P} - 1 = \dfrac{r}{100}$$
$$\Rightarrow \quad \left(\dfrac{A}{P} - 1\right)100 = r$$

28. Given, $h = \dfrac{2A}{b_1 + b_2} \Rightarrow 2A = h(b_1 + b_2)$

$\Rightarrow \quad A = \dfrac{h}{2}(b_1 + b_2)$

$\Rightarrow \quad A = \dfrac{1}{2} \times h(b_1 + b_2)$

29. Consider, $2(x - 3) = 5$

$\Rightarrow \quad 2x - 6 = 5 \Rightarrow 2x = 11$

$\Rightarrow \quad x = \dfrac{11}{2}$

Now,

$\qquad 5 - 3x = 10 \Rightarrow 5 - 10 = 3x$

$\Rightarrow \quad -5 = 3x \Rightarrow x = \dfrac{-5}{3}$

and $\quad \dfrac{1}{4}x - 2 = 7$

$\Rightarrow \quad \dfrac{1}{4}x = 9 \Rightarrow x = 36$

30. Let the depth be d.

Increase in temperature for each kilometre of depth

$\qquad\qquad = 30°C$

Givedn, temperature $= 110°C$

Accoring to the question,

$\qquad 110°C = 20°C + 30°C\, d$

$\Rightarrow \quad 110°C - 20°C = 30°C\, d$

$\Rightarrow \qquad 90°C = 30°C\, d$

$\Rightarrow \qquad d = 3$

5 Lines and Angles

2. All other options are complementary.

3. Since, $\overleftrightarrow{PQ}$ is a line, so it doesn't have an any end point.

4.
I. Line segment PQ or $\overline{PQ}$ \qquad II. Ray PQ or $\overrightarrow{PQ}$

III. Line PQ or $\overleftrightarrow{PQ}$

6. Lines IJ and GH are parallel.

7.

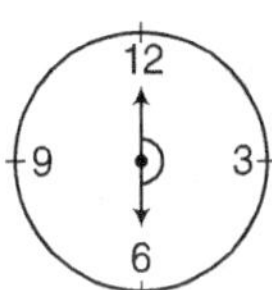

The angle formed is of measure $180°$ or straight angle.

8. In the given figure,

$\qquad 2S = 100°$ \qquad [vertically opposite angles]

$\therefore \qquad S = 50°$

9.

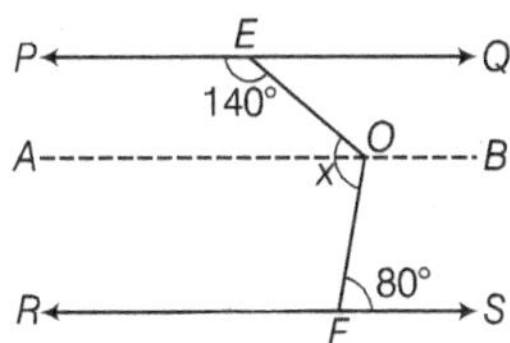

Draw $AB \parallel PQ \parallel RS$

$\therefore \qquad \angle EOA = 180° - 140°$

$\qquad$ [since, interior angles on the same side of transversal are supplementary]

$\therefore \qquad \angle EOA = 40°$

Now, $\quad \angle AOF = \angle OFS$ \qquad [alternate angles]

$\therefore \qquad \angle AOF = 80°$

$\therefore \qquad \angle x = \angle EOA + \angle AOF = 40° + 80° = 120°$

11. We have,

$\qquad \angle y + \angle y + 78° = 180°$ [linear pair]

$\therefore \qquad 2\angle y = 180° - 78°$

$\Rightarrow \qquad 2\angle y = 102°$

$\therefore \qquad \angle y = 51°$

12. A line segment has two end points. So, a line segment has a definite length.

13.

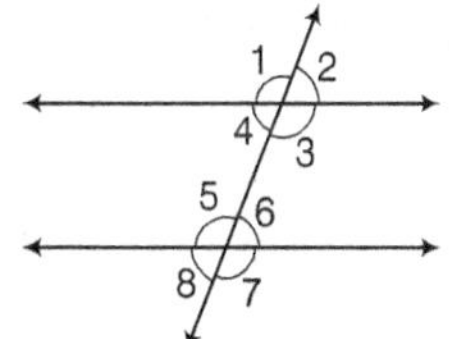

Here, $\angle 1$ and $\angle 5$, $\angle 2$ and $\angle 6$, $\angle 4$ and $\angle 8$, $\angle 3$ and $\angle 7$ are two pairs of corresponding angles.

14. Assertion (A) $\angle 1 = \angle 2$ and $\qquad \angle 5 = \angle 8$

[alternate angles, since $AB \parallel CD$]

Reason (R) True

15. We have,

$\qquad 3x + 5° + x + 15° = 180°$

$\Rightarrow \qquad 4x + 20° = 180° \Rightarrow 4x = 160°$

$\Rightarrow \qquad x = 40°$

Also, $\quad y + 20° + 4y - 15° = 180°$

$\Rightarrow \qquad 5y + 5° = 180° \Rightarrow 5y = 175°$

$\Rightarrow \qquad y = 35°$

$\therefore \qquad \angle x = 40°$ and $\angle y = 35°$

16.
I. $x = 90°$

II. $x + 60° + 90° = 180°$ \qquad [linear pair]

$\therefore \quad x + 150° = 180°$

$\Rightarrow \qquad x = 30°$

III. $x + 35° = 90°$ [complementary]

$\Rightarrow \qquad x = 55°$

17. We know that,

$\qquad \angle x = 40°$ \qquad [vertically opposite angles]

Now, $CD \parallel EF$

$\therefore \qquad \angle EOA = 180° - 40°$

$\qquad$ [interior angles on the same side of transversal]

Now, $\quad \angle y = \angle EOA$ \qquad [vertically opposite angles]

$\therefore \qquad \angle y = 140°$

18. Let the angle be x.

Then, its supplement $= (180° - x)$

According to the question,

$\qquad x - 3(180° - x) = 40° \Rightarrow x - 540° + 3x = 40°$

$\Rightarrow \qquad 4x = 580° \Rightarrow x = 145°$

19. (c) We have, $RS \parallel UT$

Also, TR is a transversal.

$\therefore \qquad \angle SRT = \angle RTU$ [alternate angles]

$\Rightarrow \qquad 89° = x + \angle CTU$

$\Rightarrow \qquad 89° = x + 39°$

$\Rightarrow \qquad x = 50°$

$\therefore \qquad \angle RTC = 50°$

20. $\angle 1 + \angle 2 = \angle 5 + \angle 4$ [vertically opposite angles]

21. By definition

22.

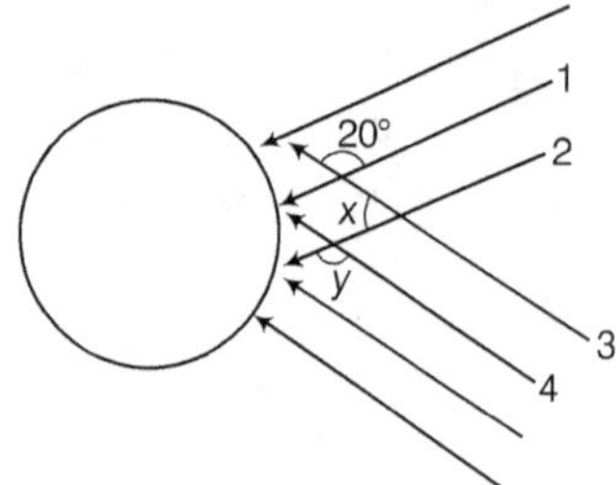

Here, ray 1 is parallel to ray 2 and ray 3 is the transversal.

$\therefore \qquad \angle x = 180° - 20° = 160°$

Also, ray 3 and ray 4 are parallel and ray 2 is the transversal.

$\therefore \qquad \angle y = 180° - \angle x = 180° - 160° = 20°$

23. If an angle is its own supplementary angle, then

$x + x = 180°$ [let the angle be x]

$\Rightarrow \qquad 2x = 180°$

$\Rightarrow \qquad x = 90°$

24.   I. $80°$ II. vertically opposite

   III. complementary   IV. $99°$

   V. parallel   VI. supplementary

   VII. transversal

25. Given, AOB is a line and

$\angle a = 40°$.

We know that,

$\angle a + 3y + 4y = 180°$ [linear pair]

$\therefore \qquad 40° + 3y + 4y = 180°$

$\Rightarrow \qquad 7y = 140°$

$\Rightarrow \qquad y = 20°$

$\therefore \qquad \angle FOE = 3y = 60°$

26. Given, $\qquad \angle XOV = 90°$ and $c : b = 7 : 3$

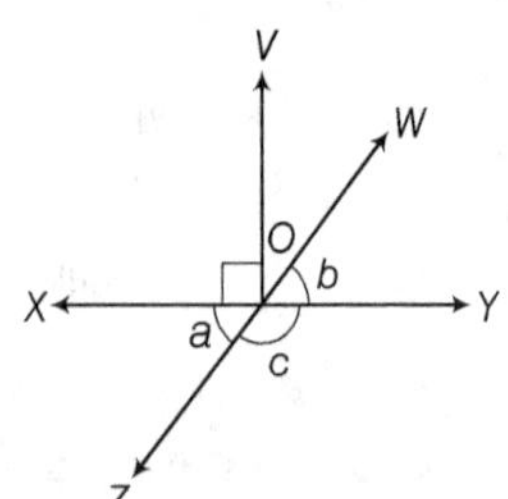

We know that,

$\angle c + \angle b = 180°$ [linear pair]

$\therefore \qquad 7x + 3x = 180°$

$\Rightarrow \qquad 10x = 180°$

$\Rightarrow \qquad x = 18°$

$b = 3 \times 18 = 54°$

Now, $\qquad \angle a = \angle b$ [vertically opposite angles]

$\therefore \qquad \angle a = 54°$

27. By definition

28. Given, $EF \parallel AO$

$\therefore \qquad \angle A = \angle CEF$ [corresponding angles]

$\therefore \qquad x = \angle CEF = 75°$

Also, $\qquad \angle OEF = 20°$

      [vertically opposite angles]

$\therefore \qquad \angle CEO = \angle CEF + \angle OEF$

$= 20° + 75° = 95°$

Now, $AC \parallel OD$ and OB is the transversal.

$\therefore \qquad \angle CEO + \angle EOF = 180°$

      [interior angles on the same side of transversal are supplementary]

$\angle EOF = 180° - \angle CEO$

$= 180° - 95° = 85°$

$\therefore \qquad y = 85°$

29. Given, $\qquad AB \parallel CD \parallel XY$ and $OC \parallel EB$

Also, $\qquad \angle ABE = 46°$ and $\angle EDC = 33°$

Now, $AB \parallel XY$

$\therefore \qquad \angle ABE + \angle XEB = 180°$

$\angle XEB = 180° - 46°$

$= 134°$

      [interior angles on the same side of transversal are supplementary]

Now, $OC \parallel EB$

$\therefore \qquad \angle BEF + \angle OFE = 180°$

      [same reason as above]

$\therefore \qquad \angle OFE = 180° - 134°$

$= 46°$

Now, $XY \parallel CD$

$\therefore \qquad \angle OFE = \angle OCD$ [corresponding angles]

$\therefore \qquad \angle OCD = 46°$

Also, $\qquad \angle YED = \angle EDC$ [alternate angles]

$\therefore \qquad \angle YED = 33°$

Now, $AB \parallel XY$

$\therefore \qquad \angle BEY = \angle EBA$ [alternate angles]

$\therefore \qquad \angle BEY = 46°$

Now, $\qquad \angle e = \angle YED + \angle BEY$

$= 33° + 46° = 79°$

30.   I. False   II. True   III. True   IV. True

6 Triangle : Properties and Congruence

A) Triangles and Its Properties

1. Orthocentre is a point of concurrence, whereas other options are line segment.

2. Sum of three angles of a triangle is 180°.

3. An equilateral triangle always has 3 acute angles which are also equal in measure.

4. If one angle is 90°, then sum of other two angles is 90° i.e. complementary.

5. All are true.

6. Given, $AB = AC$

   $\therefore \quad \angle ABC = \angle ACB$

   [angles opposite to equal sides are also equal]

   Now,

   $\angle ABC + \angle ACB = 130°$ [exterior angle property]

   $\therefore \quad x + x = 130°$

   $\Rightarrow \quad 2x = 130° \Rightarrow x = 65°$

7. I. All sides are unequal.

   II. All sides are unequal but $13^2 = 12^2 + 5^2$

   $\therefore$ It is satisfy the Pythagoras theorem.

   III. Two sides are equal i.e. isosceles triangle.

   IV. All three sides are equal i.e. equilateral triangle.

8. Given, ΔPQR with $\angle a$ and $\angle b$ as exterior angles,

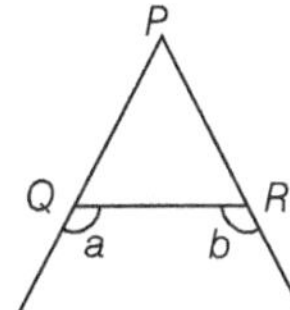

   Also, $\quad \angle Q > \angle R$

   $\Rightarrow \quad -\angle Q < -\angle R$

   $\Rightarrow \quad 180° - \angle Q < 180° - \angle R$

   $\therefore \quad \angle a < \angle b$

9.

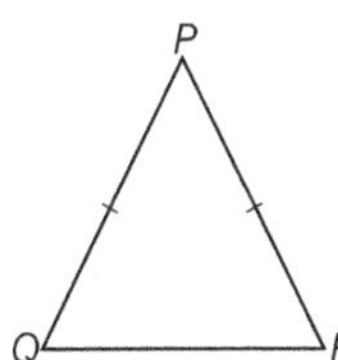

   Given, $\quad PQ = PR$

   $\therefore \quad \angle PQR = \angle PRQ$

   i.e. $\quad \angle Q = \angle R$ ...(i)

   Also, $\quad \angle P = 3\angle Q$ ...(ii)

   We have,

   $\angle P + \angle Q + \angle R = 180°$ [angle sum property]

   $\Rightarrow 3\angle Q + \angle Q + \angle Q = 180°$ [from Eqs. (i) and (ii)]

   $\Rightarrow \quad 5\angle Q = 180°$

   $\Rightarrow \quad \angle Q = 36°$

   $\therefore \quad \angle R = 36°$

10. In the given figure, $\angle PRS$ is the exterior angle.

    $\therefore \quad \angle PRS + \angle PRQ = 180°$ [linear pair]

    $\Rightarrow \quad \angle PRQ = 180° - 136° = 44°$

Also, $\quad \angle PRQ = \angle PQR$ [$\because$ angles opposite to equal sides are also equal]

$\therefore \quad \angle PQR = 44°$

We have,

$x + \angle PQR = 136°$ [exterior angles]

$\Rightarrow \quad x + 44° = 136°$

$\therefore \quad x = 136° - 44° = 92°$

11. We know, in ΔPQR,

    $\angle P + \angle Q + \angle R = 180°$ [angle sum property]

    $\Rightarrow \quad \angle P + 2\angle P = 180°$ [$\because 2\angle P = \angle Q + \angle R$]

    $\Rightarrow \quad 3\angle P = 180°$

    $\Rightarrow \quad \angle P = 60°$

12. The three angles of the triangle are $x, 2x$ and x.

    Now, by angle sum property

    $x + 2x + x = 180°$

    $\Rightarrow \quad 4x = 180°$

    $\Rightarrow \quad x = 45°$

    So, greatest angle $= 2x = 90°$

13. Third side can't be 2, because $2 + 2 < 7$.

    [sum of two sides of a triangle must be greater than third side]

15. Given, angles are in the ratio 2 : 3 : 5.

    Let the angles be $2x$, $3x$ and $5x$.

    Then, $\quad 2x + 3x + 5x = 180°$

    $\Rightarrow \quad 10x = 180°$

    $\Rightarrow \quad x = 18°$

    $\therefore$ The angles are 36°, 54°, 90°. Hence, it is a right angled triangle.

16.

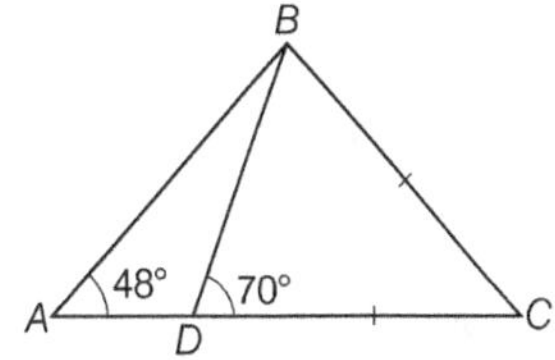

    Given, $\quad BC = CD$

    $\therefore \quad \angle CBD = \angle CDB = 70°$

    [angles opposite to equal sides are also equal]

    Also, $\quad \angle BDC = \angle BAD + \angle ABD$

    [exterior angle property]

    $70° = 48° + \angle ABD$

    $\Rightarrow \quad \angle ABD = 70° - 48° = 22°$

    So, $\quad \angle ABC = \angle ABD + \angle CBD = 22° + 70° = 92°$

17. In the given figure,

    $\angle a + 20° + 90° = 180°$ [linear pair]

    $\Rightarrow \angle a = 180° - 110° = 70°$

    Also, $\quad \angle c = \angle b$

    $\therefore \quad \angle b + \angle c = 90° + 20°$

    $\Rightarrow \quad \angle b + \angle b = 90° + 20°$ [$\because \angle c = \angle b$]

$\Rightarrow \qquad\qquad 2\angle b = 110°$

$\Rightarrow \qquad\qquad \angle b = 55°$

$\therefore \qquad\qquad \angle a = 70°,$

$\qquad\qquad \angle b = 55° \text{ and } \angle c = 55°$

18. I. > II. circumcentre III. medians
IV. hypotenuse V. AC VI. acute
VII. equilateral VIII. one

19. In the given figure,

$$OB = OC$$

$\therefore \qquad\qquad \angle OBC = \angle OCB$

$\Rightarrow \qquad\qquad \angle OCB = 42° \qquad [\because \angle OBC = 42°]$

Also, in $\triangle ABC$,

$$\angle A + \angle B + \angle C = 180°$$

$\Rightarrow 54° + (42° + 21°) + \angle C = 180°$

$\Rightarrow \qquad 54° + 63° + \angle C = 180°$

$\Rightarrow \qquad 117° + \angle C = 180°$

$\Rightarrow \qquad\qquad \angle C = 63°$

$\Rightarrow \qquad i + \angle OCB = 63°$

$\Rightarrow \qquad i + 42° = 63°$

$\Rightarrow \qquad\qquad i = 63° - 42°$

$\Rightarrow \qquad\qquad i = 21°$

20. We have,

$$\angle a + \angle b + \angle c + \angle d + \angle e + \angle x = 180° + 180°$$

$\Rightarrow \angle a + \angle b + \angle c + \angle d + \angle e + 90° = 360° \quad [\because \angle x = 90°]$

$\Rightarrow \angle a + \angle b + \angle c + \angle d + \angle e = 360° - 90° = 270° = 3 \times 90°$

21.

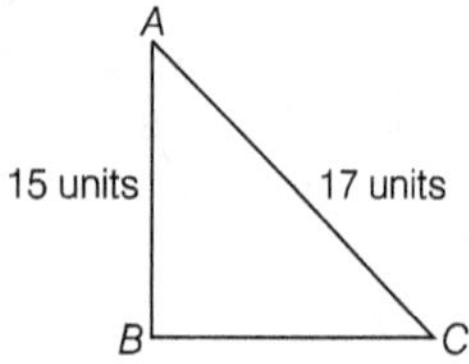

Here, AB is the pole and AC is the rope and $\triangle ABC$ is right angled triangle at B.

By using Pythagoras theorem,

$$AC^2 = AB^2 + BC^2$$

$\Rightarrow \qquad 17^2 = 15^2 + BC^2$

$\Rightarrow \qquad 17^2 - 15^2 = BC^2$

$\Rightarrow \qquad 289 - 225 = BC^2$

$\Rightarrow \qquad\qquad BC^2 = 64$

$\Rightarrow \qquad\qquad BC = 8 \text{ units}$

22. We have, the ratio angles as $3 : 3 : 4$.

Now, sum of angles $= 180°$

$\therefore \qquad 3x + 3x + 4x = 180°$

$\Rightarrow \qquad\qquad 10x = 180°$

$\Rightarrow \qquad\qquad x = 18°$

$\therefore$ Measure of angles is $54°, 54°, 72°$.

23.

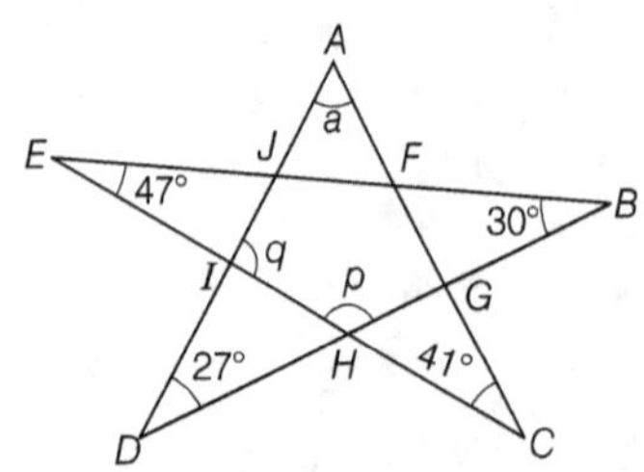

Consider $\triangle HEB$,

$$\angle p + \angle HEB + \angle HBE = 180°$$

$\Rightarrow \quad \angle p + 47° + 30° = 180°$

$\Rightarrow \quad \angle p = 180° - 77° = 103°$

$\therefore \qquad\qquad \angle DIH = 103° - 27° \qquad \text{[exterior angle property]}$

$\qquad\qquad\qquad = 76°$

Now, $\angle q = 180° - 76° = 104° \qquad\qquad \text{[linear pair]}$

In $\triangle IAC$,

$\qquad \angle q + \angle a + \angle ACI = 180° \qquad \text{[sum of three angles]}$

$\Rightarrow \quad 104° + \angle a + 41° = 180°$

$\Rightarrow \qquad\qquad 145° + \angle a = 180°$

$\Rightarrow \qquad\qquad \angle a = 180° - 145°$

$\therefore \qquad\qquad \angle a = 35°$

24.

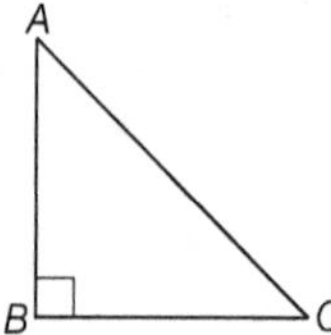

Given a right angled $\triangle ABC$,
right angle at B and $A : C = 7 : 11$

Now, $\qquad \angle A + \angle B + \angle C = 180°$

$\Rightarrow \qquad\qquad \angle A + \angle C = 90°$

$\Rightarrow \qquad\qquad 7x + 11x = 90°$

$\Rightarrow \qquad\qquad 18x = 90°$

$\Rightarrow \qquad\qquad x = 5°$

$\therefore \qquad\qquad \angle A = 35°$

and $\qquad\qquad \angle C = 55°$

25.

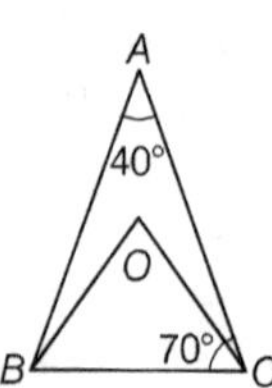

In $\triangle ABC$,

$\qquad \angle A + \angle B + \angle C = 180° \qquad \text{[angle sum property]}$

$\qquad 40° + \angle B + 70° = 180°$

$\Rightarrow \qquad 110° + \angle B = 180°$

$\Rightarrow \qquad\qquad \angle B = 70° = \angle C$

Now, OB and OC are bisectors of $\angle B$ and $\angle C$, respectively.

$\therefore \qquad \angle OBC = \angle OCB = 35°$

Now, $\qquad\qquad \angle BOC = 180° - (\angle OBC + \angle OCB)$

$\qquad\qquad\qquad = 180° - (35° + 35°)$

$\qquad\qquad\qquad = 180° - 70° = 110°$

26. By definition

27. In the given figure,

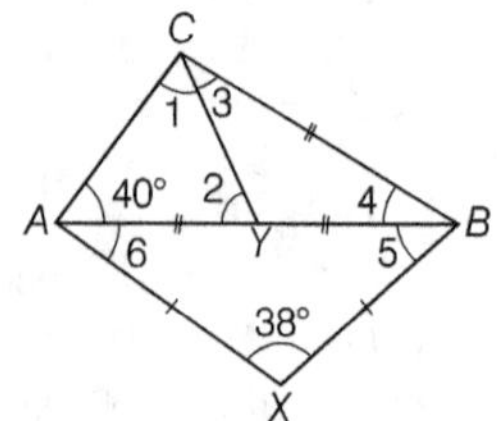

$$AY = CY$$
$$\Rightarrow \qquad \angle 1 = 40°$$

[angle opposite to equal sides are also equal]

Also, $\angle 1 + \angle 2 + \angle CAY = 180°$ [angle sum property]
$$\angle 2 = 180° - (40° + 40°) = 180° - 80°$$
$$\angle CYA = \angle 2 = 100°$$

In $\triangle CYB$,
$$\angle 3 + \angle 4 = 100 \qquad \text{[exterior angles]}$$
$$2\angle 3 = 100 \qquad [\because \angle 3 = \angle 4, \text{ since } BY = CY]$$
$$\Rightarrow \qquad \angle 3 = \frac{100°}{2} = 50°$$
$$\Rightarrow \qquad \angle 3 = \angle 4 = 50°$$

In $\triangle XAB$,
$$\angle AXB + \angle 5 + \angle 6 = 180°$$
$$\Rightarrow \qquad 38° + 2\angle 5° = 180° \quad [\because \angle 5 = \angle 6, \text{ since } XA = XB]$$
$$\Rightarrow \qquad 2\angle 5 = 180° - 38°$$
$$\Rightarrow \qquad 2\angle 5 = 142°$$
$$\Rightarrow \qquad \angle 5 = 71°$$

Now, $\qquad \angle CBX = \angle 4 + \angle 5 = 50° + 71° = 121°$

28.

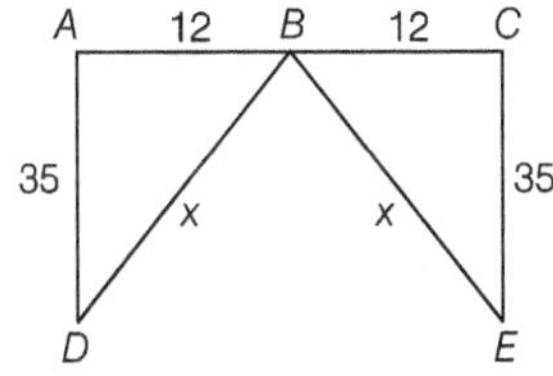

In the given figure, $\triangle DAB$ and $\triangle ECB$ are right angled triangles at A and C, respectively.

Consider $\triangle BAD$, BD is the hypotenuse.
$$\therefore \qquad BD^2 = AD^2 + AB^2$$
$$\Rightarrow \qquad x^2 = 35^2 + 12^2$$
$$\Rightarrow \qquad x^2 = 1225 + 144$$
$$\Rightarrow \qquad x^2 = 1369$$
$$\Rightarrow \qquad x = \sqrt{1369}$$
$$\Rightarrow \qquad x = 37$$

29. In the given figure,

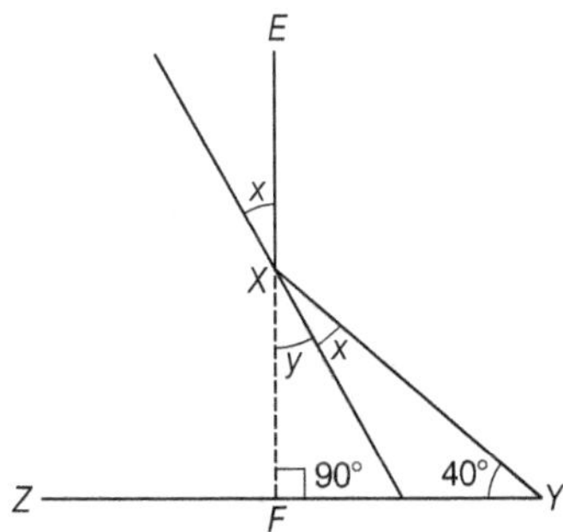

In $\triangle XFY$,

Here, $\angle XFY + \angle XYF + \angle FXY = 180°$ [angle sum property]
$$\Rightarrow \qquad 90° + 40° + \angle FXY = 180°$$
$$\Rightarrow \qquad \angle FXY = 50°$$
Now, $\qquad \angle x = \angle y$

[vertically opposite angles]
$$\therefore \qquad \angle x + \angle y = 50°$$
$$\Rightarrow \qquad 2\angle x = 50° \qquad [\because \angle x = \angle y]$$
$$\Rightarrow \qquad \angle x = 25°$$

30. I. False   II. True   III. False   IV. True   V. False

1. In the given $\triangle PSQ$ and $\triangle PSR$,
$$\angle PSQ = \angle PSR \qquad [90°]$$
$$PQ = PR \qquad \text{[given]}$$
$$PS = PS \qquad \text{[common]}$$
$$\therefore \qquad \triangle PQS \cong \triangle PRS \qquad \text{[by RHS rule]}$$

2. Other triangles are congruent.

3. All statements are true.

4. AAA is a rule for similarity of triangles.

6.

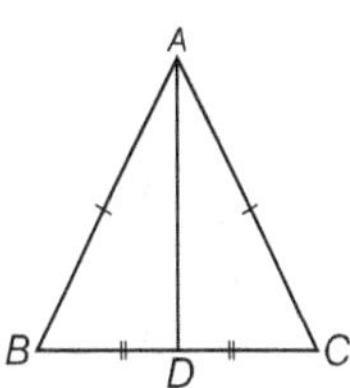

In $\triangle ABD$ and $\triangle ACD$,
$$AB = AC \qquad \text{[given]}$$
$$BD = DC \qquad [AD \text{ is the median}]$$
$$AD = AD \qquad \text{[common]}$$
$$\therefore \qquad \triangle ABD \cong \triangle ACD \qquad \text{[by SSS property]}$$

7.

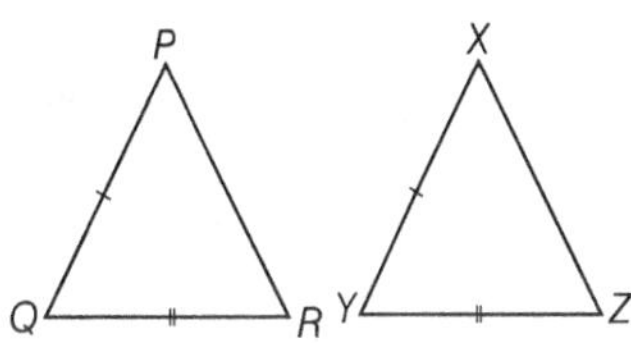

Given, $\qquad \triangle PQR$ and $\triangle XYZ$

with $\qquad PQ = XY$

and $\qquad QR = YZ$

To make $\qquad \triangle PQR \cong \triangle XYZ$
$$\therefore \qquad \angle Q = \angle Y \qquad \text{[by SAS property]}$$

8. Given $\triangle ABC$ with $AB = 3$ cm, $BC = 4$ cm, $AC = 5$ cm

and $\triangle PQR$ with $\angle Q = 90°$

Here, hypotenuse $= 5$ cm

and perpendicular $= 3$ cm

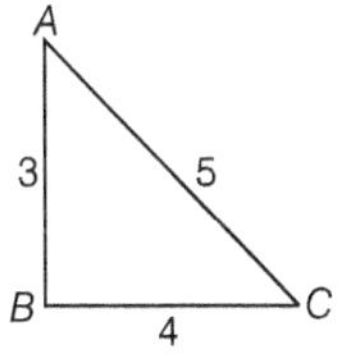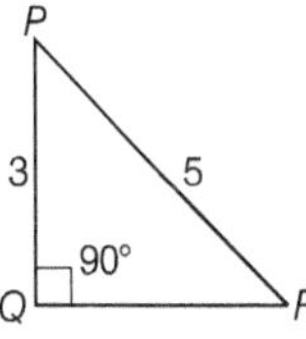

In $\triangle ABC$,
$$AB = 3 \text{ cm}, BC = 4 \text{ cm}$$
and $\qquad AC = 5$ cm

Then, $\triangle ABC$ is a right angled triangle as it satisfies the Pythagoras property. $[AC^2 = AB^2 + BC^2]$
$$\therefore \qquad \angle B = 90°$$
Also, in $\triangle PQR$, we have
$$PR = 5 \text{ cm}, \angle Q = 90°$$
and $\qquad PQ = 3$ cm

Now, consider $\triangle ABC$ and $\triangle PQR$

$$\angle B = \angle Q \qquad [90°]$$
$$AB = PQ$$
$$AC = PR \qquad [\text{hypotenuse}]$$
$$\therefore \quad \triangle ABC \cong \triangle PQR \qquad [\text{by RHS}]$$

9. Given, $\triangle ABC \cong \triangle XYZ$
   and $\triangle PQR \cong \triangle XYZ$
   $\therefore \quad \triangle ABC \cong \triangle PQR$
   $\Rightarrow \quad \angle A = \angle P \qquad [\text{by CPCT}]$
   and $\quad AB = PQ \qquad [\text{by CPCT}]$

10. 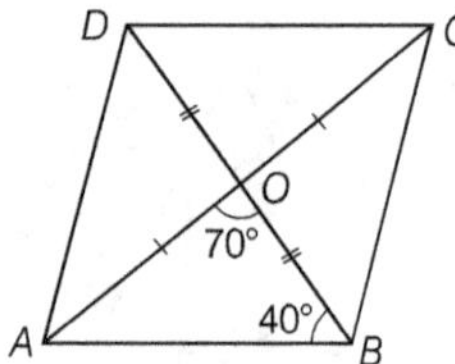

Given, $ABCD$ is a parallelogram.
$\therefore \quad AB = CD$
Consider $\triangle AOB$ and $\triangle COD$,
$$OB = OD$$
Here, $\quad OA = OC \qquad [\text{given}]$
and $\quad CD = AB$
$\therefore \quad \triangle AOB \cong \triangle COD$
In $\triangle OBA$,
$$\angle OBA + \angle AOB + \angle OAB = 180°$$
$\Rightarrow \quad 40° + 70° + \angle OAB = 180°$
$\Rightarrow \quad \angle OAB = 180° - 110° = 70°$
$\therefore \quad \angle OCD = \angle OAB = 70° \qquad [\text{by CPCT}]$

11. 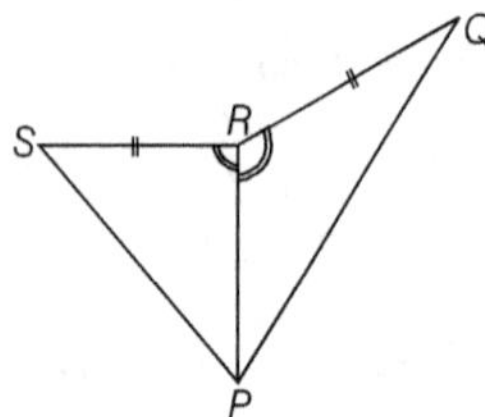

Consider $\triangle PRS$ and $\triangle PRQ$,
Here, $\quad PR = PR \qquad [\text{common side}]$
$$\angle PRQ = \angle PRS \qquad [\text{given}]$$
$$RQ = RS \qquad [\text{given}]$$
So, $\quad \triangle PRS \cong \triangle PRQ$
$\Rightarrow \quad PS = PQ \qquad [\text{by CPCT}]$
and $\quad \angle PSR = \angle PQR \qquad [\text{by CPCT}]$
So, all options are true.

12. I. ASA rule II. SSS Rule III. SAS rule

13. 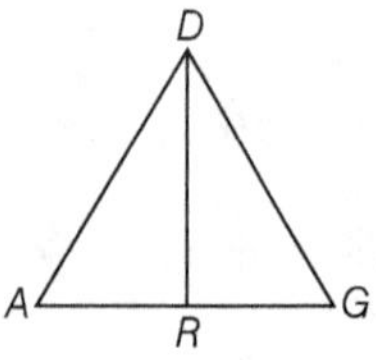

Given, $\quad DR \perp AG$
Now, to prove $\triangle DAR \cong \triangle DGR$
We can either use $DA = DG$ or $RA = RG$
As, if $\quad DA = DG \qquad [\text{assumption}]$

$$\angle DRA = \angle DRG \qquad [90°]$$
$$DR = DR \qquad [\text{common}]$$
$$\triangle DAR \cong \triangle DGR \qquad [\text{by RHS}]$$
and, if $\quad RA = RG$
We have, $\quad DR = DR$
$$\angle DRA = \angle DRG$$
$$RA = RG$$
$\therefore \quad \triangle DRA \cong \triangle DRG \qquad [\text{by SAS rule}]$

14. In the given figure,
$$MD = MC = EC = EB = AB$$
$\Rightarrow \quad DC = MD + MC = CE + EB = CB \qquad ...(i)$
and $\quad AB = EC \qquad ...(ii)$
Consider $\triangle DEC$ and $\triangle CAB$,
$$DE = CA \qquad [\text{given}]$$
$$DC = CB \qquad [\text{from Eq. (i)}]$$
$$EC = AB \qquad [\text{from Eq. (ii)}]$$
$\therefore \quad \triangle DEC \cong \triangle CAB$

15. 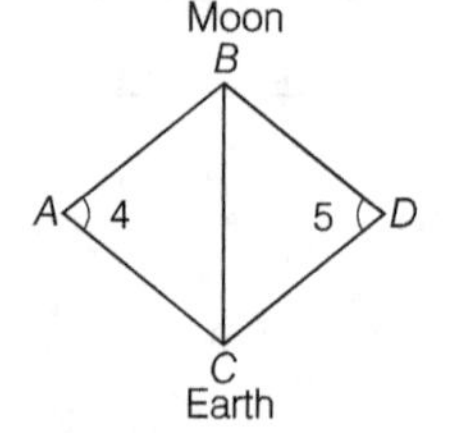

Consider $\triangle ABC$ and $\triangle DBC$,
$$AB = DB \qquad [\text{given}]$$
$$AC = DC \qquad [\text{given}]$$
and $\quad BC = BC \qquad [\text{common}]$
$\therefore \quad \triangle ABC \cong \triangle DBC \qquad [\text{by SSS rule}]$
$\Rightarrow \quad \angle 4 = \angle 5 \qquad [\text{by CPCT}]$

16. 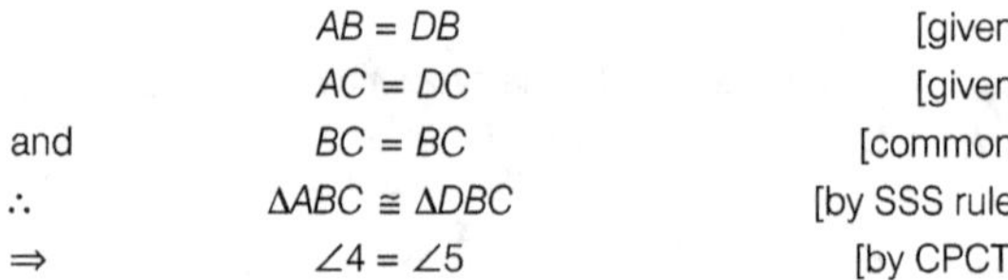

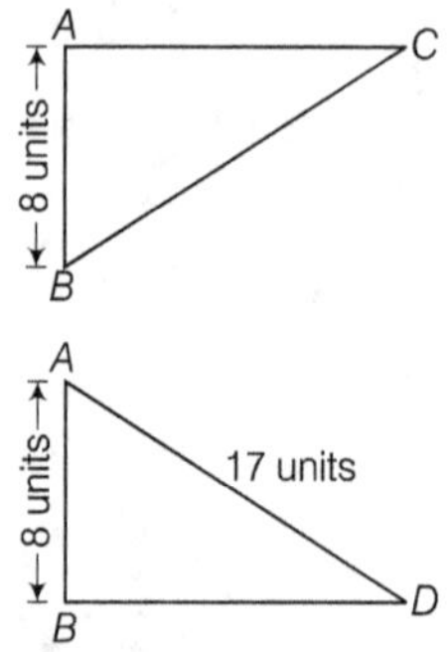

Consider, $\triangle ABD$ which is a right angled triangle.
$\therefore \quad AD^2 = AB^2 + BD^2$
$$17^2 = 8^2 + BD^2$$
$\Rightarrow \quad BD^2 = 289 - 64 \Rightarrow BD^2 = 225 \Rightarrow BD = 15$
From the given conditions,
$$\triangle ABC \cong \triangle ABD$$
$\Rightarrow \quad BC = BD \qquad [\text{by CPCT}]$
$\therefore \quad BC = 15 \text{ units}$

17. I. $\triangle ABC \cong \triangle ZXY$ II. SAS   III. Corresponding
    IV. AAA   V. four   VI. parts
    VII. congruent   VIII. same

18. I. False   II. True   III. False   IV. True

19. By property of congruence

A Percentage

1. 36% of 20 = $\dfrac{36}{100} \times 20 = \dfrac{36}{5}$

   Other options are in 9 : 10.

2. Consider, 40% of 70 = $\dfrac{40}{100} \times 70 = 28$

   and 70% of 40 = $\dfrac{70}{100} \times 40 = 28$

   ∴ Sum = 28 + 28 = 56

3. $0.047 = \dfrac{47}{1000} = \dfrac{47}{1000} \times 100 = 4.7\%$

4. Consider, $\dfrac{4500}{7500} \times 100 = 60\%$

5. Number of goats = 30

   Per cent increase = 20%

   ∴ Number of goats increased = 30 of 20% = $30 \times \dfrac{20}{100} = 6$

6. Ratio of grey tiles to white tiles = 3 : 5

   Number of white tiles used = 45

   ∴ Number of grey tiles used = $\dfrac{45}{5} \times 3 = 27$

   ∴ Total number of tiles used = 27 + 45 = 72

   Percentage of grey tiles used = $\dfrac{27}{72} \times 100 = \dfrac{3}{8} \times 100$

   $= \dfrac{300}{8} = \dfrac{75}{2} = 37.5\%$

7. Total number of shapes = 12

   Number of circles = 3

   So, required percentage = $\dfrac{3}{12} \times 100 = \dfrac{1}{4} \times 100$

   $= 25\%$

8. I. 10% of 2 km = $\dfrac{10}{100} \times 2 = \dfrac{2}{10}$ km = $\dfrac{2}{10} \times 1000$ m

   $[\because 1 \text{ km} = 1000 \text{ m}]$

   $= 200$ m

   II. 1 min = 60 s

   20 min = 20 × 60 s = 1200 s

   Required per cent = $\dfrac{144}{1200} \times 100 = 12\%$

   III. $\dfrac{7}{5}$ of 200 cm = $\dfrac{7}{5} \times 200 = 280$ cm

   Now, x% of 28 m = 280 cm

   $\Rightarrow \dfrac{x}{100} \times 28 \times 100 = 280$ cm $\qquad [\because 1 \text{ m} = 100 \text{ cm}]$

   $\Rightarrow \qquad x = 10$

   IV. 25% of x kg = 600 g

   $\Rightarrow \dfrac{25}{100} \times x \times 1000 = 600$ g $\qquad [\because 1 \text{ kg} = 1000 \text{ g}]$

   $\Rightarrow \qquad 250 x = 600$ g

   $\Rightarrow \qquad 25x = 60$ g

   $\Rightarrow \qquad x = 2.4$

9. 15% of ₹ 12 = $\dfrac{15}{100} \times 12 = \dfrac{180}{100} = ₹ 1.8$

10. Total number of pupils who attended the concert = 1600

    Per cent of pupils who were late = 5%

    ∴ Number of pupils who were late = $\dfrac{5}{100} \times 1600 = 80$

    So, the number of pupils who were punctual = 1600 − 80 = 1520

11. Consider 45% of x + 30% of 90 = 30% of 210

    $\Rightarrow \dfrac{45}{100} x + \dfrac{30 \times 90}{100} = \dfrac{30}{100} \times 210$

    $\Rightarrow \dfrac{45}{100} x + 27 = 63$

    $\Rightarrow \dfrac{45}{100} x = 63 - 27 = 36$

    $\therefore \qquad x = \dfrac{36 \times 100}{45} = 80$

12. Let the number be x.

    According to the question,

    $\dfrac{25}{100} x + 30 = x$

    $\Rightarrow \dfrac{1}{4} x + 30 = x$

    $\Rightarrow \qquad 30 = x - \dfrac{1}{4} x \Rightarrow 30 = \dfrac{3}{4} x$

    $\Rightarrow \qquad x = 40$

13. Percentage increased in number of students = 3%

    Let the students earlier be x.

    We have, 3% of x = 42

    $\Rightarrow \dfrac{3}{100} \times x = 42$

    $\Rightarrow \qquad x = 1400$

14. I. $400\% = \dfrac{400}{100} = 4$ II. $\dfrac{1}{4} = 0.25 = \dfrac{25}{100} = 25\%$

    III. $0.02 = \dfrac{2}{100} = 2\%$ IV. $6\dfrac{1}{4}\% = \dfrac{25}{4}\%$

    V. $10\% = \dfrac{10}{100} = \dfrac{1}{10}$

15. Length of rectangle = 40 cm

    Breadth of rectangle = 30 cm

    Decrease in length = 20%

    ∴ New length = (100 − 20)% of 40 = $\dfrac{80}{100} \times 40 = 32$

    New area = 32 × 30 = 960 sq cm

16. Number of men = 75

    Number of women = 60

    Difference between them = 75 − 60 = 15

    Per cent of difference = $\dfrac{15}{60} \times 100 = 25\%$

    Reason (R) True

17. A. 104% of 150 = $\dfrac{104}{100} \times 150 = 156$

    B. 100% of 150 + 4% of 150

    $= \dfrac{100}{100} \times 150 + \dfrac{4}{100} \times 150 = 150 + 6 = 156$

    ∴ A = B

18. A. 25% of $x = 400$

$\Rightarrow \dfrac{25}{100} \times x = 400 \Rightarrow x = 1600$

B. 15% of $x = 225$

$\Rightarrow \dfrac{15}{100} x = 225 \Rightarrow x = 1500$

$\therefore \qquad\qquad A > B$

19. A. Let the number be x.

According to the question, 20% of $x = 60$

$\Rightarrow \dfrac{20}{100} \times x = 60$

$\Rightarrow \qquad\qquad x = 300$

So, $\quad$ 45% of $300 = \dfrac{45}{100} \times 300 = 135$

B. $\dfrac{16}{100} = \dfrac{x}{2500}$

$\Rightarrow \dfrac{16 \times 2500}{100} = x$

$\Rightarrow \qquad\qquad x = 400$

$\therefore \qquad\qquad B > A$

20. Number of family members = 20 Per cent of O negative blood group people = 6.6%

$\therefore$ Number of people $= \dfrac{66}{100} \times \dfrac{20}{10} = \dfrac{132}{100} = 1.32 \Rightarrow 1 < 1.32 < 2$

21. Number of people who registered for blood donation camp
$= 200$

Per cent of people having B negative blood group = 1.5%

Per cent of people having B positive blood group = 8.5%

$\therefore$ Required ratio = 1.5% to 8.5%

$= \dfrac{1.5}{100} : \dfrac{8.5}{100} = 15 : 85 = 3 : 17$

22. Number of bottles having blood of AB negative group = 12

Per cent of AB negative blood group = 0.06%

Total number of bottles of blood $= \dfrac{12}{0.06} \times 100 = 20000$

$\therefore$ Number of bottles of AB positive blood group = 3.4% of 20000

$= \dfrac{34}{1000} \times 20000 = 680$

23. Energy (Kcal) requirement of man = 2500

Energy (Kcal) requirement of woman = 2000

Difference = 2500 − 2000 = 500

Required percentage $= \dfrac{500}{2500} \times 100 = 20\%$

24. Total of requirement of sugar, fat and saturates in a man
$= 120 + 95 + 30 = 150 + 95 = 245\,g$

Total of requirement of sugar, fat and saturates in a woman
$= 90 + 70 + 20 = 180$

$\therefore$ Required ratio = 245 : 180 = 49 : 36

25. Non-current assets = ₹ 20000

Current assets = ₹ 49500

Required percentage $= \dfrac{20000}{49500} \times 100 = 40.40\%$

26. Member of children below 10 y = 20%

Number of boys $= \dfrac{2}{3}$ [below 10 yr]

$\therefore$ Number of girls $= \dfrac{1}{3}$ $\qquad\qquad$ [below 10 yr]

Also, given number of girls = 22 $\qquad$ [below 10 yr]

$\therefore$ Number of children below 10 yr = 22 × 3 = 66

Total number of children who participated $= \dfrac{66 \times 100}{20}$

$= 330$

27. Percentage of English books = 34%

Percentage of French books = 42%

$\therefore$ Percentage of Spanish books = 100 − (34 + 42)

$= 100 − 76 = 24\%$

Also given, number of Spanish books = 72

$\therefore$ Total number of books $= \dfrac{72}{24} \times 100 = 300$

28. Number of English books $= \dfrac{34 \times 300}{100} = 102$

Required per cent $= \dfrac{102}{72} \times 100 = 141.67\%$

(B) ## Application Based Problems on Percentage, Profit or Loss

1. CP of TV set = ₹ 48000

Profit per cent = 15

$\therefore$ Amount of profit earned $= \dfrac{48000 \times 15}{100} = ₹\,7200$

2. In all other options, profit is earned, while in option (d) loss is being suffered.

3. Earlier price of gasoline drops = ₹ 2.00

New price of gasoline drops = ₹ 1.90

Decrease in price = ₹ 2.00 − ₹ 1.90 = ₹ 0.10

Per cent decrease in price $= \dfrac{0.10}{2.00} \times 100 = 5\%$

4. I. Given, $P = 1000$,

$r = 2\%$ and $t = 1\,yr$

$\therefore \quad SI = \dfrac{1000 \times 2 \times 1}{100} \qquad \left[\because SI = \dfrac{P \times r \times t}{100} \right]$

$= ₹\,20$

II. $P = 500$,

$r = 3\%$ and $t = 2\,yr$

$\therefore \quad SI = \dfrac{500 \times 3 \times 2}{100} = ₹\,30$

III. $P = 250$, $r = 4\%$ and $t = 4\,yr$

$\therefore \quad SI = \dfrac{250 \times 4 \times 4}{100} = ₹\,40$

5. Percentage of commission = 5%

Amount of sales = ₹ 15000

$\therefore$ Amount of commission earned $= 15000 \times \dfrac{5}{100} = ₹\,750$

6. Marks scored in Mathematics = 97

Marks scored in English = 94

Marks scored in Hindi = 46

Total marks = 237

For overall percentage to be 80%.

Total marks required to be score
$= 80\%$ of 400
$= 320$

So, marks to be scored in Science
$= 320 − 237$
$= 83$

7. CP of 1 battery = ₹ 2

SP of 4 batteries = ₹ 10

$\therefore$ SP of 1 battery $= \dfrac{10}{4} = ₹\ 2.5$

$\therefore$ Profit $= SP - CP = ₹\ (2.5 - 2.0) = ₹\ 0.5$

So, profit per cent $= \dfrac{0.5}{2} \times 100 = 25\%$

8. Given, $P = ₹\ 200$

$r = 4\%$ and $t = 3$ yr

$\therefore$ $SI = \dfrac{P \times r \times t}{100} = \dfrac{200 \times 4 \times 3}{100} = ₹\ 24$

9. Given, $r = 6\%$

$t = 2$ yr and $SI = ₹\ 12$

We have,

$$SI = \dfrac{P \times r \times t}{100}$$

$\Rightarrow \quad 12 = \dfrac{P \times 6 \times 2}{100} \Rightarrow P = ₹\ 100$

10. CP of car = ₹ 5 lakh

SP of car = ₹ 7.5 lakh

Profit $= SP - CP = (7.5 - 5)$ lakh $= ₹\ 250000$

$\therefore$ Percentage of profit (on SP)

$$= \dfrac{250000}{750000} \times 100 = \dfrac{100}{3} = 33\dfrac{1}{3}\%$$

11. CP of play station game pack = ₹ 7000

SP of play station game pack = ₹ 6090

Loss $= CP - SP = ₹\ (7000 - 6090) = ₹\ 10$

$\therefore$ Loss per cent $= \dfrac{10}{7000} \times 100 = \dfrac{1}{7}\%$

12. Number of apples = 180

Percentage of number of red apples = 40%

$\therefore$ Percentage of number of green apples $= (100 - 40) = 60\%$

So, number of green apples $= \dfrac{60}{100} \times 180 = 108$

Percentage of green apples which are bad in quality
$= 25\%$

$\therefore$ Percentage of green apples which are not bad in quality
$= (100 - 25)\% = 75\%$

So, number of green apples which are not bad

$$= \dfrac{75}{100} \times 108 = 81$$

13. Percentage of money spent on maintenance of bus stands
$= 15\%$

Amount of money spent on maintenance of bus stands
$= ₹\ 30$ lakh

Let total budget be ₹ B.

$\therefore \quad 15\%$ of $B = 3000000$

$\Rightarrow \quad \dfrac{15 B}{100} = 3000000$

$\Rightarrow \quad B = \dfrac{3000000 \times 100}{15}$

$\therefore$ Total budget $= ₹\ 20000000$

14. Let principal be ₹ P. Then, SI is ₹ $\dfrac{1}{3} P$.

According to the question, $\dfrac{1}{3} P = \dfrac{P \times 8 \times 4}{100}$

$\Rightarrow \quad \dfrac{1}{3} = \dfrac{8 \times 4}{100}$ $\hspace{1cm}$ [data inadequate]

15. Amount after 2 yr = ₹ 840

Amount of 4 yr = ₹ 920

$\therefore$ SI for 2 yr = ₹ 920 – 840 = ₹ 80

So, SI for 4 yr = ₹ 160

$\therefore$ Principle amount = ₹ (920 – 160) = ₹ 760

16. Let the total number of people be 100.

$\therefore$ Number of men = 40% of 100 = 40

and number of women = 100 – 40 = 60

Now, number of married men = 20% of $40 = \dfrac{20}{100} \times 40 = 8$

and number of unmarried women $= \dfrac{30}{100} \times 60 = 18$

$\therefore$ Total number of married people = 8 + 18 = 26

So, number of unmarried people = 100 – 26 = 74

$\therefore$ Per cent of unmarried members $= \dfrac{74}{100} \times 100 = 74\%$

17. SP of toy = ₹ 750

Profit per cent = 20%

$\therefore \quad CP = \dfrac{SP \times 100}{(100 + Profit)} = \dfrac{750 \times 100}{120} = ₹\ 625$

18. CP of VCD player = ₹ 5500

Discount per cent = 20%

$\therefore$ Buying price of VCD player

$$= \dfrac{5500 \times 80}{100} = ₹\ 4400$$

Now, profit she wants = 10%

$\therefore$ SP of VCD player

$$= CP + 10\% \text{ of } CP = CP\left(1 + \dfrac{10}{100}\right) = CP\left(\dfrac{110}{100}\right)$$

$$= \dfrac{4400 \times 110}{100} = ₹\ 4840$$

19. Let the amount received by Anish be ₹ x. Then, amount received by Anuj is ₹ (20000 – x).

Now, according to the question,

$$\dfrac{x \times 12 \times 2}{100} = \dfrac{(20000 - x) \times 8 \times 2}{100}$$

$\Rightarrow \quad 12x = 160000 - 8x$

$\Rightarrow \quad 20x = 160000$

$\Rightarrow \quad x = ₹\ 8000$

$\therefore$ Anish received ₹ 8000, whereas Anuj received ₹ 12000.

20. CP of Mr. Verma = SP of Mr. Anand = ₹ 82440

Profit earned by Mr. Anand = 20%

$\therefore$ CP for Mr. Anand $= 82440 \times \dfrac{100}{120} = ₹\ 68700$

Now, CP for Mr. Anand = SP of Mr. Qureshi = ₹ 68700

Discount offered by Mr. Qureshi = 10%

Now, CP for Mr. Qureshi $= \left(68700 \times \dfrac{100}{90}\right) = ₹\ 76333$

21. (d) Given,

SP for Mr. Qureshi

$= $ SP for Mr. Anand

$= $ SP for Mr. Qureshi = ₹ 82440

So, profit earned by Mr. Qureshi

$= ₹\ (82440 - 76333) = ₹\ 6107$

$\therefore$ Profit per cent $= \dfrac{6107}{76333} \times 100 = 8\%$

Alternate Method

Let CP of scooter (initially) be 100.

SP of scooter $= 100 - 10\%$ of $100 = 90$

Now, 90 is the CP for Mr. Anand.

$\therefore$ SP of scooter $= 90 + \dfrac{90 \times 20}{100} = 108$

Now, according to the question,

Profit percentage made by Qureshi $= \dfrac{108 - 100}{100} \times 100 = 8\%$

22. Column A

Amount Manisha has $= ₹1500$

Per cent of money spent on a watch $= 30\%$

$\therefore$ Amount of money spent $= \dfrac{30}{100} \times 1500 = ₹\ 450$

$\therefore$ Amount left $= 1500 - 450 = ₹1050$

Percentage of money spent on top $= 10\%$

$\therefore$ Amount of money spent on top $= \dfrac{10}{100} \times 1050 = ₹\ 105$

$\therefore$ Money left $= ₹1050 - ₹105 = ₹945$

Column B

Cost of computer book $= ₹\ 1500$

Loss per cent $= 15\%$

$\therefore$ SP $= $ CP $- \dfrac{15}{100}$ of CP $=$ CP $\left(1 - \dfrac{15}{100}\right)$

$\qquad = $ CP $\times \left(\dfrac{85}{100}\right) = \dfrac{1500 \times 85}{100} = ₹1275$

$\therefore$ B $>$ A

8   Algebraic Expressions

1. $-a^2b^3 = -1 \times a \times a \times b \times b \times b$

3. Consider the terms,

$$9a(2b - a) = 18ab - 9a^2$$

and $\ -6b(4a - 2b) = -24ab + 12b^2$

$\therefore$ $18ab$ and $-24ab$ are like terms.

4. $2x^2 = 2x\,(x)$

5. Consider, $[(2a^3b)^3]\,[(4a^2b^2)]$

$\qquad = [(2 \times 2 \times 2 \times a^3 \times a^3 \times a^3 \times b \times b \times b)\,(4a^2b^2)]$

$\qquad = [(8a^9b^3)\,(4a^2b^2)] = 32a^{11}b^5$

6. Consider, $\dfrac{7a - 2}{5}$

Substitute $a = 3$, we get

$$\dfrac{7 \times 3 - 2}{5} = \dfrac{21 - 2}{5} = \dfrac{19}{5}$$

7. Consider, $3y = 15$

$\Rightarrow \qquad y = 5$ and $2x = 16$

$\Rightarrow \qquad x = 8$

So, $3x + 2y = 3 \times 8 + 2 \times 5 = 24 + 10 = 34$

8. Product of two numbers be xy and difference of the product of two numbers by third number

$$= z - (x \times y)$$

9. Consider, $3h + 45 - 12 + (3 \times 5)h$

$\qquad = 3h + 45 - 12 + 15h$

$\qquad = 18h + 33 = 18 \times 10 + 33 = 180 + 33 = 213$

10. Given, C $= \dfrac{5}{9}$ (F $- 32$)

Substitute, F $= 32$, we get

$$\text{C} = \dfrac{5}{9}\,(32 - 32) = 0$$

11. Consider, $12a + 14b - 3b - 11c + 8.5a$

$\Rightarrow \qquad 12a + 8.5a + 14b - 3b - 11c$

$\Rightarrow \qquad 20.5a + 11b - 11c$

12. Number of skirts Meera has $= 4q$,

Number of skirts Tara has $= 12q$

and Number of skirts Lara has $= 2q$

Number of skirts Meera and Lara have $= 4q + 2q = 6q$

$\therefore$ Difference of number of skirts

Tara has from the combined number of skirts of Meera and

Lara $= 12q - 6q = 6q$

If $q = 5$, then $6q = 6 \times 5 = 30$

13. I. $x^2 + y^2 + 3xy$

$\qquad = 1^2 + (-2)^2 + 3(1) \times (-2) = 1 + 4 - 6 = -1$

II. $x^2 + x^2y + xy^2 + y^2$

$\qquad = (1)^2 + (1)^2 \times (-2) + 1 \times (-2)^2 + (-2)^2$

$\qquad = 1 - 2 + 4 + 4 = 7$

III. $x^2 + y^2 - 3xy$

$\qquad = (1)^2 + (-2)^2 - 3 \times 1 \times (-2) = 1 + 4 + 6 = 11$

IV. $(x^2 - y^2) = (1)^2 - (-2)^2 = 1 - 4 = -3$

14. I. Trinomial $\quad$ II. 4 $\quad$ III. $7y - 4x$ $\quad$ IV. St

V. Unlike terms

15. Required expression

$\qquad = (-2x^3 + 5x^2 - x + 8) - (5x^2 - 4x + 12)$

$\qquad = -2x^3 + 5x^2 - x + 8 - 5x^2 + 4x - 12$

$\qquad = -2x^3 + 3x - 4$

16. Required expression

$\qquad = 3x^2 + 2x + 1 - (x + x^2 + 6)$

$\qquad = 3x^2 + 2x + 1 - x^2 - x - 6 = 2x^2 + x - 5$

17. Consider, $\dfrac{pq + pr}{ps} = \dfrac{p(q + r)}{p \times s} = \dfrac{q + r}{s}$

18. Consider, $\left(\dfrac{2}{5}a^4 - 2a + 7\right) - \left(-\dfrac{3}{10}a^4 + 6a^3\right) - (2a^2 - 7)$

$\qquad = \dfrac{2}{5}a^4 - 2a + 7 + \dfrac{3}{10}a^4 - 6a^3 - 2a^2 + 7$

$\qquad = \dfrac{2}{5}a^4 + \dfrac{3}{10}a^4 - 6a^3 - 2a^2 - 2a + 7 + 7$

$\qquad = \dfrac{7}{10}a^4 - 6a^3 - 2a^2 - 2a + 14$

19. Area of rectangle $= l \times b$

Here, $\qquad l = 33y$ and $b = 10x$

$\therefore \qquad$ Area $= 33y \times 10x = 330xy$

20. Perimeter of regular pentagon $= 5l$

where, $l = $ Side $= (3x + 1)$

$\therefore \qquad$ Perimeter $= 5 \times (3x + 1) = (15x + 5)$ inch

21. $(2a^3 - 3)(5a^3 - 2)$
$= 2a^3 \times 5a^3 + 2a^3(-2) - 3 \times 5a^3 - 3 \times (-2)$
$= 10a^6 - 4a^3 - 15a^3 + 6 = 10a^6 - 19a^3 + 6$

22. Ages of two friends are in the ratio $= 2:1$
Given, sum of their ages is 51.
Let the ages be $2x$ and x.
Then, $\qquad 2x + x = 51 \Rightarrow 3x = 51$
$\Rightarrow \qquad\qquad x = 17$ and $2 \times 17 = 34$
So, the ages are 34 yr and 17 yr.

23. Given, $\qquad A = \dfrac{1}{2} b \times h$

Here, $AD \perp BC$, where $AD = 4$ cm
$\therefore \qquad\qquad \angle A = 60°$
$\qquad\qquad\qquad \angle B = 60°$
$\qquad\qquad\qquad \angle C = 60°$
So, $\triangle ABC$ is an equilateral triangle.
$\Rightarrow \qquad\qquad AB = BC = AC = 7$ cm
Now, area of $\triangle ABC = \dfrac{1}{2} \times 7 \times 4 = 14$ sq units

24. Given, $A = 10w^3 + 20w^2 - 55w + 60$,
$B = -25w^2 + 15w - 10$ and $C = 5w^2 - 10w + 20$
$\therefore A + B - C$
$= 10w^3 + 20w^2 - 55w + 60 + (-25w^2) + 15w - 10$
$\qquad\qquad\qquad\qquad\qquad - (5w^2 - 10w + 20)$
$= 10w^3 + 20w^2 - 55w + 60 - 25w^2 + 15w - 10$
$\qquad\qquad\qquad\qquad\qquad - 5w^2 + 10w - 20$
$= 10w^3 + 20w^2 - 25w^2 - 5w^2 - 55w + 15w + 10w$
$\qquad\qquad\qquad\qquad\qquad + 60 - 10 - 20$
$= 10w^3 - 10w^2 - 30w + 30$

25. Given, width of house $= x$
$\therefore \qquad$ Length of house $= 1.5x$
Area of house $= l \times b = x \times 1.5x = 1.5x^2$
Width of land $= x + 20$
Length of land $= 2 \times 1.5x = 3x$
$\therefore$ Area of land $= 3x \times (x + 20) = 3x^2 + 60x$
Remaining area of land $= 3x^2 + 60x - 1.5x^2 = 1.5x^2 + 60x$
where, $x = 30$, then area $= 1.5(30)^2 + 60 \times 30$
$= 1.5 \times 900 + 1800 = 1350 + 1800 = 3150$ sq units

26. Given, $\quad P = 2387.74t + 155211.46$
and $\quad M = 1164.16t + 75622.43$
$\therefore$ Female population, $F = P - M$
$\qquad = 2387.74t + 155211.46 - 1164.16t - 75622.43$
$\qquad = 1223.58t + 79589.03$

27. Value of $F = 247821.76 - 123456.01 = 124365.75$

28. Monthly salary of Max $= ₹\ 5445q$
Money saved by him $= 30\%$
$\therefore$ Money spent by him $= 70\%$ of $5445q = \dfrac{7}{10} \times 5445q$
Money given to parents $= \dfrac{1}{2} \times \dfrac{7}{10} \times 5445q$
Money used to buy guitar $= \dfrac{1}{2} \times \dfrac{3}{4} \times \dfrac{7}{10} \times 5445q$
where, $q = 8$, we have
$\dfrac{1}{2} \times \dfrac{3}{4} \times \dfrac{7}{10} \times 5445 \times 8 = ₹\ 11434.5$

29. I. Cost of vacuum cleaner $= ₹\ 154.25\ K$
Cost of additional pipes $= ₹\ 15.2\ K$
Cost of 3 vacuum sets $= 3 \times 154.25\ K = ₹\ 462.75\ K$
Cost of 5 additional pipes $= 5 \times 15.2\ K = ₹\ 76\ K$
$\therefore$ Total cost $= ₹\ (462.75 + 76)\ K = ₹\ 538.75\ K$

II. Original cost of both the items $= 538.75 \times 10\ [\because K = 10]$
$= ₹\ 5387.5$
Discount on vacuum sets $= 462.75 \times \dfrac{30}{100} = 138.825\ K$
$\therefore$ New price of vacuum sets
$= 462.75\ K - 138.825\ K = ₹\ 323.925\ K$
Discount on additional pipes $= 75\%$
$\therefore$ Cost of additional pipes $= \dfrac{25}{100} \times 76 = ₹\ 19\ K$
$\therefore$ Total cost $= ₹\ (323.925 + 19)\ K = ₹\ 342.925\ K$
$\qquad\qquad = ₹\ 3429.25 \qquad\qquad [\because K = 10]$
$\therefore$ Difference of cost $= ₹\ (5387.5 - 3429.25)$
$\qquad\qquad\qquad = ₹\ 1958.25$

30. Let cost of 1 dozen of eggs $= a$,
Cost of 1 bread $= b$ and Cost of 1 bottle of juice $= c$
$\therefore$ We have the expression as, $a + 3b + 5c$

31. Given, $N = 1.23t^2 - 3.21t + 27.40$
and $\qquad E = -0.109t^2 + 5.293t + 107.735$
$\therefore A = N + E = 1.23t^2 - 3.21t + 27.40$
$\qquad\qquad\qquad\qquad - 0.109t^2 + 5.293t + 107.735$
$= 1.121t^2 + 2.083t + 135.135$

32. I. False $\qquad$ II. False $\qquad$ III. True $\qquad$ IV. True

33. Given, $\qquad S_n = \dfrac{n(n + 1)}{2}$
$\therefore$ Sum of first 20 natural numbers,
$\qquad S_{20} = \dfrac{20(20 + 1)}{2} = \dfrac{20 \times 21}{2} = 210$

34. Given volume, $V = lwh = 8 \times 10 \times 6 = 480$ cu cm
and Surface area $= 2(lw + hw + lh)$
$\qquad\qquad = 2(80 + 60 + 48) = 2(188) = 376$ sq cm
Hence, volume is greater than surface area.

35. Consider,
$\qquad A\ 4$
$\qquad \underline{2\ A}$
We know that 4×4 gives 6 at unit digit and 4×9 gives 6 at unit digit.
$\therefore \qquad\qquad A \neq 2, 6$
Now, we have $94 \times 29 = 2726$
$\therefore \qquad\qquad A = 9$

36. Consider, $x + 1$
where, $x = \dfrac{x - 3}{x + 1}$
So, we have $\dfrac{x - 3}{x + 1} + 1 = \dfrac{x - 3 + x + 1}{x + 1} = \dfrac{2x - 2}{x + 1}$

37. Let the distance be x km.
Then, $\qquad \dfrac{x}{4} - \dfrac{x}{5} = \dfrac{11 + 7}{60}$
$\Rightarrow \qquad \dfrac{5x - 4x}{20} = \dfrac{18}{60} \Rightarrow \dfrac{x}{20} = \dfrac{18}{60}$
$\therefore \qquad\qquad x = \dfrac{18 \times 20}{60} = 6$ km

1. Consider, $\dfrac{1}{x^{-4}} = x^4 = x \times x \times x \times x \times x$

2. $x^y + y^x = 1^2 + 2^1 = 1 + 2 = 3$

3. Consider, $\dfrac{(a^2 b^3 c)^2}{a^4 b^6 c^2} = \dfrac{a^4 b^6 c^2}{a^4 b^6 c^2} = 1$

4. I. $a^2 \times b^2 = (ab)^2 = \dfrac{1}{(ab)^{-2}}$

   II. $a^4 \div b^4 = \dfrac{a^4}{b^4} = \left(\dfrac{a^2}{b^2}\right)^2$

   III. $(a^3)^{\frac{1}{3}} \times (b^2)^{\frac{1}{2}} = a \times b = ab$

   IV. $(ab)^5 \div (a^2 b^2) = \dfrac{(ab)^5}{(ab)^2} = (ab)^3 = a^3 b^3$

5. Consider, $\left(\dfrac{169}{225}\right)^{\frac{1}{2}} \times \left(\dfrac{125}{27}\right)^{\frac{2}{3}} \times \left(\dfrac{81}{4}\right)^{\frac{1}{2}}$

   $= \dfrac{(169)^{\frac{1}{2}}}{(225)^{\frac{1}{2}}} \times \dfrac{(125)^{\frac{2}{3}}}{(27)^{\frac{2}{3}}} \times \dfrac{(81)^{\frac{1}{2}}}{(4)^{\frac{1}{2}}} = \dfrac{(13^2)^{\frac{1}{2}}}{(15^2)^{\frac{1}{2}}} \times \dfrac{(5^3)^{\frac{2}{3}}}{(3^3)^{\frac{2}{3}}} \times \dfrac{(9^2)^{\frac{1}{2}}}{(2^2)^{\frac{1}{2}}}$

   $= \dfrac{13}{15} \times \dfrac{5^2}{3^2} \times \dfrac{9}{2}$ $[\because (a^m)^n = (a)^{m \times n}]$

   $= \dfrac{13}{15} \times \dfrac{25}{9} \times \dfrac{9}{2} = \dfrac{13}{15} \times \dfrac{25}{2} = \dfrac{13}{3} \times \dfrac{5}{2} = \dfrac{65}{6}$

6. Consider, $\dfrac{\left(\frac{-1}{3}\right)^6}{\left(\frac{-1}{3}\right)^5} + \dfrac{\left(\frac{-1}{27}\right)}{\left(\frac{-1}{9}\right)}$

   $= \left(\dfrac{-1}{3}\right)^{6-5} + \dfrac{9}{27}$ $[\because a^m \div a^n = a^{m-n}]$

   $= \dfrac{-1}{3} + \dfrac{1}{3} = -1$

7. Given, $\left(\dfrac{4}{5}\right)^3 \times \left(\dfrac{4}{5}\right)^{b+8} = \left(\dfrac{5}{4}\right)^{-11}$

   $\Rightarrow \quad \left(\dfrac{4}{5}\right)^{b+8+3} = \left(\dfrac{4}{5}\right)^{11}$ $[\because a^m \times a^n = a^{m+n}]$

   $\Rightarrow \quad \left(\dfrac{4}{5}\right)^{b+11} = \left(\dfrac{4}{5}\right)^{11}$

   $\Rightarrow \quad b = 0$

8. Consider, $\left(\dfrac{7}{9}\right)^4 \times \left(\dfrac{7}{9}\right)^{-10} = \left(\dfrac{9}{7}\right)^{-4} \times \left(\dfrac{7}{9}\right)^{2a-1}$

   $\Rightarrow \quad \left(\dfrac{7}{9}\right)^{4-10} = \left(\dfrac{7}{9}\right)^4 \times \left(\dfrac{7}{9}\right)^{2a-1}$

   $\Rightarrow \quad \left(\dfrac{7}{9}\right)^{-6} = \left(\dfrac{7}{9}\right)^{4+2a-1}$

       $\left[\because a^m \times a^n = a^{m+n}, \ a^m = \dfrac{1}{a^{-m}}\right]$

   $\Rightarrow \quad -6 = 2a + 3$

   $\Rightarrow \quad -6 - 3 = 2a$

   $\Rightarrow \quad -9 = 2a$

   $\Rightarrow \quad a = \dfrac{-9}{2}$

9. Consider, $\left(4^{\frac{4}{3}} \div 8^{\frac{2}{3}}\right) \times 2^{\frac{3}{2}} = \left[(2^2)^{\frac{4}{3}} \div (2^3)^{\frac{2}{3}}\right] \times 2^{\frac{3}{2}}$

   $= \left[(2)^{\frac{8}{3}} \div (2)^{\frac{6}{3}}\right] \times 2^{\frac{3}{2}}$

   $= (2)^{\frac{8}{3} - 2 + \frac{3}{2}}$ $\left[\begin{array}{l} \because a^m \div a^n = a^{m-n}, \\ a^m \times a^n = a^{m+n} \end{array}\right]$

   $= (2)^{\frac{16-12+9}{6}} = (2)^{\frac{13}{6}} = (2)^2 \times (2)^{\frac{1}{6}} = 4 \times (2)^{\frac{1}{6}}$

10. $9.9 \times 10^{-6} = \dfrac{9.9}{10^6} = \dfrac{9.9}{1000000} = \dfrac{99}{1000000} \times \dfrac{1}{10} = 0.0000099$

11. Given,

    $\qquad 2^x = 4^y = 8^z = 64$

    $\because \qquad 2^x = 64$

    $\Rightarrow \qquad x = 6$

    Now, $\qquad 4^y = 64$

    $\Rightarrow \qquad y = 3$ and $8^z = 64$

    $\Rightarrow \qquad z = 2$

    $\therefore \quad x + y + z = 6 + 3 + 2 = 11$

12. Consider, $\dfrac{2x^2 y}{3x} \cdot \dfrac{9xy^2}{y^4}$

    $= \dfrac{2}{3} x^{2+1-1} \cdot 9y^{1+2-4} = \dfrac{2}{3} x^2 \ 9y^{-1} = \dfrac{6x^2}{y}$

13. We have,

    $\qquad 0.000000748 = \dfrac{000000748}{1000000000}$

    $\qquad\qquad\qquad = \dfrac{748}{10^9} = 748 \times 10^{-9}$

    $\qquad\qquad\qquad = 7.48 \times 10^{-7}$

14. I. $(2^2)^3 = 2^6$ and $2^{2^3} = 2^8$

    $\therefore \qquad (2^2)^3 < 2^{2^3}$

    II. $(4^4)^{\frac{1}{2}} = 4^{\frac{4}{2}} = 4^2 = 16$

    $\qquad (2^4) = 4 \times 4 = 16$

    $\therefore \qquad (4^4)^{\frac{1}{2}} = 2^4$

    III. $\left(3^{\frac{1}{3}}\right)^9 = 3^{\frac{9}{3}} = 3^3 = 27$

    $\left(81^{\frac{1}{4}}\right)^2 = \left(3^{4 \times \frac{1}{4}}\right)^2 = 3^2 = 9$

    $\therefore \qquad (3^{\frac{1}{3}})^9 > \left(81^{\frac{1}{4}}\right)^2$

15. Given, $\quad V = \dfrac{4}{3} \pi r^3$

    Area of circle $= \pi r^2$

    Required ratio $= \pi r^2 : \dfrac{4}{3} \pi r^3 = 1 : \dfrac{4}{3} r = 3 : 4r$

16. Consider,

    $\left(\dfrac{m^3 p^5}{n^7}\right)^6 \times \left(\dfrac{m^2 n^0 p^3}{m^4 n^2}\right)^3 = \dfrac{m^{18} p^{30}}{n^{42}} \times \dfrac{m^6 p^9}{m^{12} n^6}$

    $= m^{18+6-12} \ p^{30+9} \ n^{-42-6} = m^{12} \ p^{39} \ n^{-48} = \dfrac{m^{12} p^{39}}{n^{48}}$

17. Consider, $\left(\dfrac{4^{\frac{-3}{2}} x^{\frac{2}{3}} y^{\frac{-7}{4}}}{2^{\frac{3}{2}} x^{\frac{-1}{3}} y^{\frac{3}{4}}}\right)^{\frac{2}{3}} = \left(\dfrac{(2^2)^{\frac{-3}{2}} x^{\frac{2}{3}} y^{\frac{-7}{4}}}{2^{\frac{3}{2}} x^{\frac{-1}{3}} y^{\frac{3}{4}}}\right)^{\frac{2}{3}}$

$= \left(\dfrac{2^{-3-\frac{3}{2}} x^{\frac{2}{3}+\frac{1}{3}} y^{\frac{-7}{4}-\frac{3}{4}}}{1}\right)^{\frac{2}{3}}$ $\quad [\because a^m \div a^n = a^{m-n}, a^m \times a^n = a^{m+n}]$

$= (2^{\frac{-9}{2}} x^{\frac{3}{3}} y^{\frac{-10}{4}})^{\frac{2}{3}} = 2^{\frac{-9}{2} \times \frac{2}{3}} x^{\frac{3}{3} \times \frac{2}{3}} y^{\frac{-10}{4} \times \frac{2}{3}} = 2^{-3} x^{\frac{2}{3}} y^{\frac{-5}{3}} = \dfrac{(x^2 y^{-5})^{\frac{1}{3}}}{8}$

18. Consider, $\left(\dfrac{24 a^3 b^{-8}}{6 a^{-5} b^2}\right)^{\frac{-1}{2}} = (4\, a^{3+5} b^{-8-2})^{\frac{-1}{2}}$

$\quad [\because a^m \div a^n = a^{m-n}, a^m \times a^n = a^{m+n}]$

$= (4 a^8 b^{-10})^{\frac{-1}{2}} = 4\, a^{\frac{-8}{2}} b^{\frac{-10 \times (-1)}{2}} = 4\, a^{-4} b^5 = \dfrac{4\, b^5}{a^4}$

19. Given, $5^x = 999$

Consider, $5^{x-3} = \dfrac{5^x}{5^3}$ $\quad \left[\because \dfrac{a^m}{a^n} = a^{m-n}\right]$

$= \dfrac{999}{125}$

20. Total area of land $= 2^{17}$ sq miles

Area of pieces to be cut-out $= 16^2 = (2^4)^2$ $\quad [\because (a^m)^n = a^{m \times n}]$

$= 2^8$

Number of pieces of land $= \dfrac{2^{17}}{2^8} = 2^{17-8}$ $\quad [\because a^m \div a^n = a^{m-n}]$

$= 2^9$

21. Amount spent by each household $= ₹\ 40000$

Number of such households $= 1 \times 10^8$

$\therefore$ Total amount spent

$= ₹\ 40000 \times 1 \times 10^8$

$= 4 \times 10^4 \times 10^8$ $\quad [\because 10^4 = 10000]$

$= 4 \times 10^{12}$ $\quad [\because a^m \times a^n = a^{m+n}]$

22. Given, $(5x^7 y^3 z^{-1})^2 \times (2xy^{-5})^3 \times (2y^{-3}z^2)^3$

$= 5^2 x^{14} y^6 z^{-2} \times 2^3 x^3 y^{-15} \times 2^3 y^{-9} z^6$

$= 25 \times 8 \times 8 \times x^{14+3} \times y^{6-15-9} \times z^{-2+6}$

$= 1600 \times x^{17} \times y^{-18} \times z^4 = \dfrac{1600\, x^{17} z^4}{y^{18}}$

23. $(-1)^{101} + (-1)^{102} + (-1)^{103} + \ldots + (-1)^{200}$

$= \{(-1)^{101} + (-1)^{103} + \ldots + (-1)^{199}\}$

$\qquad + \{(-1)^{102} + (-1)^{104} + \ldots + (-1)^{200}\}$

$= \{\underbrace{(-1) + (-1) + \ldots + (-1)\}}_{50\,\text{times}} + \{\underbrace{(1) + (1) + \ldots + (1)}_{50\,\text{times}}\ \}$

$= -50 + 50 = 0$

24. I. $\dfrac{6^3 \times 9^2 \times 25^2}{3^2 \times 4^2 \times 15^4} = \dfrac{2^3 \times 3^3 \times 3^4 \times 5^4}{3^2 \times 2^4 \times 3^4 \times 5^4}$ $\quad [\because (a \cdot b)^m = a^m \cdot b^m]$

$= 2^{3-4} \times 3^{3+4-2-4} \times 5^{4-4}$

$= 2^{-1} \times 3^1$ $\quad \left[\begin{array}{l}\because a^m \div a^n = a^{m-n}, \\ a^m \times a^n = a^{m+n}\end{array}\right]$

$= \dfrac{3}{2}$

II. $\dfrac{3^8 \times 16^2 \times 7^5}{81^2 \times 2^5 \times 49^2}$

$= \dfrac{3^8 \times (2^4)^2 \times 7^5}{(3^4)^2 \times 2^5 \times (7^2)^2} = \dfrac{3^8 \times 2^8 \times 7^5}{3^8 \times 2^5 \times 7^4}$ $\quad [\because (a^m)^n = (a)^{m \times n}]$

$= 3^{8-8} \times 2^{8-5} \times 7^{5-4}$ $\quad \left[\because \dfrac{a^m}{a^n} = a^{m-n}, a^0 = 1\right]$

$= 1 \times 2^3 \times 7 = 8 \times 7 = 56$

III. $\dfrac{15^4 \times 21^3}{3^3 \times 5^2 \times 7^3} = \dfrac{5^4 \times 3^4 \times 3^3 \times 7^3}{3^3 \times 5^2 \times 7^3}$

$= 5^{4-2} \times 3^{4+3-3} \times 7^{3-3} = 5^2 \times 3^4 \times 1 = 5^2 \times 3^4$

25. Three most populous states

$=$ Beijing + California + New York

$= 2 \times 10^9 + 124 \times 10^9 + 276 \times 10^9$

$= 402 \times 10^9 = 4.02 \times 10^{11}$

26. Total population of Tokyo, Texas and New York

$= 8 \times 10^6 + 19 \times 10^6 + 26 \times 10^6 = 53 \times 10^6$

Total population of Brazil, California and Beijing

$= 9 \times 10^6 + 40 \times 10^6 + 57 \times 10^6 = 106 \times 10^6$

$\therefore$ Required ratio $= \dfrac{53 \times 10^6}{106 \times 10^6} = \dfrac{1}{2}$

27. Uranus distance from Sun (farthest) $= 3.004 \times 10^9$

Uranus distance from Sun (closest) $= 2.749 \times 10^9$

Total distance $= 3.004 \times 10^9 + 2.749 \times 10^9 = 5.753 \times 10^9$

Average distance $= \dfrac{5.753 \times 10^9}{2} = 2.8765 \times 10^9$

28. Consider,

$7^4\left[\left(\dfrac{6}{7}\right)^2 + \left(\dfrac{6}{7}\right) - \left(\dfrac{6}{7}\right)^3\right] + (-7)^3\left[\left(\dfrac{6}{7}\right) + 1 - \left(\dfrac{6}{7}\right)^2\right] \times 6$

$= 7^4 \times \dfrac{6}{7}\left[\dfrac{6}{7} + 1 - \left(\dfrac{6}{7}\right)^2\right] + (-7)^3 \times 6\left[\dfrac{6}{7} + 1 - \left(\dfrac{6}{7}\right)^2\right]$

$= 7^3 \times 6\left[\dfrac{6}{7} + 1 - \left(\dfrac{6}{7}\right)^2\right] - 7^3 \times 6\left[\dfrac{6}{7} + 1 - \left(\dfrac{6}{7}\right)^2\right] = 0$

29. Consider, $\left(\dfrac{a^{5b-3} \times a^{3-2b}}{a^{4b-6} \times a^{2b-9}}\right)^{\frac{-8}{6}} = \left(\dfrac{a^{5b-3+3-2b}}{a^{4b-6+2b-9}}\right)^{\frac{-8}{6}}$

$= \left(\dfrac{a^{3b}}{a^{6b-15}}\right)^{\frac{-8}{6}}$ $\quad [\because a^m \div a^n = a^{m-n}, a^m \times a^n = a^{m+n}]$

$= (a^{3b-6b+15})^{\frac{-4}{3}} = (a^{-3b+15})^{\frac{-4}{3}}$

$= (a^{-b+5})^{-4} = a^{4b-20}$

30. Mass of Earth $= 5.9 \times 10^{24}$ kg

Mass of Pluto $= 13 \times 10^{21} = 1.3 \times 10^{22}$

Required difference $= 5.9 \times 10^{24} - 1.3 \times 10^{22}$

$= (5.9 \times 10^2) \times 10^{22} - 1.3 \times 10^{22}$

$= 590 \times 10^{22} - 1.3 \times 10^{22}$

$= 588.7 \times 10^{22} = 5.887 \times 10^{24}$

31. Consider, $\left(\dfrac{p^{a^4}}{p^{b^4}}\right)^{\frac{1}{a^2+b^2}} \times \left(\dfrac{p^{b^4}}{p^{c^4}}\right)^{\frac{1}{b^2+c^2}} \times \left(\dfrac{p^{c^4}}{p^{a^4}}\right)^{\frac{1}{c^2+a^2}}$

$= (p^{a^4-b^4})^{\frac{1}{a^2+b^2}} \times (p^{b^4-c^4})^{\frac{1}{b^2+c^2}} \times (p^{c^4-a^4})^{\frac{1}{c^2+a^2}}$

$= p^{\frac{(a^2-b^2)(a^2+b^2)}{a^2+b^2}} \times p^{\frac{(b^2-c^2)(b^2+c^2)}{b^2+c^2}} \times p^{\frac{(c^2-a^2)(c^2+a^2)}{c^2+a^2}}$

$= p^{a^2-b^2} \times p^{b^2-c^2} \times p^{c^2-a^2}$

$= p^{a^2-b^2+b^2-c^2+c^2-a^2} = p^0 = 1$

1. 
2. 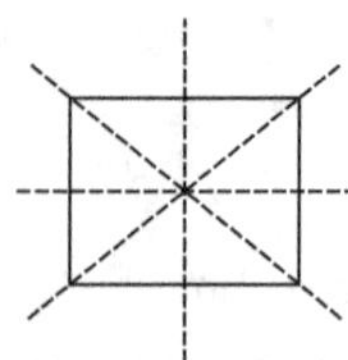
3. Only figure (a) is a closed figure.
4. 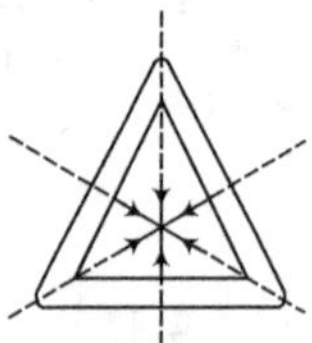

   All letters have vertical lines of symmetry.
5. Both figures (A) and (D) are net of the cube.
6. An equilateral triangle has order of rotational symmetry equal to 3.
7. 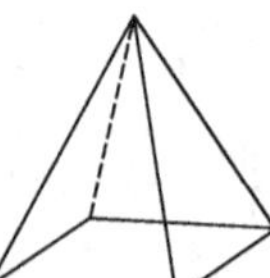

   Three lines of symmetry.
8. 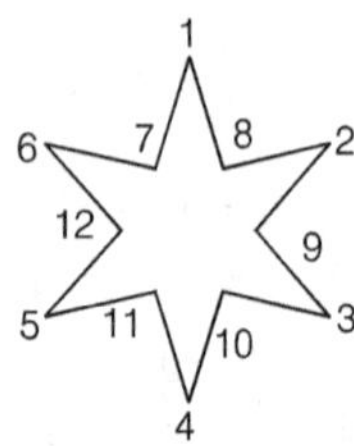

   The figure formed is a pyramid.
9. 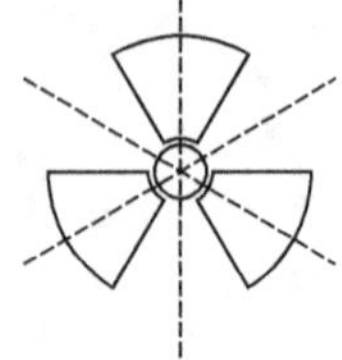

   So, it has 12 corners.
10. The solid figure has 3 faces.
11. I. Rectangle has order of symmetry equal to 2.
    II. This figure has no order of symmetry.
    III. It has 6 order of symmetry.
12. It has order of symmetry equal to 2.
13. 

    It has 3 lines of symmetry.
14. A pyramid is formed (triangular).
15. The given figure has 10 as the order of symmetry. So, it has 10 faces.
16. From the given net, we get
    1 is opposite to 3.
    2 is opposite to 4.
    5 is opposite to 6.
    Figure (a) doesn't satisfy the given condition.
17. 18 cubes are needed to make given figure.
18. 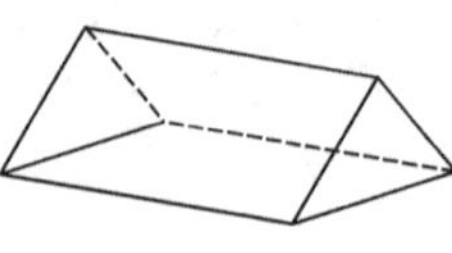

    It has 3 as the order of symmetry.
19. The given figure has 2 lines of symmetry i.e. vertical and horizontal.
20. The given figure has 3 as the order of symmetry.
21. I. It has one line of symmetry.
    II. It has no line of symmetry.
    III. It has four lines of symmetry.
22. The order of symmetry of the given figure is 6.
23. The given figure has the following conditions :
    1 is opposite to 3.
    2 is opposite to 4.
    5 is opposite to 6.
24. Number of faces in the given solid = 8
25. Prism is formed by the given net.

    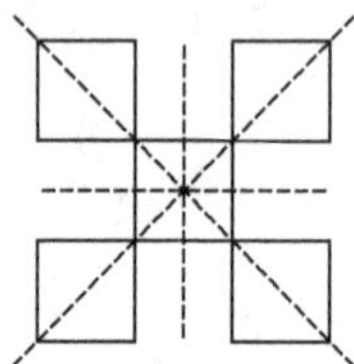

26. 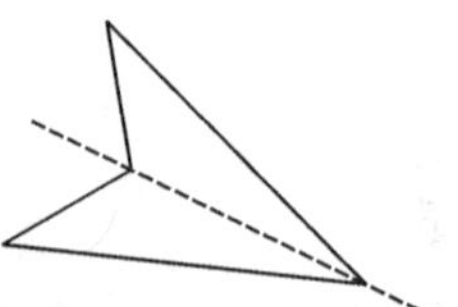

    It has 4 lines of symmetry.
27. Other figures have more than one line of symmetry, except figure (b).

31. I. isometric   II. regular   III. net   IV. cuboid